Amish-Country COOKBOOK

Volume 2
SECOND EDITION

Edited by Bob & Sue Miller

Evangel Publishing House

Nappanee, Indiana 46550

Amish-Country Cookbook: Volume 2
Second Edition

Evangel Publishing House
P.O. Box 189
2000 Evangel Way
Nappanee, IN 46550-0189
Telephone (800) 253-9315
www.evangelpublishing.com

Scripture quotations are from The Holy Bible, King James Version.

Cover design by Jim Ferm
Interior book design by Ramona Severn
Text illustrations by Susan G. Yoder

LCCN 2001094022
ISBN 1-928915-21-3

Printed in the United States of America
10 9 8 7 6 5 4 3 2 1

Publisher's Preface

BOB AND SUE MILLER grew up in a small Amish community in Sugarcreek, Ohio. Christian teaching and good home cooking were part of their upbringing, a heritage which continued when they established their own home.

In 1968, the Millers purchased property on U.S. 20 in Middlebury, Indiana. Back then it was a 24-hour truck stop named Everrett's Highway Inn. But the Millers saw other possibilities. After renovation, the restaurant reopened on January 1, 1971 as Das Dutchman Essenhaus, a six-day-a-week Amish restaurant complete with Amish and Mennonite cooks and wait-staff.

The history of Das Dutchman Essenhaus is a story of growth—growth of a family as well as a business. When the Millers moved to Indiana, they had two small children. Today, their family includes five adult children with their spouses and seven grandchildren. The Essenhaus has grown from a staff of 24 to nearly 450 during the tourist season. What began as a small restaurant has expanded into one of Indiana's largest and finest restaurants with a baker, a country inn, numerous shops, and a wholesale food business.

Guests to the Essenhaus restaurant, flagship of the corporation, enjoy the barnlike structure supported by heavy oak beams, each hewn and hand-fitted by Amish craftsmen. The decor is replete with old wood stoves, horse collars, rustic farm tools, quilts, and antique furniture.

On a busy day, nearly six thousand people enjoy a family-style meal here. Many stop by the bakery before leaving to purchase homemade favorites like apple cinnamon bread, chocolate chip cookies, noodles, dressings, and red raspberry cream pie.

Over the years, the Essenhaus grounds and services have expanded to include charming village shops, Amish country tours, and buggy rides along the well-kept lawns and gardens. The facilities include a windmill, a children's playground, a petting zoo, a miniature golf course, and a covered bridge with scenic trails. Many more acres of the lake-dotted Essenhaus property have yet to be developed, except in the minds of the Millers.

Bob and Sue are dedicated to Jesus Christ and seek to operate the Essenhaus by Christian values. They believe that providing excellent service, good measure, and quality food to their guests reflects their conviction that God desires all of his creation to live in harmony.

After enjoying a memorable dining experience, many guests ask about the unique recipes prepared in the Essenhaus kitchens. The Millers have responded by compiling three cookbooks containing their own original recipes and others gathered from their employees, many never published before. **Amish-Country Cookbook: Volumes 1-3** will help you create the good taste of Das Dutchman Essenhaus right in your home.

Who Are The Amish?

THE AMISH are one of the most colorful and distinctive religious groups in North America. Who are these people that wear plain clothing and ride in buggies? What are they really like? Why do they embrace such distinctive practices?

It is difficult to describe THE Amish because there are more than a dozen different Amish groups—each with its own customs—across North America. The buggy tops of some groups are white, others are yellow, but most are black or grey. Some groups only permit open buggies. Farmers in some groups milk their cows by hand, but most do not. Some women bake their own bread, but many buy it in stores. Even within the same Amish affiliation, some local congregations may permit the use of power lawn mowers while others do not. Some adults till the soil while others work in factories, and still others operate their own businesses.

It is tempting to assume that the Amish are all alike, as if all 180,000 of them were pressed from the same cultural cookie cutter. However, social customs vary from one settlement to another, though most Amish communities do share some basic values and practices regardless of their affiliation.

Growth and Expansion

The Amish are growing. Many of their communities double about every twenty years. Today approximately 180,000 children and adults live in twenty-three different states. About two-thirds of them reside in Ohio (49,000), Pennsylvania (41,000), and Indiana (33,000). Smaller settlements can be found in twenty other states, mostly east of the Mississippi River. Following the big three, the next five most populous states are Wisconsin (10,000), Michigan (8,000), Missouri (6,000), New York (5,000), and Kentucky (5,000).

Amish growth is fueled by sizeable families and strong retention. Typical families have six to nine children and, in some of the groups, ten or more. The average Amish person has at least seventy-five first cousins, many of whom live within several miles. Large families, however, are not enough to make the Amish population grow. Young people must be persuaded to join the church as adults, and indeed most of them do. On average, 85 percent request baptism and join the church between the ages of sixteen and twenty-two.

Deciding about church membership is a crucial step for Amish youth. Those who join are expected to follow the rules of the church for the rest of their life. If they are baptized and later violate church standards (e.g., by driving a car or buying a television), they will be asked to confess their transgression publicly before the church. If they refuse, they will face excommunication and likely some form of shunning. Some youth join the church because it is the natural thing to do; others weigh the consequences carefully because joining entails a lifelong commitment.

On the local level, the Amish are organized into more than thirteen hundred local church districts in 250 geographical settlements. Large settlements such as those in Holmes County, Ohio; Lagrange, Indiana; or Lancaster, Pennsylvania have 100 or more church districts. New settlements, on the other hand, may have only one or two church districts.

About twenty-five to thirty-five families live in a church district. This basic social unit of Amish society serves as parish, precinct, shop, and club. The families meet every other Sunday for a three-hour worship service in their homes. Services rotate among the homes of a district throughout the course of a year. A bishop, deacon, and two ministers typically serve as unpaid leaders in addition to their regular occupations. They receive no theological training and serve for life. Religious, social, and family life revolve around face-to-face interaction in the local district which forms the heart of Amish life.

Religious Roots

Amish roots reach back to the Anabaptist movement that emerged in Switzerland, Germany, and the Netherlands during the Protestant Reformation of the sixteenth century. They were nicknamed "rebaptizers" or "Anabaptists" by their opponents because they baptized adults who already had been baptized as infants in the Catholic Church. The Anabaptists believed that baptism should be reserved for adults who confessed Jesus Christ as Lord and fully understood the consequences of their decision.

Early Anabaptists emphasized the authority of the Bible for daily living, the separation of church and state, and the importance of following the teachings of Jesus in everyday life. Heeding Jesus' call to love our enemies, many of them espoused pacifism and refused to wield the sword or even retaliate against their persecutors. Indeed, thousands of Anabaptists were killed for their religious beliefs. Government officials as well as Catholic and Protestant leaders hunted the despised Anabaptist "heretics," who were considered a threat to civic order. Those who were caught received the capital punishment of their day—burning at the stake. The bloody stories of Anabaptist martyrs who died for their faith are told in the *Martyrs Mirror*. This 1,100-page book is found in many Amish homes today. The severe persecution shaped strong convictions among many Anabaptists that the church should be separate from the evils of the world around it.

The *Amish* name comes from Jakob Ammann, a Swiss Anabaptist leader who converted to the Anabaptist faith more than one hundred and fifty years after its beginning. He introduced several practices, including shunning, that led to a division among the Swiss Anabaptists in 1693. Ammann's followers became known as Amish. Many other Anabaptists were eventually called Mennonites after Menno Simons, a prominent Dutch Anabaptist leader.

In addition to the Amish and Mennonites, Hutterite and Brethren groups also trace their roots to the early Anabaptists. With a few exceptions, most of the Amish came to the Americas in two waves, in 1730-70 and in 1817-60. The first migration settled in Pennsylvania and eventually moved to Ohio, Indiana, and other states. Many in the second wave went directly to Ohio, Illinois, Indiana, and Iowa.

Current Beliefs and Values

As members of the larger Christian faith, the Amish endorse basic Christian beliefs—the authority of the Bible, salvation through Jesus Christ, the church as the body of Christ, a belief in heaven and hell, and so forth. The Amish also subscribe to an Anabaptist confession written in 1632 in the Netherlands. The language of Amish spirituality emphasizes the importance of living in community, in contrast to the individualistic language of American Evangelicalism.

Beyond their basic Christian beliefs, the Amish accent some distinctive values that shape their identity. Here are a few:

Separation from the world is a key belief that undergirds many unusual Amish customs. Based on biblical admonitions such as "love not the world" (1 John 2:15) and "be ye not conformed to this world" (Rom. 12:2), the Amish teach that Christians should live apart from the larger society. Followers of Jesus, the Amish believe, should walk on the straight and narrow way of moral purity, not the broad way that glorifies violence, sex, entertainment, and pleasure.

Speaking a dialect known as Pennsylvania German or Pennsylvania Dutch helps to clarify the line of distinction between the Amish and the larger world. Separation from the world, however, does not mean a wall of social separation. Many Amish interact freely with their non-Amish neighbors.

Church authority is another important Amish emphasis. For the Amish, the church is a redemptive community whose authority spans their total way of life. Each member participates in a local congregation (called a "church district") with specific geographical boundaries formed by a road, a stream, or a township line. The regulations of the local church district govern many aspects of daily life including dress, the use of technology, entertainment, and education. Their entire way of life reflects their religious commitments. Religion is not practiced only in special segments of the week, as is often the case in modern society; religious values permeate the entire fabric of their life.

Obedience is a cardinal Amish virtue. Children are expected to obey their parents without question. Talking back or challenging a parent or teacher is not tolerated. Younger people are expected to respect and honor their elders. Married women follow the lead of their husbands in major decisions related to family and church. Younger ministers accept the guidance and wisdom of older ministers and bishops. Obedience to traditional customs and authority undergirds the harmony of Amish communities.

Unlike most of American culture, which celebrates individual rights and freedom, the Amish emphasize *humility*. Members are expected to deny personal and selfish interests for the sake of their community. They believe the welfare of the community supersedes the rights of the individual. The church discourages activities that highlight individual achievement or call undue attention to oneself because self glory may lead to pride, arrogance, and spiritual downfall. Unbridled individualism will surely lead to pride (the most dreaded Amish fear) and disturb the harmony and equality of community.

The rejection of individualism undergirds a number of Amish practices. Posing for photographs is forbidden. Using make-up and wearing jewelry, wedding rings, and wrist watches is strictly taboo. The plain clothing worn by the Amish underscores their separation from the world and also nurtures humility. Plain dress is a collective badge of group identity, but it also discourages individuals from buying fancy clothing and designer fashions, which would be extravagant.

Amish communities hold *traditional wisdom* in high regard. Elders are reluctant to change practices that have successfully served their community in the past. Amish folk are likely to try one of their grandmother's herbal remedies before running off to visit a doctor. They are reluctant to have their members study science or take up professional occupations, but they are willing to pick some of the fruits of modern progress. For example, they use the services of outside experts—veterinarians, dentists, doctors, lawyers, and accountants. At the same time, they are more likely to tap the wisdom of seasoned elders than to seek the advice of a consultant, therapist, or financial planner. Many customs are entrenched in long-standing traditions that are resistant to change.

A Basic Education

The Amish emphasize learning practical skills that will directly help them to make a living. Until the middle of the twentieth century, most Amish youth attended rural one-room public schools. The rise of large consolidated schools worried many Amish parents because they feared that big schools would expose Amish youth to alien ideas and friends that could lead them away from the church.

In some communities, harsh confrontations erupted between Amish parents and government officials when parents refused to send their offspring to consolidated schools. Indeed, some parents were jailed in the 1950s and 1960s for keeping their children at home. In 1972, the United States Supreme Court favored the Amish with a ruling that permits their youth to end formal schooling after eighth grade.

Today, most Amish youth attend private, one-room schools where they are taught by Amish teachers and surrounded by Amish peers. In a few communities, Amish children attend small, rural public schools operated for the Amish. The vast majority, however, attend approximately twelve hundred private schools operated by Amish parents. One teacher is responsible to teach all eight grades. Classes are conducted in English. Science, sex education, and religion are not taught in Amish schools. Practical subjects like reading, writing, spelling, and basic math are emphasized.

School regulations and practices vary somewhat from state to state. Amish parents support their own schools as well as pay public school taxes. After completing eighth grade, young people learn technical and vocational skills by working in apprenticeships in the homes, shops, or farms of their parents or relatives. The practical skills gained through Amish education prepare young people for successful lives in Amish society.

The Puzzles of Amish Technology

Some Amish practices are puzzling at first glance. Why may they hire and ride in cars but not drive them? Why is electricity from a battery preferable to energy from a public utility line? And why would God smile on a tractor at the barn but not in the field?

The Amish use of technology varies greatly from settlement to settlement. Despite public misconceptions, the Amish do use modern technology. They are not antiques in a nineteenth-century museum. Some new forms of technology, such as gas barbeque grills and chain saws, are used without reservation. Other types of technology which they fear will hurt their community are rejected outright. Examples include television, radio, video players, cell phones, personal computers, and use of the Internet. Outsiders are often perplexed by how the Amish adapt technology in specials ways to serve their community.

For example, they believe that owning cars would pull their community apart. Horse and buggy transportation limits mobility and keeps the community close together. A symbol of individualism and independence, private automobiles would encourage mobility and eventually fragment the community. Nevertheless, as families spread to new settlements and as more Amish became involved in business, the use of motor vehicles became more attractive. So many groups struck a compromise. They permitted members to hire vehicles (with a driver) for special needs, but not to own and drive them. This practice of hiring "taxis" flourishes in settlements that are involved in business. More conservative groups frown on this compromise.

As public utility lines spread across the country in the first half of the twentieth century, the Amish feared that tapping electricity from the lines would tie them too directly to the outside world, make them dependent on it, and provide too easy access to unnecessary conveniences. Since they already had been using batteries, they decided simply to use 12-volt electricity from batteries for small tools and appliances. This compromise continues in many communities today. Many farms and businesses also have diesel engines to produce air and hydraulic pressure. This so-called "Amish Electricity" operates heavy equipment, pumps water, operates fans, and powers washing machines. Without 110-volt electrical current, Amish homes are remarkably quiet. They have no noisy microwaves, air conditioners, televisions, videos, and CD players.

Tractors are not used in fields because they would encourage large-scale farming, steal work from Amish youth, and possibly lead to the use of cars. However, tractors are often used at barns for high power needs—such as to blow silage, chop fodder, and pump liquid manure.

Telephones in homes are discouraged because they provide another direct connection to the outside world. Strangers could enter a home via a telephone call at any moment. Moreover, face-to-face visiting is the social glue that holds an Amish community togther. If one can talk on the phone, why visit? In many settlements, members may use public phones or one in the home of a neighbor, but not install one in their own home. In more progressive settlements, a "community telephone" for several families is permitted. In some cases, individual phones for business outside the home are permissible.

Thus, the Amish do use technology. They try to control it so that it supports rather than tears down their community. Some Amish practices that look silly from the outside are actually ingenious compromises that allow them to use technology, but with restraints, so that it serves the welfare of the community. They often make a distinction between using and owning technology. For example, it may be acceptable to use a public pay phone but not to install a phone in the home. These many compromises create the riddles that enable the Amish to tap the power of technology without sacrificing their community life and identity.

Amish Food and Cooking Practices

The Amish are known for their beautiful gardens and hearty tables. Some of their food traditions such as pie-baking trace back to their roots in Switzerland. Other food habits can be tracked to Germany as well as colonial America. Food practices vary considerably from settlement to settlement, but most Amish families have gardens and preserve large quantities of food—often by canning. Yet, not all food is home grown. Prepared foods such as instant pudding, snack foods, pizza, and soft drinks may be purchased at stores.

In some regions of the country, favorite Amish foods include shoofly pie—eaten as coffee cake with breakfast—snitz (dried apple) pie, applesauce, cornmeal mush, chicken pot pie, homemade noodles, and mashed potatoes smothered with gravy. Snitz pie is a staple at the fellowship meal following Sunday services in some regions. It is not unusual for a mother and her daughters to bake more than thirty pies for a fellowship meal. Noon meals during the week, often called "dinner," are the hearty meal of the day for farm workers.

Some Amish kitchens are equipped with fine cabinetry and have state-of-the-art stoves and refrigerators powered by bottled gas. In more conservative communities, cooking is done on wood stoves and ice is used for refrigeration. Generally speaking, the responsibilities for gardening, food preservation, and cooking fall to the women. Husbands sometimes help to prepare the garden for planting and help to harvest vegetables. Some men help to cook at large social gatherings like weddings or reunions, which may involve two large meals in a day. In recent years, some progressive families have begun hosting outside visitors in their homes for sumptuous Amish meals. This is often done to provide a sideline income as well as to extend a hand of hospitality to outsiders.

Occupations and the Future

Farming has long been the trademark of Amish life. This began to change in the last third of the twentieth century as farmland became more expensive and commercial agriculture became more competitive. Tourist markets and various business opportunities offered Amish people new ways of making a living. In some of the more rural areas, the bulk of Amish families are still tilling the soil. However, in many settlements the majority of households are no longer farming. Agriculture and sideline business are often mixed together. In some areas of Indiana, for example, Amish men work in large recreational vehicle factories.

In many settlements, the Amish have developed hundreds of small private businesses. These enterprises make fine indoor furniture, lawn furniture, gazebos, and storage sheds. Other Amish entrepreneurs operate greenhouses, construction crews, and machine shops. Amish women produce and sell lovely quilts, food preserves, and a wide assortment of handicrafts. Some of businesses are actually owned and operated by Amish women. The plentiful products of these shops are shipped and sold around the world by commercial distributors.

This growing Amish involvement in business signals an important social change that will likely alter Amish life and culture in the years to come. Business involvements will impact child-rearing practices, gender roles, leisure activities, lifestyles, the use of technology, and the speaking of English. Such involvements will bring broader exposure to the outside world. All of these changes will likely modify the traditional understanding of what it means to be separate from the world as the Amish interact with their non-Amish neighbors more frequently.

Donald B. Kraybill
Messiah College
GRANTHAM, PA

For Further Reading

Kraybill, Donald B. *The Riddle of Amish Culture, Revised Edition*. Baltimore, Md.: The Johns Hopkins University Press, 2001.

Kraybill, Donald B. and Carl Bowman. *On the Backroad to Heaven: Old Order Hutterites, Mennonites, Amish and Brethren*. Baltimore, Md.: The Johns Hopkins University Press, 2001.

Kraybill, Donald B. and Steve Nolt. *Amish Enterprise: From Plows to Profits*. Baltimore, Md.: The Johns Hopkins University Press, 1995.

Nolt, Steve. *A History of the Amish*. Intercourse, Pa.: Good Books, 1992.

Scott, Steve. *Why Do They Dress That Way?* Intercourse, Pa.: Good Books, 1986.

Table of Contents

BAKING CHART

Slow oven	250° - 325°
Moderate oven	350° - 375°
Moderate hot oven	375° - 400°
Hot oven	400° - 450°
Very hot oven	450° - 500°
Pastry Shell	450° - 12 to 15 min.
Custard pie	450° - 10 min.
reduce to	350° - 25 min.
Two crust pies with uncooked filling	450° - 10 min.
reduce to	350° - 30 to 40 min.
Two crust pies with cooked filling	440° 450° - 30 min.
Meringue	350° - 10 to 12 min.
Yeast bread loaf	400° - 425° - 40 to 45 min.
Sweet rolls	375° - 15 to 20 min.
Biscuits	450° - 12 to 15 min.
Muffins	425° - 20 to 25 min.
Corn bread	425° - 20 to 30 min.
Gingerbread	425° - 40 to 50 min.
Angel and sponge cakes	325° - finish at 375°
Loaf cake	350° - 375° - 40 to 50 min. depending on size
Layer cake, or cup cakes	350° - 375° - 20 to 30 min.
Cookies	350° - 425° - 6 to 12 min. depending on size

Laura Miller (Grill Cook)

ABBREVIATIONS

c.	- cup	sm.	- small
T.	- tablespoon	pt.	- pint
t.	- teaspoon	med.	- medium
pkg.	- package	gal.	- gallon
lb.	- pound	sq.	- square
qt.	- quart (4 cups)	approx.	- approximately
lg.	- large (29 oz.)	min.	- minutes
oz.	- ounce		

SERVES 100 PEOPLE

Bakes beans	5 gals.	Meat loaf	24 lbs.
Beef	40 lbs.	Milk	6 gals.
Beets	30 lbs.	Nuts	3 lbs.
Bread	10 loaves	Olives	1¾ lbs.
Butter	3 lbs.	Pickles	2 qts.
Cakes	8	Pies	18
Carrots	3 lbs.	Potatoes	35 lbs.
Cheese	3 lbs.	Potato salad	12 qts.
Chicken pot pie	40 lbs.	Roast pork	40 lbs.
Coffee	3 lbs.	Rolls	200
Cream	3 qts.	Salad dressing	3 qts.
Fruit cocktail	2½ gals.	Scalloped potatoes	5 gals.
Fruit juice	4 #10 cans	Soup	5 gals.
Fruit salad	12 qts.	Tomato juice	4 #10 cans
Ham	40 lbs.	Vegetable	4 #10 cans
Hamburger	30 to 36 lbs.	Weiners	25 lbs.
Ice cream	4 gals.	Vegetable salad	20 qts.
Lettuce	20 heads	Whipping cream	4 pts.

Betty A. Hershberger (Grill Cook)

EQUIVALENT MEASURES

Dash or speck	=	less than 1/8 t.
3 t.	=	1 T.
4 T.	=	¼ c.
5⅓ T.	=	⅓ c.
8 T.	=	½ c.
10⅔ T.	=	⅔ c.
12 T.	=	¾ c.
16 T.	=	1 c.
2 c.	=	1 pint
4 c.	=	1 quart
4 quarts	=	1 gallon
8 ozs.	=	1 cup
4 ozs.	=	¼ lb.
16 ozs.	=	1 lb.

CONTENTS OF CANS

SIZE	AVERAGE CONTENTS
No. 1½ flat	1 c.
8 oz.	1 c.
No. 300	1¾ c.
No. 1 tall	2 c.
No. 303	2 c.
No. 2	2½ c.
No. 2½	3½ c.
No. 3 cylinder	5¾ c.
No. 10	12 c.

Lydia Ann Miller

EQUIVALENTS

BAKING ITEMS

Bread Crumbs, Dry	1 cup	= 3 to 4 dried bread slices
Soft	1 cup	= 1½ fresh bread slices
Flour, all purpose	1 lb.	= 4 cups
Gelatin, unflavored	1 envelope	= 1 tablespoon
Graham Cracker Crumbs	1 cup	= 13 square graham crackers finely crushed
Margarine		
Solid Regular	1 stick	= 8 tablespoons
		= ½ cup
		= ¼ lb.
Soft	1 container	= 1 cup
		= ½ lb.
Marshmallows	1 regular marshmallow	= 10 miniature
	100 to 110 miniature marshmallows	= 1 cup
Nuts, chopped (peanuts, pecans, walnuts)	4½ ozs.	= 1 cup
Sugar		
Brown	1 lb.	= 2¼ cups packed
Confectioners	1 lb.	= 4½ cups sifted
Granulated	1 lb.	= 2¼ cups

CHEESES

Natural Chunk or Process Cheese	4 ozs.	= 1 cup shredded or cubed
Cottage	1 lb.	= 2 cups
Cream	8 ozs.	= 1 cup

FRUITS AND VEGETABLES

Apples	3 medium (1 lb.)	= 3 cups sliced
Coconut	3½ oz. can shredded	= 1⅓ cups
Lemon or Lime	1 medium	= 2 to 3 tablespoons juice = 1 tablespoon grated rind
Onion	1 medium	= ½ cup chopped
Orange	1 medium	= ⅓ to ½ cup juice = 1 to 2 tablespoons grated rind
Potatoes	3 medium (1 lb.)	= 2¼ cups mashed

RICE AND PASTAS

Macaroni, uncooked	4 ozs. (1 cup)	= 2 cups cooked
Noodles, uncooked	4 ozs. (1½ to 2 cups)	= 2 cups cooked
Rice		
Precooked	1 cup	= 2 cups cooked
Uncooked	1 cup	= 3 cups cooked
Spaghetti, uncooked	1 lb.	= 6½ cups cooked

COOKING TERMS

BASTE: Spoon liquid over meat or other foods during cooking to add flavor and prevent drying of the surface. The liquid may be melted fat, meat drippings or sauce.

BEAT: Thoroughly combine ingredients and incorporate air with a rapid regular motion.

BLEND: Thoroughly combine two or more ingredients or prepare food in an electric blender.

BOIL: Cook in liquid in which bubbles rise continually to the surface and break.

CHILL: Refrigerate until cold.

CHOP: Cut into pieces of random size.

COAT: Cover surface of food evenly.

COOL: Allow to come to room temperature.

CREAM: Soften a fat, such as margarine, by beating with a spoon or mixer. This usually refers to blending a sugar and a fat together.

CUBE: Cut into pieces of uniform size and shape, usually ½ inch or larger.

CUT IN: Combine solid fat with dry ingredients by using a pastry blender or two knives in a scissor motion until particles are of desired size, i.e., coarse crumbs.

DASH: Add less than 1/8 teaspoon of an ingredient.

DOT: Evenly distribute small amounts of an ingredient such as margarine or preserves.

Breads, Rolls, Doughnuts & Cereals

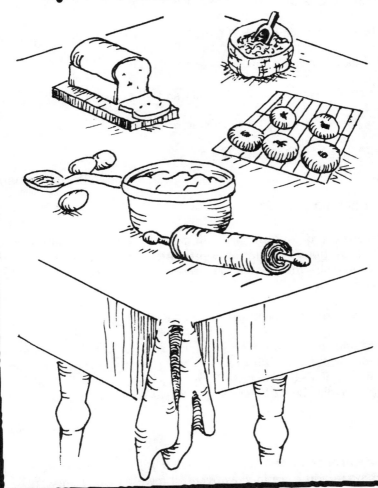

TABLE OF SUBSTITUTIONS

1 c. bottled milk equals ½ c. evaporated milk, plus ½ c. water.

1 c. sour milk equals 1 c. sweet milk into which 1 T. vinegar or lemon juice has been added.

1 square chocolate equals 3 T. cocoa.

1 T. cornstarch equals 2 T. of flour for thickening gravies.

1 t. baking powder equals ¼ t. soda plus ½ t. cream of tartar.

1 t. baking powder equals 1 t. soda with ½ c. sour cream or milk.

½ t. baking powder equals 1 egg

1 c. heavy cream equals ¼ c. milk and ¼ c. lard.

1 T. Clear-Jel equals 1 T. cornstarch

Butter, size of walnut equals 1 T.

Katie Miller (Gift Shop)

A RECIPE TO LIVE BY

Blend one cup of love and one half cup of kindness, add alternately in small portions one cup of appreciation and 3 cups of pleasant companionship into which has been sifted three teaspoons of deserving praise.

Flavor with one teaspoon carefully chosen advise.

Lightly fold in one cup of cheerfulness to which has been added a pinch of sorrow. Pour with tender care into small clean hearts and let bake until well matured. Turn out on the surface of society. Humbly invoke God's blessing and it will serve all mankind.

Katie Miller (Gift Shop)

A stale loaf of bread tastes almost fresh if you wrap it in a wet towel, set on a pan and bake in slow oven till towel is almost dry.

Breads, Rolls, Doughnuts & Cereals

APPLE FRITTER BATTER

2 c. milk
3 eggs
1 t. baking powder

½ t. salt
2 c. flour

Mix well. Dip sliced apples in batter. Fry in butter.

Mary Yoder (Bakery)

BRAN MUFFINS

1 c. wheat bran
1 c. boiling water

Let set for a few minutes, then add:

½ c. oleo or shortening
2 eggs
2½ c. flour
½ t. salt

1¼ c. sugar
½ qt. buttermilk
2½ t. soda

Mix all together in order given. Put in muffin tins and bake at 400° till nice and brown and top springs back when lightly touched.

Mary Esther Miller (Bakery Manager)
Elsie Miller (Grill Cook)

1

BREAKFAST CEREAL

10 c. quick rolled oats
1 pkg. coconut
2 c. raw sugar
1 c. corn oil

1 can wheat germ
4 c. all-bran
1 T. salt

Mix and put in pans. Toast 20 min. in oven at 350°, stirring twice during that time. Add Grapenuts to the mixture for a variation.

Alma Hershberger (Bakery)

BLUEBERRY MUFFINS

4 c. flour
1 t. salt
2 eggs, well beaten
¾ c. oil
2 T. sugar

6 t. baking powder
½ c. sugar
2 c. milk
2 c. blueberries

Sift together flour, baking powder, salt and ½ c. sugar. Combine eggs, milk, and oil. Add all at once to flour mixture. Stir until dry ingredients are moist, but still lumpy. Fold in blueberries. Fill greased muffin pans ⅔ full. Sprinkle with 1 T. sugar. Bake in hot oven (400°) about 25 min.

Mary Esther Miller (Bakery)

The greatest objectives are reached by the heart, not by the head.

DILLY BREAD

1 T. yeast
1 c. cottage cheese, lukewarm
1 T. minced onion
2 t. dill seed
¼ t. soda
2¼ to 2½ c. flour

¼ c. water
2 T. sugar
1 T. butter
1 t. salt
1 egg, unbeaten

Soften yeast with water. Combine cottage cheese, sugar, onion, butter, dill seed, salt, soda, egg and softened yeast in mixing bowl. Add flour to form a stiff dough, beating well after each addition. Cover, let rise in warm place until light and double in size (50-60) min. Stir down dough. Turn into well greased pans. Let rise until light. Bake 30-40 min. at 350° or until golden brown. Brush with butter and sprinkle with salt. Makes 3 small loaves.

Mary Esther Miller (Bakery)

"Yes" can say "I love you." But when said with a set jaw and narrowed eyes, it can mean "I hate you."

DUTCH APPLE BREAD

2 c. flour
3 t. baking powder
2 T. sugar
1 t. salt

1 egg
1 c. milk
2 T. butter or shortening

Sift flour and add baking powder, salt, and sugar. Sift again. Cut softened butter into dry ingredients as for pastry. Add beaten egg and milk. Beat thoroughly until well blended. Spread in a greased shallow pan 8×12. Press apple slices over the top and sprinkle with sugar and cinnamon. Bake at 400° for 25-30 min.

Ida Weaver (Cook)

REQUIREMENTS OF AN 1869 KITCHEN—"If parents wish their daughters to grow up with good domestic habits, they should have, as one means of securing this result, a neat and cheerful kitchen," say the Beechers.

A kitchen should always, if possible, be entirely above ground and well lighted.

It should have a large sink, and with a drain running underground so that all the premises may be kept sweet and clean.

If flowers and shrubs be cultivated around the (kitchen) door and windows, and the yard near them be well turfed, it will add much to the kitchen's agreeable appearance.

The walls should be cleaned often and whitewashed to promote a neat look and pure air. The floor of a kitchen should be painted, or where it is better, covered with an oil cloth.

He who is on the road to Heaven should not be content to go alone!

DINNER ROLLS

Mix together:

1 pkg. yeast
1 T. sugar

Beat in 3 eggs with 1 c. warm water.

Add:

½ c. sugar
½ c. shortening
½ t. salt
5 c. flour

Knead well. Let stand in refrigerator overnight, divide in 2 parts and roll out in 12″ circle, cut into 16 wedges. Roll up starting with wide side, let rise 3-4 hours. Bake at 400° for 15 min. Brush with butter, serve while warm.

Meredith Mast (Dishwasher)

COFFEE CAKE

1 c. butter
1½ c. sugar
3 eggs
3½ c. flour
½ t. baking soda

½ t. baking powder
½ t. salt
1 t. vanilla
¾ c. sour cream

Cream together the butter, sugar, and eggs. Sift dry ingredients and add to creamed mixture. Add sour cream and vanilla.

Crumb Mixture:

1 c. brown sugar
1 T. flour
2 t. cinnamon

4 T. butter
½ c. nuts, chopped

Mix these ingredients thoroughly. Place half of dough in a greased 9"x13" pan. Top it with half of the crumb mixture. Put the remaining dough on top and cover with the remaining crumbs. Bake at 300° 40-45 minutes.

Mary Yoder (Baker)

CAKE DOUGHNUTS

½ c. butter
3 eggs, beaten
pinch of salt
6 t. baking powder

2 c. sugar
2 c. milk
½ t. nutmeg
1 c. flour

Cream together the butter and sugar. Add the rest of the ingredients, using enough flour to make a soft dough. Roll, cut, and fry in deep fat. Sprinkle the doughnuts with sugar while they are hot.

Rose Schrock (Baker)

Be kindly affectioned one to another with brotherly love; in honour preferring one another; Not slothful in business; fervent in spirit; serving the Lord; Rejoicing in hope; patient in tribulation; continuing instant in prayer; Distributing to the necessity of the saints; given to hospitality.

Rom. 12:10-13

FLUFFY RAISED DOUGHNUTS

Scald 2 c. of milk and cool to lukewarm.

Add:

1 cake yeast	2 eggs, well beaten
½ c. lard	2 t. salt
½ c. sugar	7 c. flour

Knead until smooth. Let rise until doubled, then roll out and cut with doughnut cutter. Let rise again and fry in hot fat.

Millie Whetstone (Cook)

Pray earnestly; you can't expect a thousand-dollar answer to a ten-cent prayer!

GRANOLA

Mix:

4¼ lbs. oatmeal	2 lbs. brown sugar
1½ c. corn oil	½ c. honey
1½ lb. coconut	2 lbs. almonds
2 lbs. raisins	2 t. salt
1 t. cinnamon	4 t. vanilla

Bake at 225° for 1½ hours, stirring every 15 min.

Mary Esther Miller (Bakery)

Perk up a simple meal with an ounce or two of godly conversation.

GLAZED POTATO DOUGHNUTS

1 pkg. active dry yeast
¼ c. warm water
1 c. milk (scalded)
¼ c. shortening
¼ c. sugar
1 t. salt

¾ c. mashed potatoes
2 eggs, beaten
5 to 6 c. sifted flour
1 lb. powdered sugar
6 T. water
1 T. vanilla

Dissolve yeast in warm water. Combine milk, sugar, shortening and salt. Cool until lukewarm. Stir in dissolved yeast, potatoes, and eggs. Gradually add enough flour to make soft dough. Turn onto lightly floured surface, knead until smooth. Place in lightly greased bowl, cover bowl. Let rise in a warm place until doubled (1 to 1½ hours). Now roll the dough to ½" thickness, cut with 3" doughnut cutter. Cover, let rise until double (about 30 min.). Meanwhile stir powdered sugar, water and vanilla together. Fry cutout doughnuts in deep hot fat at 375°. Drain on absorbent paper. Drop hot doughnuts into glaze. Place on a cooking rack until glaze is set. Yields about 3½ dozen.

Laura Anna Miller (Grill Worker)

HOMEMADE BISCUITS

3 c. flour
¼ lb. melted oleo
1 c. milk

5 t. baking powder
pinch of salt

Fold all together, but do not over mix. Roll out to approximately¼- 3/8" thick. Cut with biscuit cutter, butter top side and bake at 350° for approximately 10-12 min. or until golden brown.

Lydia Ann Miller (Head Cook)

MOCK ECLAIRS

1 box yellow cake mix
1 box vanilla pudding
chocolate fudge topping

Mix and bake cake as directed on package in 13×9×2 pan. Cut into sixteen 4½×1½ inch pieces. Cut each piece in half lengthwise. Spread one tablespoon pudding between cake pieces and top with chocolate fudge topping. Store in refrigerator until ready to use.

Polly Yoder

MUFFINS

Preheat oven to 400°.

1 egg	½ c. sugar
½ c. milk	2 t. baking powder
¼ c. oil	½ t. salt
1½ c. flour	

Beat egg and stir in milk and oil. Add other ingredients and mix until flour is moistened. Batter will be lumpy. Fill greased muffin cups ⅔ full. Bake 20 min. For blueberry muffins, add blueberries to batter before baking.

Doris Miller (Waitress)
Esther Nisley (Pie Baker)

FAVORITE QUICK SUPPER

Measure 3 c. flour into bowl; answer doorbell. Take bowl off small son's head; sweep up flour. Measure 3 c. flour into bowl, add shortening. Change baby's diaper, wash shortening from son's hand and face. Add ¼ c. shortening to flour, mix well. Rock crying baby for 10 minutes. Answer doorbell. Put son in tub and scrub well. Scrape flour and shortening mixture from floor, adding enough tears to relieve tension. Open 1 can beans and serve with remaining strength.

OLD RECIPE - PAPOOSES

Sift together and set aside:

1 c. sifted flour   ½ t. salt
1½ t. baking powder

Cream together:

½ c. sugar   2 T. fat
1 t. vanilla

Add 1 egg to the sugar mixture and beat until smooth. Add about half of the flour mixture and combine. Add ⅓ c. of milk and the remaining flour, and mix. In a saucepan, which has a tight-fitting cover, heat 2 c. of maple syrup to boiling, then turn heat down so syrup simmers. Drop dough by spoonfuls into the hot syrup, cover the pan, and cook for 20 min. Serve at once.

                              Kathy Sue Yoder (Busser)

QUICK-BREAD ENGLISH MUFFINS

1½ c. whole wheat flour   ½ c. cornmeal
1 t. salt (optional)   2½ t. baking powder
½ c. dried milk powder   2 T. vegetable oil
2 T. honey   1½ c. water

Mix dry ingredients together. Add oil and honey. Add one cup water, stir until all ingredients are moist. Add remaining water as necessary to produce a batter thicker than pancake batter, but still spreads. Bake in covered skillet in 4" rings.

                              Carolyn Mast (Waitress)

If a task is once begun
Never leave it till it's done
Be the labor great or small
Do it well or not at all.

TOMMY LOMIES BISCUITS

2 large c. flour
4 t. baking powder
4 T. shortening

¾ c. milk
1½ T. sugar

Mix and knead, cut or drop. Bake in 400° oven for 20 min.

Betty Miller (Pie Baker)

PANCAKES

2 eggs
6 T. cooking oil or oleo
4 t. baking powder

2 t. sugar
1 t. salt
2 big cups flour

Add milk till batter is thin. Drop by spoonfuls on hot greased griddle, turning when pancakes puff and bubble.

Esther Nisley (Pie Baker)
Mary Ann Schlabach (Waitress)

 What a beautiful world when your heart gets involved.

PANCAKES

1 heaping c. New Rinkle flour
½ t. soda
⅓ or ½ c. vegetable oil
1 T. sugar

2 t. baking powder
1 egg, beaten
½ t. salt
milk

Variation: use ½ or ⅓ c. whole wheat flour with rest of pastry flour.

Doris Miller (Waitress)

Children seldom misquote you; they repeat word for word what you SHOULD NOT have said!

RAISED DONUTS

½ c. sugar
½ c. oil
2 T. yeast
2 eggs, beaten

2 t. salt
3 c. water
1 t. nutmeg
8 c. flour

Dissolve yeast in 1 c. warm water. Beat eggs and add sugar, oil, salt, 2 c. hot water, nutmeg and some flour. Then add yeast mixture and the rest of flour. Let rise 1½ hour, working down every ½ hour. Roll out ½" thick and cut. Cover and let rise ½ hour. Fry in hot fat about 400° till nice and brown. Glaze while hot.

Rose Schrock (Baker)

RAISED DOUGHNUTS

6 egg yolks, beaten
3½ c. scalded milk
1 c. lard
12-13 c. Robin Hood flour

1 c. sugar
1 c. mashed potatoes
3 pkg. yeast (soaked in ½ c. lukewarm potato water)

Mix all together and let rise double in size. Punch down and let rise double again. Roll and cut and let rise again. Deep fry (in lard). Glaze while still warm.

Glaze: powdered sugar and warm water.

Mabel Hershberger (Cashier)

11

HOMEMADE PANCAKES

Mix:

1¼ c. flour	3 T. sugar
3 t. baking powder	

Add:

1 egg	1 c. milk
3 T. oleo	

Mix well and fry as any other pancakes. You can mix a larger batch of the dry ingredients (flour, sugar and baking powder), then store and add egg, milk and oleo when ready to use.

Lydia Ann Miller (Cook)

What they leave IN their children should concern parents more than what they leave TO them.

WHOLE WHEAT MUFFINS

2 c. whole wheat graham flour	1 t. soda
½ t. salt	4 T. sugar
1½ c. sour milk or buttermilk	1 egg, beaten
3 T. melted lard	½ c. raisins

Combine flour, salt, and sugar. Add sour milk, egg and lard. Add raisins and soda. Bake in hot oven (375°) for 25 min. Makes 12 gems. This is a very old recipe, used by my grandmother. We like to break these apart and eat them with sugar and milk, also fresh fruit.

Mary Ann Schlabach (Waitress)

WHEAT BREAD

Mix together and let set 20 min.

4 c. Wheat Chex
2 c. water (almost boiling)
1 stick oleo

2½ c. scalded milk
1 c. sugar
1 T. salt

Add rest of ingredients and beat till smooth..

2 pkgs. dry yeast dissolved in
½ c. warm water

1 T. sugar
9 c. flour

This mixture will be sticky. Bake at 325° for 35-45 min.

Betti Kauffman (Cashier-Hostess)

WAFFLES

3 c. flour
1 t. salt
2 t. sugar

½ c. melted butter
2 c. milk
4 eggs, separated

Beat egg yolks, add milk and beat 1 min. Add dry ingredients and melted butter and beat again. Fold in stiffly beaten egg whites. Bake on hot waffle iron.

Edna Slabach (Cook)

STIR FRY PANCAKES

3 eggs
1 c. milk
1 c. flour

½ t. salt
½ t. baking powder

Pour all ingredients into a blender and blend well. Melt ½ stick of butter in an electric frying pan at 425°. Pour all of the batter into pan and stir while frying.

Ginger Yoder (Waitress)

13

SOURDOUGH STARTER

2 c. flour
2 c. warm water
1 pkg. yeast

Mix together and let set uncovered overnight in a warm place. Put in covered container and keep refrigerated. Feed once or twice a week with:

1 c. milk
1 c. flour
¼ c. sugar

Mix together first and then add to starter. After feeding do not use for 24 hours.

Mary Esther Miller (Bakery Manager)

Sitting still and wishing
Makes no person great.
The good Lord sends the fishing
But you must dig the bait!

SOURDOUGH BISCUITS

1 c. starter
⅓ c. cooking oil
¾ t. soda
¼ t. salt
1 c. flour

Mix starter and oil, add dry ingredients and mix well. Drop by table-spoon on an ungreased cookie sheet. Bake at 350° for 10-15 min.

Mary Esther Miller (Bakery Manager)

SOURDOUGH BANANA NUT LOAF

1 c. sourdough starter	2 c. flour
1 c. mashed bananas	2 t. baking powder
½ c. shortening	1 t. baking soda
1 c. sugar	1 t. salt
2 eggs	½ c. nuts, chopped

Cream together the shortening, bananas, and sugar. Add starter and eggs. Mix well. Add dry ingredients and nuts. Pour into 2 greased and floured loaf pans. Bake at 350° for 40 minutes.

Mary Esther Miller
(Bakery Manager)

APPLE ROLLS

4 c. flour	1 t. salt
¼ c. sugar	2 T. + 2 t. baking powder
3 T. shortening	milk
butter	apples, peeled and chopped

Syrup:

3 c. sugar	2 c. hot water
2 t. flour	1 t. salt

Combine syrup ingredients in sauce pan and keep on low heat. Stir together remaining dry ingredients and cut in shortening till crumbly. Add enough milk to make a soft dough. Roll out, then spread with butter and sprinkle with chopped apples. Roll dough up into a log and slice. Place rolls in pan, pour hot syrup over them, and bake at 350° for 45 minutes.

Rose Schrock (Baker)

CAKE MIX ROLLS

2 pkg. yeast	butter
2 c. warm water	brown sugar
1 pkg. yellow cake mix	cinnamon
4 c. flour	

Dissolve yeast in warm water. Add cake mix and flour, then mix. Let dough rise until double in bulk. Roll out and spread with butter and brown sugar. Sprinkle with cinnamon. Roll up into a log and slice. Place rolls in baking pan and let rise again. Bake at 350° for 10-20 minutes.

Carolyn Yoder (Baker)

COCOA ROLL

6 eggs, separated
⅓ c. cocoa
½ t. baking powder
1 t. vanilla

¾ c. sugar
¼ c. flour
pinch of salt

Beat egg yolks until thick, then add sugar. Combine cocoa, flour, baking powder, and salt. Add to egg yolks with vanilla. Beat egg whites until stiff, then gently fold in batter. Spread in pan. Grease jelly roll pan, line with waxed paper and grease again. Bake at 350° for 20-25 min.

Melissa Hershberger (Bakery Cashier)

Serving the Lord is much like riding a bicycle—either you keep moving forward, or you fall down.

FRENCH BREAKFAST PUFFS

½ c. sugar
⅓ c. shortening
1½ t. baking powder
½ t. salt
¼ t. nutmeg
½ c. milk

1 egg
1½ c. flour
½ c. sugar
6 T. butter
1 t. cinnamon

Cream shortening, ½ c. sugar, egg. Sift flour, baking powder, salt and nutmeg. Add to creamed mixture. Alternate with milk, beating well after each addition. Fill greased muffin tins ⅔ full. Bake at 350° for 20-25 min. Remove from pan immediately. Dip in melted butter and then sugar, cinnamon mixture till top is coated. Makes 12.

Edna Borntrager (Cook)

JELLY ROLL

3 eggs
⅓ c. water
1 t. vanilla
1 c. cake flour
½ c. sugar

1 t. baking powder
¼ t. salt
⅔ c. jelly or jam
powdered sugar

Heat oven to 375°. Line 15½ × 10½ × 1 inch jelly roll pan with waxed paper, grease. Beat eggs in small bowl until thick and lemon colored, about 5 minutes. Pour eggs into large mixer bowl, beat in sugar gradually. Blend in water and vanilla on low speed. Add flour, baking powder and salt gradually, beating until batter is smooth. Pour into pan, spreading batter to corners. Bake 12-15 min., or until wooden pick inserted in center comes out clean. Loosen cake from edges of pan, invert on towel sprinkled with powdered sugar. Carefully remove paper. While cake is hot, roll in towel. When almost cool, unroll. Beat jelly slightly with fork to soften, spread over cake. Roll up, sprinkle with powdered sugar. Serves 10.

Marlene Eash (Cook)

LONG JOHNS

Dissolve 1 pkg. yeast in ¼ c. lukewarm water. Heat 1 pint milk to boiling point. Add to hot milk ½ c. sugar, ½ c. lard, 1 t. salt. Let cool to lukewarm. Then add yeast mixture. Add 6 c. Robin Hood flour. Cover and let rise. Work it down, let rise again, then roll out and cut in pieces. Let rise and fry in deep fat.

Filling

Mix 1½ rounded t. flour and ½ T. sugar. Then mix with ½ c. milk and cook. When cold, add ½ t. vanilla. Cream ½ c. white sugar and ½ c. Crisco. Then add flavor and milk mixture. Add 1¼ c. or more powdered sugar, cream well. When Long Johns are cooled, cut tops and fill with filling.

Ada Schrock (Cook)

TWIST CINNAMON ROLLS WITH CARAMEL ICING

2 c. scalded milk
2 c. warm water
4 pkg. yeast
½ lb. margarine
4 eggs, beaten

12-13 c. flour
1 c. sugar
½ t. salt
1 t. nutmeg

Place yeast in bowl, add 2 c. warm water and sprinkle 2 t. sugar over top. Stir slightly. Scald milk with approx. ⅓ c. of the sugar. Place margarine in bowl and pour hot milk over it to melt. Stir. Cool slightly, add salt, beaten eggs and ⅔ c. sugar mixed with nutmeg. Also add yeast mixture. Stir in approx. 12-13 c. flour. Knead. Keep dough quite sticky. Let rise till double. Grease 4 pizza pans and set aside. Divide dough into 12 equal parts. Roll out one part to fit in a pizza pan—spread with melted butter, or margarine and sprinkle with cinnamon and brown sugar. Do this two more times. You will have 3 layers of dough on each pan. Place a glass in the middle of the pan, as a guideline, and cut 1½ inch pie wedges to the rim of the glass. Pick up a pie wedge and give it a couple of twists then lay down again. Do this all around the pan. Let rise and bake at 325° for 20-25 min. Turn rolls out of pans and turn right side up to cool. While hot, ice with caramel icing.

Caramel Icing

½ lb. margarine
1 c. brown sugar

½ c. milk or cream

Boil until smooth. Add 3½ c. powdered sugar while warm and beat well.

Rose Borntrager (Hostess)

I can be about as happy
As I make up my mind to be;
For it's not so much what happens
As what's in the heart of me!

OATMEAL ROLLS

1 c. oatmeal   2 c. boiling water
3 T. butter

Pour boiling water over oatmeal and butter. Let stand for 20 min. In another bowl mix and add to first mixture:

⅔ c. brown sugar   1 T. white sugar
1½ t. salt   2 pkg. yeast, softened in
4 c. white flour   ⅓ c. warm water
1 c. whole wheat flour

Add nutmeg and orange peel if desired. Let rise to double size twice, then form into rolls or bread. Let rise again (double size). Bake for 20-30 min. at 350°.

Mabel Hershberger (Cashier)

SWEET BUNS

Mix together in large bowl:

¼ c. sugar   2 T. shortening
1½ t. salt   1 c. milk (scalded)

Let cool till lukewarm and add:

1 pkg. dry yeast. Stir till dissolved. Let stand 5 min. Sift 3½ c. flour and add ½ to first mixture. Beat 100 strokes (important). Add 1 egg and beat thoroughly. Add rest of flour and mix well. Let rise until double (1-2 hrs.). Shape into cinnamon rolls or whatever shape you choose. Let rise 1-2 hrs. Bake 10-15 min. at 400°.

Ida Weaver (Cook)

APPLE BREAD

1 c. sugar	½ t. salt
½ c. shortening	2 c. apples, chopped (about
2 eggs	4 medium apples)
1 t. vanilla	½ c. nuts, chopped
2 c. flour	1 T. sugar
1 t. baking powder	¼ t. cinnamon
1 t. baking soda	

Preheat oven to 350°. Grease and flour 9×5×3 inch pan. Mix 1 c. sugar, shortening, eggs and vanilla. Stir in dry ingredients until smooth. Add apples and nuts. Mix well. Spread into pan. Mix 1 T. sugar and cinnamon. Sprinkle over batter. Bake for 50-60 min. Remove from pan. Cool before slicing.

Esther Nisley (Bakery)

APPLE BREAD

2 c. brown sugar	1 c. butter
4 eggs	3 c. grated apples
4 c. flour	1 t. salt
2 t. soda	1 t. vanilla
3 T. buttermilk	2 c. pecans
2 t. cinnamon	

Cream sugar and butter. Add eggs and beat well. Add apples—mix in dry ingredients, buttermilk and vanilla. Add pecans. Put in loaf pans and bake at 350° for 45 min. or till done. Delicious! Top can be sprinkled with sugar and cinnamon mixed together.

Elizabeth Miller (Cleaning)

 "A word of advice—don't give it."

When things get rough, remember—it's rubbing that brings out the shine!

BANANA BREAD

1 c. shortening	2 c. sugar
4 eggs	6 bananas, crushed
½ c. nuts	4 c. flour
2 t. soda	2 t. salt

Cream shortening and sugar. Add eggs, bananas, nuts, and flour which has been sifted with soda and salt. Place in loaf pan. Bake at 350° for 50-60 min. This is good to freeze in foil.

Mary Esther Miller (Bakery)
Wilma Weaver (Waitress)
Esther Nisley (Pie Baker)

BANANA BREAD

Mix together:

1 c. brown sugar	2 c. mashed bananas
1 c. white sugar	3 t. vanilla
1 c. vegetable oil	½ c. wheat germ
3 eggs	3 c. flour
2 t. soda	1 t. salt
½ t. baking powder	1 c. walnut bits

Bake at 350° for 40-45 min. The same recipe can be used for pumpkin or zucchini bread. Add cinnamon for pumpkin bread.

Ruth Ann Bontrager (Busser)
Lydia Gingerich (Cashier-Bakery)

BROWN BREAD

Dissolve 1 pkg. yeast in ½ c. warm water. Scald 1½ c. rich milk, add 4 T. brown sugar, 1 T. salt, and 2 T. butter. Cool to lukewarm, then add yeast and water, and 1¾ c. graham flour, and 3¼ c. (Robin Hood) flour. Mix then knead 10 minutes. Cover and let rise in warm place till double in bulk. Turn out and knead thoroughly. Place in well greased pans. Cover and let rise till light, about 1 hour. Bake in a 350° oven for about 1 hour.

Lizzie Ann Bontrager (Cook)

BREAD

1st   Mix and set aside:

¾ c. warm water	2 T. yeast
½ t. sugar	

2nd

2½ c. very warm water	½ c. sugar
2 T. salt	⅓ c. oil

Mix together these 4 ingredients. Beat in 2 c. whole wheat flour with egg beater. Then add yeast solution and beat in 2 more cups of flour (white) with egg beater. Then rest of flour I mix by hand (using 2 c. brown flour and 8½ c. white flour all together). Sometimes it doesn't take that much flour. I just add enough so it isn't sticky at all. Put in greased tupperware bowl with lid and let rise 1 hour. Punch down and let rise ½ hour, repeat 2 more times every ½ hour. Divide in 4 parts and roll out with rolling pin, then put in pans and let rise till 1" above pans. Bake in preheated oven for 25 min. at 350° or nice-n-brown bag. When done, take out of pans and grease top. Then when cooled off a little, put in plastic bags. Also prick the bread as soon as you put it in pans.

Norine Borkholder (Cook)

CRANBERRY BREAD

Mix together:

2 eggs
4 T. hot water

4 T. melted butter
1 c. orange juice

Add:

4 c. flour
1 t. salt
1 t. soda

2 c. sugar
3 t. baking powder
2 c. sliced cranberries

Add nuts if desired. Makes 3 or 4 small loaves. Bake at 325° for 1 hour or until done.

Mary Esther Miller (Bakery)

CORN BREAD

¾ c. sugar
1 c. shortening
2 eggs
1 c. sour milk
1 t. cream of tartar

1¼ c. corn meal
1 c. flour
1 t. soda
1 t. salt

Mix all ingredients and pour into greased pans. Bake at 400° for 20-25 min.

Lillian Miller (Cashier-Hostess)

Hardening of the heart ages people more quickly than hardening of the arteries!

ENGLISH MUFFIN BREAD

5½ c. flour
¼ t. soda
2 pkg. yeast
2 c. milk

1 T. sugar
1½ t. salt
½ c. water

Mix 3 c. flour and dry ingredients. Heat milk and water. Beat together, add rest of flour and mix well. Grease 2 loaf pans and sprinkle with corn meal. Divide dough for 2 pans. Let rise for 45 min. Bake for 45 min. in 350° oven.

Mabel Hershberger (Cashier)
Rosa Borntrager (Dutch Country Gifts)

BOHEMIAN KOLACKES (Bread Rolls)

½ c. milk
2 pkg. dry yeast
½ c. warm water
¾ c. butter

1 t. salt
4 egg yolks
4½ c. all-purpose flour
½ c. sugar

Topping:

2 T. melted butter

2 T. powdered sugar

Scald milk, cool to lukewarm. Dissolve yeast in the warm water. Cream butter, sugar, salt and egg yolks. Add yeast, milk and 1½ c. flour. Stir in enough remaining flour to make a soft dough. Place in a lightly greased bowl, turn dough to grease top. Cover and let rise in warm place until doubled. Stir down, turn onto lightly floured board and divide in 24 pieces of equal size, shape each into a ball. Cover and let set 10-15 min. Place 2″ apart on greased cookie sheet. Press dough from center outward to make a hollow. Fill each hollow with filling (jam) of your choice. Cover and let rise in a warm place until doubled. Bake at 350° for 15-18 min. or until lightly browned. Brush tops of rolls with melted butter and sprinkle lightly with powdered sugar, or glaze with a thin frosting mixture.

Edna Borntrager (Cook)

FRENCH BREAD

1 heaping T. butter	1 heaping T. salt
1 heaping T. sugar	2 c. boiling water
1 T. dry yeast	⅔ c. lukewarm water

About 6 to 6½ c. unbleached hard-wheat white flour

In a large mixing bowl combine the butter, salt, and sugar and 2 c. boiling water. Stir a little as it dissolves. Sprinkle the yeast over ⅔ c. lukewarm water in a bowl and allow it to dissolve. When the butter mixture is also lukewarm, combine the two and mix well. Add 4 c. of flour gradually. Beat it vigorously with a wooden spoon for about 10 min. Then add flour until the dough is too stiff to mix with a spoon. Turn it out on a floured board and knead until it is satiny smooth and elastic. Let it rise in a warm place for about 1½ hours. Punch it down and let it rise about 1 hour. Prepare the baking sheet by buttering it and sprinkling yellow cornmeal lightly over the butter.

Divide the dough into 3 parts and shape each into a long slender loaf. Do this by rolling it into a rectangle 14×8. Roll up the long side and seal the seam. Let them rise until almost double. Brush the tops with cold water and cut diagonal slits across the top with a very sharp knife. Bake them at 400° for 45 min., brushing them with cold water every 15 min. This helps make the crisp hard crust for which french bread is famous.

Carolyn Mast (Waitress)

HONEY WHEAT BREAD

2 T. yeast	⅓ c. vegetable oil
1 c. lukewarm water	⅓ c. honey
½ t. sugar	1 T. salt
2 c. hot water	1½ c. whole wheat flour
1½ c. bread flour	

Beat well, add yeast mixture and 6 c. of bread flour and knead well, about 10 min. Let rest 15 min., knead, let rise about 1 hour. Knead again and let rise 1 hour. Then divide into 3 loaves and rise 1½ hours. Bake at 350° for 30 min.

Fannie Yoder (Cook)

NO-KNEAD BREAD

3 pkg. dry yeast
2 eggs
10 c. flour
4 t. salt

3¾ c. warm water
6 T. soft margarine
6 T. sugar

For wheat bread, use 5 c. white flour and 5 c. whole wheat flour.

Dissolve yeast in warm water; add remaining ingredients one by one. Mix by hand until moist. Seal in tupperware fix-n-mix bowl until seal pops off. Divide into 4 equal parts and put each into greased bread pan. Cover with towel and let rise ½ hour. Bake at 350° for about ½ hour. Makes 4 loaves.

Betty Miller (Pie Baker)
Lydia Ann Miller

 Will power is the ability to eat one salted peanut.

PUMPKIN BREAD

1½ c. sugar
1⅔ c. flour
¼ t. baking powder
1 t. soda
½ t. cloves
½ c. salad oil

1 c. pumpkin
2 eggs
½ c. nuts (optional)
¾ t. salt
½ t. cinnamon
½ c. water

Combine all ingredients and mix for 3 min. Then fold in nuts. Spread mixture in a well greased loaf pan. Bake at 325° for 1 hour and 20 min. Makes one loaf.

Betti Kauffman (Cashier-Hostess)

GOOD BREAD

Mix together:

1½ c. warm water
2 T. yeast (rounded)
1 t. sugar

Mix together:

5 c. hot water
⅔ c. vegetable oil
¾ c. sugar
¼ c. salt
21 c. flour

Measure 5 c. flour, then add yeast mixture. Add the rest of flour. Mix thoroughly. Let rise 1 hour, then work down. Let rise again for ½ hour, then roll out and put into pans. Let rise and bake at 350° for 30 min. or until golden brown.

Rose Schrock (Baker)

PERFECT WHITE BREAD

1 pkg. active dry yeast
2 T. sugar
1 T. shortening
¼ c. warm water

2 c. milk, scalded
2 t. salt
5¾ to 6¼ c. flour

Soften active dry yeast in warm water. Combine hot milk, sugar, salt, and shortening. Cool to lukewarm. Stir in 2 c. of the flour, beat well. Add the softened yeast, mix thoroughly. Add enough of remaining flour to make a moderately stiff dough. Turn out on lightly floured surface. Knead till smooth and satiny (8 to 10 min.). Shape in a ball; place in lightly greased bowl, turning once to grease surface. Cover, let rise in warm place till double in size. Punch down. Cut dough in 2 portions. Shape each into a smooth ball. Cover and let rest 10 min. Shape in loaves. Place in 2 greased 9 × 5 × 3 loaf pans. Cover and let rise till double. Bake in hot oven at 400° for 35 min. or till done. If tops brown too fast, cover loosely with foil for the last 15 min. Makes 2 loaves.

Patty Kauffman (Grill Worker)

Yes, worry is a killer. People are dying from it every day.

PINEAPPLE TEA RING

2 pkgs. dry yeast
¼ c. very warm water
1 t. sugar

Dissolve yeast in water. Add sugar.

½ c. sugar
¼ c. shortening

1 c. hot scalded milk
1 t. salt

Combine in large bowl. Stir in 2 unbeaten eggs and softened yeast. Gradually add 5-5½ c. flour to make a stiff dough. Knead and cover bowl. Let rise then roll out. Spread with filling. Roll up beginning at long end and shape into a ring. Let rise. Bake at 350° for 20 min.

Filling:

1½ c. crushed pineapple
¾ c. sugar
1 T. cornstarch

Cook until thick.

Wanita Mast (Busser)

It's not the hours you put in, but what you put in the hours that counts!

WHOLE WHEAT BREAD

Soften 1 pkg. dry yeast or 1 T. dry yeast with ¼ c. warm water plus 1 t. sugar. Combine:

½ c. brown sugar
1 T. salt

3 T. shortening
1 c. boiling water in large bowl, add ¾ c. cold water - cool to lukewarm

Stir in softened yeast. Gradually add 4 c. whole wheat flour and 1½ to 2 c. white flour to form a soft dough. Knead lightly on floured surface 7 to 10 min. Place in greased bowl and cover. Let rise in warm place about 2 hours. Punch down, let rise for 30 min. Divide dough in half. Shape in 2 loaves. Let rise in warm place until light and double in size. About 1¼ to 1½ hours. Bake at 350° for 30 to 40 min. Remove from pans.

Fannie Yutzy (Pie Baker)

A close look at the "chips" may reveal flaws in the "block"!

ZUCCHINI BREAD

Beat together:

3 eggs
1 c. oil
2 c. sugar

Add 3 c. shredded zucchini. Sift and add 1 t. salt, soda, baking powder, cinnamon and 3 c. flour, 1 c. coconut and 1 c. nuts (can also add ½ c. raisins). Bake 1 hour at 350°. Makes 2 loaves bread.

Barbara Bainter (Cleaning Service)

Salads &
Salad Dressings

BED BATH FOR A PERSON TO TAKE BY HIMSELF—For elderly cold-blooded and weakly persons, this should be excellent.

Wring a towel lightly out of cold water, place by the bedside and, after you are in bed, and thoroughly warm, pass the towel over the entire body, if you are able to bear it, or over a part of your body if you are not—but do this under your bedclothing. Do not take it off.

The heat of the body turns the moisture from the towel into a vapor which, in being thus drawn out, takes any ache with it and promotes sleep. This is manifestly better than no bath at all where the water and air cannot be borne at the same time.

You are often sorry for saying a harsh word, but you will never regreat saying a kind one.

"A KITCHEN PRAYER"

Bless my little kitchen Lord
I love its very look
And guide me as I do my best
Especially when I cook.

May the food that I prepare
Be seasoned from above
With thy blessings and thy grace
But most of all thy love.

So bless my little kitchen Lord
And those who share my bread
Bless its homey atmosphere
And all of those I've fed.

Mary Miller (Waitress)

Salads & Salad Dressings

AVOCADO SALAD

1 pkg. lime jello
1 c. cold water or fruit juice
¼ c. sugar
1 ripe avocado

1 c. hot water
1 - 8 oz. pkg. cream cheese
1 sm. can mandarin oranges
  (drained)

Mix the jello and chill until it begins to thicken. In the meantime, mix the softened cream cheese with the sugar. Add the mashed avocado and orange slices. Mix with the thickened jello and chill until firm.

Leora Kauffman (Purchasing)

The probability of life originating by accident is comparable to the possibility of the unabridged dictionary resulting from an explosion in a print shop!

ANGEL HASH SALAD

2 T. Sure-Jel®
1 c. pineapple juice
1 c. whipped cream

½ c. sugar
2 egg yolks

Cook together the Sure-Jel®, sugar, pineapple juice, and egg yolks until thick, stirring constantly. Cool and add the whipped cream. Pour over:

2 c. apples, diced
4-5 bananas, sliced
¼ c. nuts, chopped
maraschino cherries (garnish)

1 lg. can chunk pineapple,
    drained
marshmallows and grapes
    (optional)

Mary Esther Miller (Baker)
Laura Ann Miller (Grill Cook)
Katie Miller (Gift Shop)
Denise Henke (Waitress)

If thine enemy be hungry, give him bread to eat; and if he be thirsty, give him water to drink: For thou shalt heap coals of fire upon his head, and the LORD shall reward thee.

Prov. 25:21-22

APPLE SALAD

approx. 24 apples, chopped
4 c. celery, chopped
5 oz. miniature marshmallows
1⅓ c. salad dressing
5⅓ c. whipped topping

3 bananas, sliced
2 c. chunk pineapple,
    drained
¼ c. sugar

Blend fruit and marshmallows. Mix salad dressing, sugar, and whipped topping in a bowl, pour over the fruit mixture, and toss gently.

Lydia Ann Miller
(Head Cook)

BROCCOLI SALAD

1 head broccoli (ground or chopped)
1 small onion (chopped)
8 pieces bacon fried and broken up
⅓ c. slivered almonds
raisins (optional)

Dressing:

1 c. salad dressing
⅓ c. sugar
1 T. vinegar

Don't put dressing on till ready to serve.

Esther Nisley (Bakery)
Fannie Yoder (Cook)
Edna Borntrager (Head Cook, evening)
Jil Kauffman (Waitress)

BOONES SALAD

1 can (20 oz.) cut up peaches or any other fruit
1 box (3½ oz.) instant pistachio pudding mix
1 container (9 oz.) non-dairy whipped topping
1 c. miniature marshmallows
½ c. finely cut up walnuts

Drain peaches, cut in tiny pieces, reserve syrup. Place pudding mix in a large bowl, add six tablespoons of the syrup and make a soft paste, add topping and mix well. Add drained fruit, mix very well until mixture is fluffy and increased in volume. Refrigerate until thoroughly chilled.

Sharon Miller (Cook)

Why not add a smile to your speech today?

BLUEBERRY SALAD

2 small boxes black raspberry jello
1 medium can crushed pineapple
1 can blueberries
1 small can coconut
8 oz. cream cheese
½ pt. sour cream

Dissolve jello in 2 c. boiling water. Drain ½ c. juice from pineapple and ½ c. juice from blueberries. Mix with jello and stir well. Add pineapple and blueberries. Mix well and let set.

Mix cream cheese, sour cream, ½ t. vanilla, ½ c. powdered sugar. Pour on top of jello and sprinkle with coconut. Keeps real well.

Mary Miller (Waitress)

BEAN 'N BACON SALAD

2 cans (16 oz.) whole green beans, drained
¼ c. chopped onion
⅓ c. salad oil
¼ c. vinegar
½ t. salt
¼ t. pepper
4 hard boiled eggs, chopped
¼ c. mayonnaise or salad dressing
1 t. prepared mustard
2 t. vinegar
¼ t. salt
4 slizes bacon, crisply fried
  and crumbled
crisp greens
paprika

Combine beans, onions, salad oil, ¼ c. vinegar, ½ t. salt and the pepper; toss lightly. Cover and chill. Mix remaining ingredients except bacon, greens and paprika. Just before serving, drain bean mixture and add to 2nd mixture. Serve on greens and top with bacon and paprika. Serves 6.

Barbara Bontrager (Cashier)

BAKED CHICKEN SALAD

3 c. chopped cooked chicken
1½ c. celery slices
1 c. shredded sharp Cheddar
1 T. chopped onion
1½ c. crushed potato chips

1 T. lemon juice
1½ t. salt
dash of pepper
tomato slices

Combine chicken, celery, ½ c. cheese, onion, lemon juice, seasonings and enough mayonnaise to moisten; mix lightly. Spoon into 1½ quart casserole; top with tomatoes. Bake at 350° for 35 min. Top with combined remaining cheese and chips; continue baking until cheese is melted. Serves 6.

Sue Miller (Manager)

CAULIFLOWER BROCCOLI SALAD

1 head cauliflower, separated
1-2 tomatoes, chopped

1-2 heads broccoli, separated
1-2 carrots, chopped

Mix together:
1 c. Hellman's Mayonnaise
½ t. Beau Monde
½-1 pkg. Hidden Valley Ranch
    Dressing

1 c. sour cream
1 T. parsley flakes

Pour mixture over cauliflower, broccoli, tomatoes, carrots for desired coverage. The mixture also makes a great vegetable dip.

Janet Lantz (Waitress)

CHICKEN SALAD

8 c. cooked chicken, cut up
    in small pieces
8 eggs, cooked and chopped
¼ t. salt
¼ c. sugar

4 c. chopped celery
3 c. salad dressing
1 t. vinegar
1 t. (scant) mustard

Put all together and mix. Serve on chef salads or in sandwiches.

Evelyn Yoder (Cook)
Lydia Ann Miller (Head Cook)

CREAMY CUCUMBER SALAD

Slice 4 large cucumbers and put them in leftover pickle vinegar to marinate. Drain well and make creamy dressing.

2 c. mayonnaise
½ c. vinegar

1 c. sugar

Add:

chopped celery
onions
grated carrots

Rosa Borntrager (Dutch Country Gifts)

CREAMY COLE SLAW

Dressing:

1 c. salad dressing
1 T. celery seed
1 t. salt

½ c. sugar
2 T. vinegar

Blend well and pour over 1 head of chopped or shredded cabbage. Variation: add 1 c. pineapple, crushed, ½ c. pecans and 2 c. miniature marshmallows.

Lydia Ann Miller (Cook)

CRANBERRY SALAD

6 oz. pkg. raspberry jello
1 c. sugar
½ c. nuts, chopped
1 c. crushed pineapple

3 c. hot water
2 apples, chopped
½ pkg. cranberries

Dissolve jello in hot water, add sugar, apples, nuts, pineapple and cranberries. Put in cool place till set.

Lydia Ann Miller (Head Cook)

CORN SALAD

12 large ears sweet corn
2 onions, chopped
5 stalks celery, diced
2 small, or 1 large, head cabbage,
    grated coarsely

1 pint vinegar
1 c. prepared mustard
¾ t. tumeric

Simmer for 30 min. A little water may be added to cook. Thicken with 1 T. cornstarch. Ladle into jars and seal at once.

Mary Ellen Yutzy

COTTAGE CHEESE SALAD

1 lb. marshmallows
½ c. milk

Melt above over low heat; then add:

1 lg. pkg. cream cheese, cut up
1 pint small curd cottage cheese

Stir a little and cool; then add:

1 #2 can crushed pineapple, well drained
½ c. nuts

Fold in 1 cup cream, whipped.

Mary Esther Lehman (Busser)
Mary Esther Mast (Waitress)
Doris Miller (Waitress)

The best exercise for the heart is to reach down and pull other people up!

COOL AS A CUCUMBER SALAD

1-2 cucumbers, pared and sliced
½ t. salt
1 c. sour cream or yogurt
1 t. dill weed
¼ t. dry mustard

1½ T. vinegar
1 T. sugar
1 green onion, snipped
½ t. celery seed

Combine all ingredients except cucumbers, mixing well. Pour over cucumbers. Refrigerate for several hours.

Barbara Bontrager (Cashier)

CHINESE CHICKEN SALAD

½ lb. diced chicken
1 head lettuce
2 t. toasted almonds
2 t. sesame seeds
3 t. vinegar
½ pkg. wonton's skins

2 t. sugar
1 t. salt
1 t. accent
½ t. pepper
¼ c. oil
onion salt (desired amount)

Mix and serve. Fry wontons and serve separate.

Betti Kauffman (Cashier-Hostess)

CHICKEN SALAD

Add to 2 c. boiled, chopped chicken:

1 - 8 oz. can of water chestnuts
½ c. sliced celery
¾ c. mayonnaise
1½ t. curry powder
⅓ c. slivered toasted almonds

1 lb. seedless green grapes
#9 can pineapple bits
¾ c. sour cream
2 t. lemon juice

Serve on lettuce leaf.

Mary Ellen Campbell (Waitress)

CARROT SALAD

1 pkg. orange gelatin
3 oz. pkg. cream cheese, softened
¾ c. grated carrots
1 small can crushed pineapple, drained (save juice)

Cream together cream cheese and gelatin. Add 1 c. hot water, stir until dissolved, add juice from pineapple, let gel slightly. Add crushed pineapple, carrots and a container of Cool Whip. Put into mold and chill until firm.

Edith Herschberger (Cashier)

DILLY TUNA SALAD

1½ c. cottage cheese
1 - 6½ oz. can tuna, drained, flaked
⅓ c. low calorie thousand island
   or French dressing
¼ c. chopped celery
¼ c. chopped green pepper
¼ c. chopped onion
¼ t. dill weed
salt and pepper
lettuce

Combine cottage cheese, tuna, dressing, celery, green peppers, onion and dill weed; mix lightly. Season to taste. Chill. Serve on lettuce. 4 servings.

For variety, add shredded carrot or chopped cucumber, and serve with sliced tomatoes or in tomato cups.

Sue Miller (Manager)

EASY SUMMER SALAD

1 - 3 oz. box jello (any flavor)
1 small box small-curd cottage cheese
1 container Cool Whip
1 small can drained fruit

Stir together Cool Whip, dry jello and cottage cheese. Then add the drained fruit. Nuts or marshmallows may also be added, if desired.

Lizzie Ann Bontrager (Cook)

EGG SALAD

6 large hard boiled eggs, diced   ½ c. celery, diced
⅔ c. salad dressing   pinch of salt and pepper

Mix all together. Makes about 5 sandwiches.

Doris Miller (Waitress)

FREEZER SLAW

1 head cabbage, shredded   1 t. salt
1 T. sweet pepper, finely chopped
1 carrot, grated fine

Let stand 1 hour. Then squeeze out juice. Make heavy syrup of:

1 c. vinegar   1 t. mustard seed
1 t. celery seed   ½ c. water
2 c. sugar

Mix all together and boil 1 min. Let stand till lukewarm. Pour over cabbage mixture and mix well. Put in boxes and freeze. Can be refrozen.

Susanna Miller (Cook)

FRUIT SALAD

1 small can mandarin oranges with juice
1 large can crushed pineapple in own juice
1 large can fruit cocktail in light syrup
1 large can lemon instant pudding mix
1 banana
lemon juice
whipped topping

Pour oranges, pineapple and fruit cocktail together in a large bowl. Add lemon pudding mix and mix well. Juice will absorb into pudding. Refrigerate covered. Just before serving, slice one banana with lemon juice, and then add to fruit. Top with whipped topping.

Barbara Bontrager (Cashier)

GREEN JELLO SALAD

1 large box lime jello in 1 c. boiling water. Add 2 c. water and pineapple juice. Cool and add:
2 c. crushed pineapple (drained)
½ c. nuts
1 pt. Riches topping, whipped
1 pt. cottage cheese
½ c. sugar
1 - 8 oz. cream cheese

Mix jello, boiling water and pineapple juice. Then cool. Whip the Riches topping and add the sugar and remaining ingredients.

Doretta Mast (Dishwasher)

HEAVENLY SALAD

2 - 3 oz. pkgs. lemon jello
1 c. cold water
16 lg. or 1½ c. sm. marshmallows
2 lg. apples, diced and unpeeled

2 c. hot water
½ c. nuts
1 - 9 oz. can crushed pineapple, drained

Dissolve jello (as usual) in hot water; add marshmallows and stir until melted. Stir in cold water and chill until partially set. Add remaining ingredients. Turn into flat dish about 9×13. Some prefer to use all hot water at one time to dissolve the jello.

Topping:

¾ c. sugar
2 eggs

½ pt. whipped cream
2 T. lemon juice

Cook sugar, eggs and lemon juice in double boiler or over very slow heat, stirring constantly. When cold, add the whipped cream and spread on jello.

Betti Kauffman (Cashier-Hostess)

HERITAGE FRUIT SALAD

1 - 32 oz. fruit salad, drained
1 c. strawberry halves
1 c. melon balls
1 banana, sliced
coconut cream dressing

Combine fruit; chill. Serve with:

Coconut Cream Dressing:

⅓ c. salad dressing or mayonnaise
1 T. honey
⅓ c. heavy cream, whipped
3 T. flaked coconut

Combine salad dressing and honey; mix well. Fold in whipped cream and coconut. Chill. 6 servings.

Sue Miller (Manager)

The bravest battle that ever was fought,
Shall I tell you where and when?
On the maps of the world you'll find it not,
It is fought by the mothers of men.

IRMA'S LETTUCE SALAD

1 head lettuce
8 strips bacon
cheese, grated
½ head cauliflower
onions, chopped

Dressing:

1 c. salad dressing
½ c. sugar
salt
1 T. vinegar

Pour on lettuce mixture.

Marlene Eash (Cook)

44

ITALIAN SPAGHETTI SALAD

1 lb. box extra thin spaghetti
1 - 10 oz. jar Italian dressing

Kroger salad seasons
  (about ½ jar or 1 oz.)

Cut up fresh vegetables:

broccoli
tomatoes

green peppers
onions

Cook spaghetti and rinse with cold water. Mix altogether and marinate overnight.

Rosa Borntrager (Dutch Country Gifts)

ITALIAN RICE SALAD

Cook 1½ c. rice till done. Cool. Blend ¾ c. Italian dressing and ¾ c. mayonnaise together. Chop fresh vegetables to make 1½ c. (like carrots, celery, peppers, onions, radishes, frozen peas, etc.). Add dressing, blend in rice, toss well. Pack in mold or bowl. Chill. Unmold on a plate of lettuce leaves.

Edna Borntrager (Cook)

LIME COTTAGE CHEESE SALAD

1 pkg. lime jello
1 c. boiling water
2 c. tiny marshmallows
dash of salt

1 - 9 oz. can crushed pineapple
1 c. small curd cottage cheese
1 c. cream whipped

Dissolve jello in boiling water, add marshmallows and let melt. Stir in salt and pineapple. Chill until slightly thickened. Fold in cottage cheese and whipped cream. Turn into 8 x 8 pan.

Rosie Eash (Waitress)
Mary Ellen Yutzy

LIME SALAD

2 c. flour
½ c. brown sugar
½ c. chopped walnuts
1 c. butter

Mix and press in oblong pan and bake 12-15 min. at 350°.

Drain 1 can crushed pineapple. Place juice in saucepan, bring to a boil. Dissolve 1 small box lime jello in the juice. Cool. Cream 1 (8 oz.) pkg. cream cheese with 1 c. sugar. Blend in jello (before it jells). Stir in pineapple. Whip 1 c. cream and mix all together. Put on top of baked crust. Chill, cut in squares and serve.

Laura Anna Miller (Grill Worker)

Can you remember the last time someone shouted at you? What was your reaction?

For most people, when you are shouted at, you shout back. And there is only one proven method to keep someone from "hollering" during a disagreement. Keep your voice low! It will almost always act to control the voice of the other person.

MACARONI SALAD

6 c. raw macaroni, cooked
   and cooled
1½-2 c. onions, chopped
1 T. relish
1 T. celery seed
approx. 1½ quarts salad dressing

2 c. celery, chopped
8 eggs, cooked and chopped
1 T. mustard
pinch of salt
approx. 1 c. sugar

Season to taste.

Lydia Ann Miller (Head Cook)

MARSHMALLOW CHEESE SALAD

1 lb. marshmallows
1 pt. creamed cottage cheese
1 can crushed pineapple, drained
1 - 8 oz. pkg. Philadelphia
   Cream Cheese

½ c. milk
1 c. whipped cream
1 c. chopped nuts

Melt marshmallows and milk in the top of a double boiler. Cream the two cheeses and add the melted marshmallows, slightly cooled. When above mixture is no longer warm, add well drained pineapple and nuts. Fold in whipped cream. Chill.

Edna Borntrager (Head Cook, evening)

MARINATED VEGETABLE SALAD

broccoli
cauliflower
celery
carrots

radishes
cherry tomatoes
green onions
green pepper

Add other vegetables if you like, but not lettuce as it will wilt. Marinate in dressing overnight or several hours.

Dressing: Mix in blender

1 c. oil
⅓ c. vinegar
parsley (optional)
2 t. oregano leaves

1 t. salt
½ t. pepper
onion (optional)
2 cloves garlic or ¼ t. powder

Edna Borntrager (Head Cook, evening)
Joyce Schrock (Waitress)
Rosa Borntrager (Dutch Country Gifts)

It's a little too much to save
And a little too much to dump—
And ther's nothing to do but eat it.
That makes the housewife plump!

ORANGE SALAD

1 box tapioca pudding
1 box (3¾ oz.) instant vanilla
    pudding
3 c. water

1 box (3 oz.) orange gelatin
2 small cans mandarin oranges,
    drained
1 container (8 oz.) Cool Whip®

Mix puddings, gelatin, and water together and boil for 10 minutes. Cool completely. Add oranges and Cool Whip®. Put into bowl and refrigerate.

Barbara Bontrager (Cashier)
Doretta Mast (Dishwasher)

POTATO SALAD

4 qt. potatoes, peeled
    cooked and diced
2 c. celery, chopped
8 eggs, hard-boiled and chopped
1½-2 c. onion, chopped
2 T. pickle relish

1 T. salt
1 c. sugar
2 T. mustard
1 t. celery seed
1-1½ qt. Miracle Whip® dressing

Combine potatoes, celery, eggs, and onion in a very large bowl. Mix remaining ingredients to make a dressing; add more or less seasoning to taste. Vinegar also may be added for a more sour flavor. Chill before serving. Makes 1½ gal. potato salad.

Lydia Ann Miller
(Head Cook)
Ruth Elaine Miller (Waitress)
Esther Nisley (Pie Baker)

ORANGE JELL-O® SALAD

1 large box orange Jell-O®
1 can (9 oz.) crushed pineapple,
    drained (save juice)
1¾ c. milk

1 can mandarin oranges, drained
1 small box instant
    lemon pudding
1 container (8 oz.) Cool Whip®

Dissolve Jell-O® in 2 c. boiling water, then add pineapple juice and enough cold water to make 2 cups liquid. Mix with mandarin oranges and crushed pineapple and chill in 9"x13" dish. Beat 1¾ c. milk and lemon pudding until thick, then fold in Cool Whip®. Spread on top of firm Jell-O®.

Rosie Eash (Waitress)

PEANUT CRUNCH SLAW

4 c. shredded cabbage
1 c. celery
½ c. sour cream
½ c. mayonnaise
1 t. salt
¼ c. chopped green onion
¼ c. chopped green pepper
½ c. chopped cucumber
1 T. butter
½ c. salted peanuts, chopped
2 T. Parmesan cheese

Toss cabbage and celery together; chill. Mix sour cream, mayonnaise, salt, onions, green peppers and cucumber; chill. Just before serving, melt butter in small skillet; add peanuts and heat until lightly browned. Immediately stir in cheese. Toss chilled vegetables with dressing. Sprinkle peanuts on top.

Denise Henke (Waitress)

PINEAPPLE CHEESE DELIGHT

Mix:

2 pkgs. lemon jello
3½ c. boiling water
1 can drained crushed pineapple
12 marshmallows (quartered)

Cook and cool:

1 can pineapple juice
½ c. sugar
1½ T. flour
1 egg

Add 1 c. whipped cream with sugar and flavoring. Pour over set jello mixture and top with grated County Line cheese.

Fannie Yoder (Cook)

PINEAPPLE AND CHERRY SALAD

1 - 3 oz. pkg. cherry jello
1 - 8 oz. pkg. cream cheese
2 T. powdered sugar
1 small can crushed pineapple

¼ c. salad dressing
¼ c. maraschino cherry juice
¼ c. maraschino cherries, chopped
1 c. heavy cream, whipped

Dissolve jello and let cool. Add salad dressing to cream cheese mixing until smooth and well blended. Add cherry juice, sugar and jello. Mix well. Chill until slightly thickened. Add fruit. Fold in whipped cream. Pour into a 1½ quart ring mold and chill until firm.

Betti Kauffman (Cashier-Hostess)

PRETZEL SALAD

1 c. crushed pretzels
1 stick butter or oleo
¼ c. sugar
1 c. crushed pineapple

½ c. sugar
2 T. cornstarch
1 pkg. Dream Whip
3 oz. cream cheese

Combine pretzels, butter and ¼ c. sugar. Press in 8×8×2 pan. Bake at 325° for 8 min. Combine pineapple and cornstarch and sugar in saucepan. Cook until thick. Cool and spread over pretzel mixture. Whip Dream Whip and add cream cheese. Spread over pineapple mixture. Chill.

Edna Slabach (Cook)

If you find your son going down the wrong track, perhaps it's because you didn't "switch" him soon enough!

It's true that people are affected much more by the tone of your voice and the look on your face than by any selected set of words.

RIBBON SALAD

First Layer:

2 (3 oz.) pkg. lime gelatin
2 c. cold water

2 c. hot water

Put in 9×13 pan to set.

Second Layer:

1 (3 oz.) pkg. lemon gelatin

1 c. hot water to dissolve gelatin

Add:
¼ lb. miniature marshmallows

1 (8 oz.) pkg. cream cheese

When starting to set add:
½ c. crushed pineapple
Put on first layer, let set.

1 c. whipped topping

Third Layer:

2 (3 oz.) pkg. cherry gelatin
2 c. cold water

2 c. hot water

When starting to set, pour on second layer.

Lydia Ann Miller (Head Cook)
Ella Bontrager (Cook)

SIX-LAYER 24 HOUR SALAD

Fix day or evening ahead:

1 layer shredded lettuce   1 small layer green onions
1 layer peas (frozen, slightly cooked)

Mix together and spread over the above layers:

1 c. sour cream   1 c. mayonnaise
1 T. sugar

Sprinkle Parmesan cheese on top. Fry bacon and crumble on top. Put in tupperware and cover. Refrigerate.

Patty Neufeld (Waitress)

7-LAYER SALAD

1½ head lettuce   1 lb. bacon, fried and broken
1 medium onion, chopped   1 lb. Cheddar cheese
1 pint frozen peas   8 hard-boiled eggs

Dressing:

3 c. mayonnaise   ½ c. milk
½ c. sugar   mustard to taste

Put above ingredients in layers, put dressing on top and let stand overnight in refrigerator. Lettuce will not wilt if you don't stir dressing through.

Jil Kauffman (Waitress)

Life's most perplexing problems usually come in the form of people.

SOUR KRAUT SALAD

Mix together:

3½ c. kraut, drained
1 lg. green pepper, chopped

1 c. celery, chopped
1 onion, chopped

Boil ¼ c. water and 1 c. sugar together. Then cool. Pour over kraut mixture. Let set overnight. Drain. Mix the following and pour over kraut:

1 c. salad oil
1 c. sugar
½ c. vinegar

¾ t. salt
1 t. celery salt
1 t. powdered mustard

Edna Borntrager (Head Cook, evening)

STRAWBERRY JELLO SALAD

2 boxes (3 oz.) strawberry jello   1 c. boiling water

Mix these together and add:

1½ pint or 1 quart frozen strawberries
1 lb. 4 oz. can crushed pineapple
2 large bananas, mashed

Maurice Berkey (Controller)

SUNSHINE MACARONI SALAD

2 c. (7 oz.) elbow macaroni, cooked and drained
½ lb. Velveeta cheese, cubed
½ c. celery slices
½ c. ham cubes
2 T. chopped pimiento
1 T. chopped green pepper
Miracle Whip salad dressing

Combine macaroni, Velveeta cheese, celery, ham, pimiento, and green pepper. Add enough salad dressing to moisten. Mix well. Chill. Makes 6 servings.

Polly Yoder (Bakery)

SWEET AND SOUR CARROTS

5 c. carrots, cooked and sliced
1 green pepper, sliced
1 c. sugar
½ c. oil
1 t. dry mustard

1 sliced onion
1 can tomato soup
1 t. pepper
¾ c. vinegar
1 t. Worcestershire sauce

Mix together last seven ingredients and bring to a boil. Then add onion and green pepper and pour over carrots. Marinate overnight.

Joyce Schrock (Waitress)
Julianna Bontrager (Waitress)

TACO DIP

1 can refried beans with green chilies

Combine:

3 medium avocados, mashed
¼ t. pepper
½ t. salt
2 T. lemon juice

Combine:

1 pkg. taco seasoning mix
1 c. mayonnaise
1 c. sour cream

Combine:

1 pkg. (8 oz.) Cheddar cheese, shredded
¼ c. chopped black olives
1 c. chopped tomatoes
½ c. green onions

Layer in order into 9×13 pan. Serve with tortilla chips.

Esther Hershberger
Mary Miller (Waitress)

TACO SALAD

Fry 1 lb. hamburger, then add 1 pkg. taco seasoning according to directions on package. Cut up as for tossed salad: 1 head lettuce, 4 tomatoes, 1 onion, 4 oz. shredded cheese, 1 can kidney beans and ½ c. crushed taco flavored chips. Prepare each food separately, mix just before serving and serve with French dressing.

Dressing:

⅓ c. ketchup
½ c. cooking oil
½ c. white sugar
¼ c. vinegar

1 T. onion salt
½ t. salt
½ t. paprika
1 T. lemon juice

Put all ingredients in a jar and shake up. May be stored in refrigerator for weeks.

Laura Anna Miller (Grill Worker)

THREE LAYER SALAD

1st layer:

3 eggs
1 c. sugar

3 T. flour
1 c. pineapple juice

Cook till thickens. Pour into 9×13 pan and chill.

2nd layer:

1 - 8 oz. pkg. cream cheese

1 c. whipping cream

Chill till set.

3rd layer:

2 boxes lemon or lime jello
(follow instructions on box)

Add:

1 can crushed pineapple, drained
½ c. nuts

Alice Weaver (Waitress)

TUNA APPLE SALAD

1 - 4 oz. can of tuna
½ c. chopped celery
¼ c. raisins
lettuce

2 c. diced apples
½ c. mayonnaise
1 T. lemon juice

Drain the tuna and break into pieces. Combine the rest of the ingredients except the lettuce. Chill thoroughly and serve on a bed of lettuce.

Leora Kauffman (Purchasing)

VEGETABLE SALAD

Drain:

1 can French-style green beans
1 can tiny green peas

1 can kidney beans
1 small jar pimientos, chopped

Chop:

4 stalks celery
1 green pepper

1 medium onion

Combine thoroughly:

1 c. salad oil
½ c. vinegar
1 c. sugar

1 T. salt
1 t. paprika

Combine dressing with vegetables. Cover and refrigerate overnight or several hours.

Barbara Bontrager (Cashier)

WONDER SALAD

2 boxes lemon jello
2 c. boiling water
24 marshmallows dissolved in hot jello

Let cool and add:

4 stalks celery, chopped
1 c. crushed pineapple
½ c. salad dressing
½ c. nut meats (optional)

2 c. carrots, shredded
2 c. cottage cheese
1 c. whipped cream

Mix all together and put in pan. Refrigerate this. Fills 9×12 pan.

Susanna Miller (Cook)

GOOD SALAD DRESSING FOR POTATO SALAD

2 c. Miracle Whip
1½ c. sugar
1 can Pet Milk
4 large T. mustard
1 T. salt

potatoes
celery
1 onion
4 to 6 eggs

Mix altogether and put in jar and keep in refrigerator and it will keep for weeks. Use as needed.

Doretta Mast (Dishwasher)

Why does everyone want to be in the front of the bus, the rear of the church, and the middle of the road?

POPPY SEED DRESSING

1½ c. buttermilk   1 c. salad dressing

Add a dash of each: salt, lemon juice, sugar, onion salt, and ½ c. poppy seeds. Blend ingredients well and serve over lettuce.

Elsie Miller (Grill Cook)

CREAMY ITALIAN DRESSING

1 c. real mayonnaise   ½ small onion, chopped fine
2 T. red wine vinegar   1 T. sugar
¾ t. Italian seasoning   ¼ t. salt
¼ t. garlic salt or powder   1/8 t. pepper

Mix well. Makes 1 pint.

Sue Miller (Manager)

CREAMY POPPY SEED DRESSING

½ c. dairy sour cream   2 T. milk
1 t. chopped chives   ¾ t. poppy seeds
¼ t. salt   ¼ t. pepper
1 T. vinegar

Mix well. Makes 1 pint.

Sue Miller (Manager)

So live that when you come to die even the undertaker will be sorry!

Meat, Poultry & Main Dishes

THE MIRACLE OF THE LOAVES AND FISH

When Jesus then lifted up his eyes, and saw a great company come unto him, he saith unto Philip, Whence shall we buy bread, that these may eat? And this he said to prove him: for he himself knew what he would do. Philip answered him, Two hundred pennyworth of bread is not sufficient for them, that every one of them may take a little.

One of his disciples, Andrew, Simon Peter's brother, saith unto him, There is a lad here, which hath five barley loaves, and two small fishes: but what are they among so many?

And Jesus said, Make the men sit down. Now there was much grass in the place. So the men sat down, in number about five thousand. And Jesus took the loaves; and when he had given thanks, he distributed to the disciples, and the disciples to them that were set down; and likewise of the fishes as much as they would.

When they were filled, he said unto his disciples, Gather up the fragments that remain, that nothing may be lost. Therefore they gathered them together, and filled twelve baskets with the frangments of the five barley loaves, which remained over and above unto them that had eaten.

Then those men, when they had seen the miracle that Jesus did, said, This is of a truth the prophet that should come into the world.

John 6:5-14

And Jesus said unto them, I am the bread of life: he that cometh to me shall never hunger; and he that believeth on me shall never thirst.

John 6:35

THE CURE CALLED "WORK"

If you are rich, work.
If you are burdened with seemingly unfair responsibilities, work.
If you are unhappy, continue to work;
Idleness gives room to doubts and fears.
If sorrow overwhelms you and loved ones seem not true, work.
If disappointments come, work.
If faith falters and reason fails, just work.
When dreams are shattered and hopes seem dead,
Work, work as if your life were in peril;
It really is.

No matter what ails you, work.
Work faithfully and work with faith.
Work is the greatest material remedy available.
Work will cure both mental and physical afflictions.
Work!

Source Unknown

Meat, Poultry & Main Dishes

BAKED BAR-B-Q

1½ lb. hamburger
1 c. canned milk
3 T. brown sugar
½ c. water
½ c. cooked carrots
¾ c. oatmeal

3 medium onions
1 c. ketchup
2 T. vinegar
1 T. Worcestershire sauce
½ c. cooked celery
salt to taste

Fry hamburger and onion until brown. Mix all together and bake 1 hour at 300°. Serves approximately 6 to 8 people.

Fannie Yutzy (Pie Baker)

BAKED BEANS

3 c. cooked navy beans
½ c. brown sugar
5 slices Velveeta cheese
2 t. mustard

1 c. cream
½ c. ketchup
3 t. butter

Add a little onion salt and pepper, add ham, weiners, bacon or bologna. Bake 1 hour at 350°.

Millie Whetstone (Cook)

BAKED BEANS

2 lbs. navy beans
1 T. salt
½ lb. bacon

1 quart tomato juice
1½ c. brown sugar
1 small onion

Wash beans, place in large cooking pan twice the size of amount of beans. Fill pan with cold water and allow beans to soak overnight. In the morning, add salt and simmer approximately 2 hours until tender. You may need to add 1 c. water in the second hour. Cut up and brown bacon with chopped onion. Add bacon and 2 T. drippings and brown sugar and tomato juice to beans and place in baking pan. Bake 3-4 hours at 350°. Cover for about half of the baking time. You may add hot dogs the last 30 min. of baking time.

Rosa Borntrager (Dutch Country Gifts)

It is a great thing to do little things well.

BAKED CHICKEN

1 frying chicken, cut in serving size pieces
1 c. very fine bread crumbs
¼ c. flour
1 t. accent
½ t. salt
¼ t. powdered sugar
¼ t. seasoned salt
¼ t. paprika
¼ t. garlic salt
½ c. margarine

Dip the chicken into melted margarine and then into crumb mixture. Bake on cookie sheet for 45 min. at 350°.

Leora Kauffman (Purchasing)

BARBEQUED CHICKEN

4 T. ketchup
4 T. brown sugar
1 T. lemon juice
½ t. paprika

2 t. Worcestershire sauce
5 T. water
½ t. prepared mustard
½ t. chili powder

Heat and blend these ingredients thoroughly. Soak chicken pieces in Tender Quick overnight. Dip in sauce and place in roaster. Pour remainder of sauce on meat. Cover with foil. Bake in a 350° oven for 1½ hours, or until done.

Ella Bontrager (Cook)

BAKED CHICKEN

1½ c. sour cream
1 t. Worcestershire sauce
2 t. celery salt
dash of garlic salt

2 T. lemon juice
½ t. paprika
1 t. salt

Roll chicken pieces in this mixture, then roll in bread crumbs. Bake at 375° till done.

Mary Ellen Campbell (Waitress)

BAKED CHICKEN LOAF

1 - 4 lb. hen, cooked
1 T. minced parsley
¼ t. pepper
2 eggs

2 c. soft bread crumbs
½ t. salt
1 c. milk
2 T. melted butter or margarine

Remove chicken meat from bones; chop finely. Mix chicken, 1¾ c. crumbs, parsley, salt, pepper, milk and eggs; stir in butter. Pour into loaf pan or oblong baking dish; sprinkle remaining crumbs over top. Bake at 325° for 45 min. Cut into squares. Serve with mushroom sauce. Yield: 8 servings.

Sauce:
1 can mushroom soup mixed with 1 c. water or milk.

Lydia Ann Miller (Head Cook)

BEANS AND MEATBALLS

2 c. dried beans
1 t. dry mustard
½ c. honey
½ lb. bacon

1 t. salt
1 t. ginger
2 T. chopped onion

Soak the beans overnight. Drain, add fresh water and cook slowly until tender. Drain, but reserve liquid. Place half the bacon in a casserole dish. Add the beans, then remaining ingredients which have been combined with 1½ c. of bean liquid. Make and press meatballs down into beans. Lay remaining bacon on top. Bake in 300° oven for 1½ to 2 hours. Serves 6.

Leora Kauffman (Purchasing)

MEAT BALLS

½ lb. ground beef
3 T. chili sauce
1 t. salt
2 T. chopped onions
¼ c. hot milk

½ lb. ground smoked ham
2 T. brown sugar
1 T. soy sauce
2 slices white bread
1 egg beaten

Pour hot milk over bread and mix thoroughly. Add remaining ingredients and shape into small meatballs.

Leora Kauffman (Purchasing)

BARRY'S CASSEROLE

2 lbs. hamburger
1 large onion
1 can cream of chicken soup

2-3 large potatoes
3-4 carrots, grated fine
grated cheese

Press raw hamburger in a casserole pan. Grate onion over hamburger. Add layer of sliced raw potatoes, grate carrots to cover potatoes. Put soup over carrots. Add a large amount of grated cheese on top. Bake at 350° for 1 hour.

Martha Miller (Cook)

BATTER-DIPPED FISH

3 c. flour
1 egg, beaten
2 T. paprika
1 t. red pepper
4 T. Lawry's salt

1½ c. milk
½ t. salt
1 t. sage
1 t. thyme
1 T. chili powder

Beat all ingredients together, dip fish in batter and deep fry.

Sue Bontrager (Grill Cook)

BAKED LASAGNA

1 lb. ground beef
1 T. parsley flakes
1½ t. salt
2 (6 oz.) cans tomato paste
1 clove garlic, minced
1 T. basil
2 c. tomatoes

2 (12 oz.) cottage cheese
2 t. salt
2 T. parsley flakes
2 eggs, beaten
½ t. pepper
1 (10 oz.) pkg. lasagna noodles
1 lb. mozzarella cheese

Brown meat slowly, add next 6 ingredients to meat. Simmer uncovered until thick, 45 min. to 1 hour. Cook noodles until tender, drain. For lasagna, combine cottage cheese with next 4 ingredients, place noodles, cottage cheese mixture, mozzarella cheese and meat in layers. Bake at 375° for 30 min. Serves 6 to 8.

Lydia Ann Miller (Head Cook)

If you don't know where you're going, you'll never recognize your destination when you arrive.

BEEF AND POTATO LOAF

Arrange evenly in greased 2 quart baking dish:

4 c. thinly sliced, peeled raw potatoes
1 onion

Sprinkle with 1 t. salt and pepper and 1 t. parsley flakes.

Mix:

1 lb. ground beef
½ c. cracker crumbs or oatmeal
1 t. salt
1/8 t. pepper

Spread evenly over potatoes. Decorate top with more catsup if desired. Bake at 350° for 1 hour. Serves four.

Rosa Hochstetler (Cook)

 A "tight" driver is much more dangerous than a loose wheel!

BEEF STICK

2 lb. hamburger
½ t. garlic salt
1 T. liquid smoke
1 c. water

¼ t. pepper
3 T. Tender Quick
¼ t. onion salt

Mix all ingredients. Separate into 2 rolls. Wrap in foil. Refrigerate for 24 hours. Cover rolls wrapped in foil with water and bring to boil. Boil ½ hr. and turn rolls over. Boil another ½ hr. Poke holes in foil to drain water. Cool before slicing.

Esther Hershberger

BEEF STROGANOFF

Brown:

2 lbs. ground beef
2 garlic cloves, minced
2½ t. salt

2 medium onions, chopped
small can mushrooms, drained

Stir into meat and simmer:

1 c. chicken bouillon
1½ c. sour cream, mixed with
4 T. flour

small can tomato sauce

Pour over cooked noodles or rice.

Dot Chupp (Secretary)

Slice left-over hot dog buns into sticks, butter them, sprinkle with garlic powder and Parmesan cheese, then toast in oven. Crumble them over salads.

BREAKFAST CASSEROLE

3 potatoes, cooked, sliced
¼ c. minced onion
½ c. cottage cheese
½ t. salt

6 slices bacon or 12 oz. sausage
1 c. shredded Swiss cheese
5 eggs, beaten

Fry bacon and onion together. Combine all ingredients. Put in 9×9 inch pan. Bake at 350° for 30 min. Serves 8.

Ellen Miller (Cashier, Gift Shop)

BREAKFAST PIZZA

1 lb. bulk pork sausage
1 c. hash browns
1 c. shredded Cheddar cheese

1 pkg. (8) refrigerated crescent rolls
or homemade pizza dough

5 eggs beaten with ¼ c. milk, ½ t. salt, 1/8 t. pepper. Place crescents or pizza dough in 12" pizza pan. Brown sausage and spoon on crust. Sprinkle with potatoes, top with cheese and pour egg mixture over all. Bake at 375° oven for 25-30 min. Serves 6-8 servings.

Rosa Borntrager (Dutch Country Gifts)
Lyle Coblentz (Dishwasher)

Spiritual enthusiasm is contagious; remember, more people chase fire engines than ice carts!

BEEF STEW

2 lbs. beef chunks, cut in 1" cubes
2 T. shortening or cooking oil
4 c. water
2 t. salt
2 medium onions, sliced
½ t. pepper
½ t. paprika
6 medium sliced carrots

4 medium cubed potatoes
1 - 16 oz. can of tomatoes
2 T. parsley, cut up
1 c. whole kernel corn
¾ c. green beans or lima beans
½ c. peas
½ c. water
¼ c. flour

In dutch oven brown the meat, half at a time, in the shortening or oil. Return all meat to the pan. Add 4 c. water, onions, salt, pepper, and paprika. Briing to a boil. Reduce heat and simmer, covered, 1¼ hours. Add carrots, potatoes, tomatoes, and parsley. Simmer, covered, for 30 min. or until vegetables are tender. Stir in corn, beans and peas. Cook for 10 min.

Combine the ½ c. water and flour. Stir into meat mixture. Cook until stew is thickened and bubbly. Cook 2 more min. Makes 6 to 8 servings.

Rosalie Bontrager (Essenhaus Country Inn Manager)

BAKED BROCCOLI

Mix:

2 eggs
3 T. flour

1 t. salt
½ t. onion powder

Add:

1 c. cottage cheese

1 c. American cheese

Add:

20 oz. broccoli - if frozen, steam apart. Water chestnuts may also be added. Bake for 45 min. or until set in a 350° oven.

Julianna Bontrager (Waitress)

BROCCOLI AND RICE

1 c. rice
1 can mushroom soup
½ c. buttered crumbs
pepper to taste

1 can Cheddar soup
1 pkg. frozen chopped broccoli
1 T. melted oleo

Cook rice and season as directed on package. Add soups to rice. Do not dilute soup. Stir until well mixed. Add the raw frozen broccoli. Stir well. Place in buttered baking dish. Top with buttered bread crumbs. Bake at 325° for about 1 hour. Do not cover. Makes 6-8 servings.

Denise Henki (Waitress)

Remember, the fellow looking down his nose at others usually has the wrong slant!

BROCCOLI, HAM AND CHEESE SKILLET

¾ lb. fresh broccoli, cut into small florets or
10 oz. pkg. frozen broccoli 2 ripe tomatoes, sliced
½ c. water 2 T. vegetable oil
3 or 4 slices baked ham, cut in strips 1 T. butter, cut in tiny pieces
½ c. shredded Cheddar cheese salt and pepper
1 ½ t. wheat germ (optional)

If using fresh broccoli, place in a 9" skillet, add water, cover and cook over moderate heat for 7 to 8 min., or until tender. (Cook frozen broccoli according to pkg. directions just until thawed and separated.) Drain broccoli thoroughly. Add oil to skillet. Arrange broccoli around edge of skillet. Place tomatoes in center. Top with ham and cheese; dot with butter. Cover and cook over low heat for 8 min. Remove from heat and let stand for 10 min. before serving. Sprinkle with wheat germ, if you like, and also salt and pepper. Makes 2 servings.

Edith Herschberger (Cashier)

 Stop living on Grumble Corner and move to Thanksgiving Street.

CALICO BEANS

1 large can pork and beans ½ c. brown sugar
1 can kidney beans ½ c. catsup
1 can butter beans ½ t. salt
¼ to ½ lb. bacon 2 T. vinegar
1 lb. ground beef or sausage 1 medium onion, diced

Drain kidney and butter beans, saving the liquid. In skillet brown bacon, ground beef and onion. Combine all 3 cans of beans with browned ingredients. Arrange in greased baking pan. Combine brown sugar, catsup, vinegar and salt into a sauce. Pour over ingredients in baking pan. If dish is too dry, add some of the liquid saved from the beans. Bake in 350° oven for 1 hour.

(optional) 1 - 10 oz. frozen lima beans

Barbara Bontrager (Cashier)
Rosa Borntrager (Dutch Country Gifts)

CHIPPED BEEF CASSEROLE

¼ lb. cut up chipped beef
2 hard-boiled eggs, diced
1 c. milk
2 T. grated onion

1 c. uncooked elbow macaroni
1 c. condensed cream of mushroom
½ lb. or 2 c. grated Cheddar cheese

Mix all ingredients and pour into 1½ to 2 qt. casserole dish. Cover and refrigerate overnight. Bake uncovered at 350° for 30 min. or until hot. Makes 4 to 6 servings.

Edna Fern Schmucker (Pie Baker)

CURRY AND RICE

1 lg. onion, chopped
3 lg. buds garlic
1 lb. meat cut in small pieces
  (chicken, beef or any raw meat)

2 med. potatoes
1½ c. tomato puree
4 t. curry powder
2 tomatoes

Put meat and onions and potatoes in skillet with a little cooking oil and stir-fry till meat and potatoes are done; add salt, tomato puree, tomatoes, curry powder, garlic and simmer for approx. 1 hour. Serve over cooked rice.

Lydia ann Miller (Head Cook)

CREAMED EGGS ON TOAST

4 eggs, hard boiled
¼ c. flour
½ t. salt

¼ c. margarine
2 c. milk
6 slices bacon, fried

Melt margarine and blend in flour. Add milk and salt, stirring continuously. Slice eggs and crumble in bacon. Serve with toast.

Ruth Elaine Miller (Waitress)

71

CORN AND BROCCOLI

4 cans cream style corn   8 eggs, beaten
1½ bags of broccoli #1 bag

Top with:

Croutons or toasted bread crumbs. Season with sour cream and chives. Bake at 250° for 1½ to 2 hours. Very delicious!

Betti Kauffman (Cashier-Hostess)

Your future does not depend on someone's opinion of you.

CHOW MEIN NOODLE CASSEROLE

Combine:

1 (5 oz.) can chow mein noodles
1 (10¾ oz.) can cream of mushroom soup
1 (10¾ oz.) can cream of celery soup
¼ c. milk
1-2 cans (5 oz.) chunk chicken or tuna. Mushrooms and almonds may also be added. Bake from 45 min. to 1 hour at 350°. Serves 4 to 6.

Julianna Bontrager (Waitress)

If you want honor—try humility.
If you want respect—try listening.
It really works!

CHICKEN CACCIATORE

1 large onion, sliced
2 - 6 oz. cans tomato paste
1 t. salt
1 clove garlic, minced
½ t. basil
1 bay leaf

2½ to 3 lbs. cut-up fryer
1 - 4 oz. can drained mushrooms
¼ t. pepper
1 to 2 t. oregano leaves
½ t. celery

Place onoin in crockpot. Add chicken. Mix remaining ingredients and pour over chicken. Cook on low for 7 to 9 hours. High at 3 to 4 hours. Good served over hot buttered spaghetti. May also be cooked in the oven.

Betty Graber (Waitress)

CHICKEN AND VEGETABLES OVER RICE

Stir fry in a skillet or wok, with a little salad oil.

2 c. chopped celery
2 c. chopped onions

2 c. mushrooms

Then add: 4 c. cooked chicken parts cut up. After celery and onions are tender, add:

3 T. soy sauce
1 T. oleo

salt and pepper to taste
½ c. milk

Remove from heat and serve over flakly rice.

Rice:

1 c. rice
pinch of salt

2 c. cold water

Bring to boil, stir once. Cover tightly and simmer for 15-20 min. Remove from heat and serve.

Lydia Ann Miller (Head Cook)

CHINESE MEATBALLS

Cook rice to serve 8 people. Prepare and reserve, ready to fry:

1 cucumber, peeled and sliced   2 stalks celery, sliced
2 green peppers, sliced   1 large onion, sliced
2 large tomatoes, cut in wedges
1½ c. pineapple chunks, drained (reserve juice)

Season, shape into small balls and fry:

1½ lb. ground beef

Combine and pour over meatballs:

¾ c. brown sugar   ¾ c. vinegar
3 T. soy sauce   ½ t. ginger
2 to 3 T. cornstarch   juice from pineapple

Allow sauce to thicken, then reduce heat and simmer for 20 min. In separate skillet stir-fry vegetables in small amount of hot oil until crisp, adding tomatoes and pineapple last. (Vegetables should be removed from heat before they have lost bright, crisp color).

Serve on large platter with rice in the center, meatballs around edge, vegetables over rice and sauce over all.

Carolyn Mast (Waitress)

CHINESE HAMBURGER

1½ lb. ground beef   1 medium can Chinese vegetables
1 c. diced celery   ½ c. diced green peppers
onions to suit taste   ⅔ c. shaved almonds
1 can cream of mushroom soup   1 can cream of chicken soup
1 t. soy sauce   1 small can water chestnuts
1 small can mushrooms

Brown beef, onions, celery, green peppers. Cook till vegetables are tender. Mix together canned vegetables and soup. Salt and pepper to taste or garlic. Bake in 2 quart casserole dish at 350° for 30 min. Then sprinkle Chinese noodles on top.

Patty Kauffman (Grill Worker)

CHINESE CHICKEN

white of chicken, cut up in bite size pieces
4 green peppers
1 can bamboo shoots
12 mushrooms
3 T. salad oil
2 T. soy sauce
1 T. cornstarch, mixed with water

Heat skillet with oil. Put in chicken and fry till white, stirring constantly. Add soy sauce, and mushrooms and cook for 2 min. Add bamboo shoots and fry for 2 min. Then add green peppers and fry for 3 min. Tilt skillet and add cornstarch, baste to juice, then mix in. (You have to keep stirring constantly. Can be put on to of chow mein noodles. Serve with rice.

Mabel Hershberger (Cashier)

Daddy bought a little car
And feeds it gasoline.
And everywhere that Daddy goes
He walks—his son is sixteen.

CHICKEN SUPREME

2 c. cooked, diced chicken meat
2 c. milk
1 medium onion, diced
¼ t. pepper

2 c. uncooked macaroni
2 cans cream of chicken soup
½ t. salt
3 T. melted cheese

Mix all ingredients together except cheese. Put in a greased casserole and refrigerate overnight. Remove from refrigerator several hours before baking. Bake at 350° for 1½ hours. Top with cheese during the last part of baking.

Usually I cook the macaroni, drain water off. Mix everything together and bake for only 45 min. to an hour. Takes less milk if macaroni is cooked.

Laura Anna Miller (Grill Worker)

CHICKEN POT PIE

1 can chicken, drained
or 1 medium chicken, cooked
2½ c. diced potatoes
1 pint peas

½ c. carrots
1 can biscuits

Cook chicken, take out bones and cut in medium size pieces. Put carrots and potatoes in chicken broth, cook until almost done. Add peas and chicken. When done thicken with cornstarch and water. Pour in baking dish or pan. Put one can biscuits on top and bake at 375°, or until biscuits are done.

Marlene Eash (Cook)
Susanna Miller (Cook)

CHICKEN GRAVY

1 pt. chicken broth
1 T. chicken base

1 pt. water

Heat till it steams, but not to boiling point. Meanwhile make a white sauce of 3 oz. cornstarch, 1 egg and a little milk. Add to hot broth and bring to boiling, stirring constantly. Remove from heat. Don't over-cook or it may get thin again. Add a few drops of yellow food coloring if you like.

Lydia Ann Miller (Head Cook)

A handful of safety pins and a few threaded needles stuck to the inside of your suitcase will come in handy when you pop a button off or your hem comes undone.

CHICKEN NOODLE CASSEROLE

1 qt. chicken broth
1 T. chicken base
1 pt. chicken, cooked, boned, and diced
1 can (10¾ oz.) cream of chicken soup
½ qt. water
½ lb. noodles
1 can (10¾ oz.) cream of mushroom soup
2 c. frozen peas and carrots
½ lb. cheese, shredded

Heat the broth, chicken base, and water to boil. Then add noodles and cook till the noodles are tender. Put in 4-qt. baking dish and add the other ingredients.

Season to taste, adding a bit of salt if desired. Top with cheese and bake for approximately ¾ hr. at 350° or until hot.

Lydia Ann Miller (Head Cook)
Meredith Mast (Dishwasher)

And they shall build houses, and inhabit them; and they shall plant vineyards, and eat the fruit of them. They shall not build, and another inhabit; they shall not plant, and another eat: for as the days of a tree are the days of my people, and mine elect shall long enjoy the work of their hands. They shall not labour in vain, nor bring forth for trouble; for they are the seed of the blessed of the LORD, and their offspring with them.

Isa. 65:21-23

CHICKEN MACARONI CASSEROLE

1 lb. macaroni, cooked
1 can cream of mushroom soup
2 c. milk
bread crumbs (optional)
2 c. chicken, cooked, boned and diced
1 can cream of chicken soup
Velveeta® cheese, sliced

Put macaroni, cheese, and meat in a cassrole dish by layers. Dilute soup with milk and pour over macaroni mixture. Top with toasted bread crumbs if desired. Bake at 350° for 45 minutes to 1 hour.

Bertha Miller (Gift Shop)

CHICKEN DIVAN

¾ lb. boned, skinned chicken
1 c. water
1 pkg. (10 oz.) Bird's Eye
  deluxe broccoli
1½ c. minute rice

2 t. oil
1 T. dry sherry wine
1 can (10¾ oz.) condensed
  cream of chicken soup
1 T. grated Parmesan cheese

Brown chicken in oil, stirring occasionally. Add water, wine, broccoli and soup. Bring to a full boil. Separate broccoli pieces. Stir in rice, cover. Remove from heat and let stand 5 min. Sprinkle with cheese. Makes 4 servings.

Patty Kauffman (Grill Worker)

CHICKEN CARUSO AND RICE

2 chicken breasts, skinned, boned, and cut in thin strips
garlic salt and pepper
3 T. butter or margarine
1 jar (15½ oz.) spaghetti sauce
1 t. Italian seasoning
2 c. sliced celery
3 c. hot cooked rice

Season chicken with garlic salt and pepper. Saute in butter about 2 min. Stir in spaghetti sauce and Italian seasoning. Cover and simmer for 10 min. Add celery; continue cooking until it's tender and crisp. Serve over beds of fluffy rice. Sprinkle with grated Parmesan cheese, if desired. Makes 6 servings.

Betti Kauffman (Cashier-Hostess)

Keep vegetables colorful: add a pinch of baking soda to cooking water.

CHICKEN CASSEROLE

Casserole crust:

4 c. soft bread crumbs
¼ t. pepper
¼ t. sage

½ t. celery salt
2 T. minced onion
¼ c. butter, melted

Combine ingredients for crust. Press into greased baking dish. Bake for 15 min. at 375°. Meanwhile mix casserole filling.

6 T. butter
6 T. flour
¼ t. celery salt
2 c. milk

1/8 t. pepper
2 c. flaked or cooked chicken
½ t. salt
cooked potatoes and peas

Melt butter gradually, stirring constantly. Stir in flour, celery salt, pepper and salt. Add milk gradually. Stir in flaked meat, potatoes and peas. Pour over crumb crust. Slightly crush 2 c. rice cereal and mix with 1 T. butter. Sprinkle over filling and bake at 425° for 1 hour.

Wilma Weaver (Cook)

CHICKEN BROCCOLI CASSEROLE

Combine:

2 - 10 oz. pkgs. of broccoli
   with cheese
½ stick butter, melted
1 T. lemon juice

4 chicken breasts, cooked
   and deboned
½ c. longhorn cheese, shredded
2 cans of cream of chicken soup
1 c. mayonnaise
2 t. curry powder (optional)

Place in pan and add on top 1½ c. bread crumbs browned in ½ c. butter. Place in refrigerator from 12 to 24 min. Bake at 350° for 25-30 min. if the mixture is at room temperature, and 40-50 min. if it is cold.

Sue Miller (Manager)
Edna Borntrager (Head Cook, evening)

CHICKEN BROCCOLI DISH

Cook until tender 3 chicken breasts. Reserve for later. Boil 1 fresh bunch of broccoli in salted water until tender, but crisp (color is still bright green). Line 9×13 dish with broccoli spears so heads are at edges. To make gravy, brown ¼ c. butter, ¼ c. flour, 2 c. chicken broth. When thick, add ½ c. light cream. Pour ½ of gravy over broccoli; add ½ c. Parmesan cheese to the remainder of the gravy. Slice chicken in long pieces and place on next. Pour the rest of the gravy on top, and sprinkle with Parmesan cheese and parsley. Bake at 350° for 20 min.

Carolyn Mast (Waitress)

CHEESEBURGER PIE

1 lb. ground beef	½ t. salt
½ c. tomato sauce	¼ t. pepper
¼ c. onion, chopped	½ c. soft bread crumbs

Mix all together and spoon into unbaked pie crust. Press down. Then make a cheese topping to put on top.

Cheese Topping:

1 c. grated cheese	1 egg, beaten
⅓ c. milk	½ t. mustard
½ t. Worcestershire sauce	

Mix these ingredients together and spread over pie. Bake at 375° for about 35 min.

Rose Schrock (Baker)

What did the mama broom and the papa broom say to the baby broom? "Go to sweep."

BAKED CHICKEN BREASTS

4 whole chicken breasts, split, skinned and boned
1 can undiluted mushroom soup
½ t. white pepper
8 slices uncooked bacon
4 oz. dried beef
1 c. sour cream

Wrap each breast in bacon. Cover bottom of 9×13 greased baking dish with dried beef. Arrange chicken on top, mix soup, sour cream and pour over chicken. Bake uncovered at 275° for 2½-3 hours or until fork tender.

Jan Bontrager (Waitress)

CHICKEN BAR-B-Q

2⅓ to 3½ lbs. chicken
1 c. catsup
½ t. pepper
1 medium onion finely chopped
1 T. Worcestershire sauce

½ c. oleo
1 t. salt
¼ t. garlic salt
⅓ c. lemon juice or vinegar

Boil all together except the lemon juice and Worcestershire sauce. Add these two when removed from heat. Pour over chicken and roast, covered tightly for 2 hours or till tender.

Fannie Yoder (Cook)

CORN PONE

½ c. sugar
1 egg
½ c. cornmeal
1 c. flour

2 t. baking powder
½ c. milk
½ c. melted butter
pinch of salt

Stir butter in last. Put in 9×9 pan and bake at 350-400° for 20 min. or till done.

Doris Miller (Waitress)

CHILI BEEF SUPREME

1 lb. ground beef
1 envelope onion soup mix
2 soup cans water
1 c. sour cream

1 T. butter
2 cans (11 oz.) condensed chili
 beef soup
1 T. flour
1 T. chili powder

Brown meat in butter. Add soup mix, chili beef soup and water. Bring to boil. Simmer 5 min. Stir flour into sour cream. Stir into chili mixture along with chili powder. Simmer 5 min. but do not boil. More water can be added to suit your taste.

Bertha Bontrager (Pie Baker)

Forget what others think. It's time to bake your own fortune cookie!

DEEP DISH TACO SQUARES

½ lb. ground beef
½ c. sour cream
⅓ c. mayonnaise
1 or 2 med. tomatoes, thinly sliced
½ c. chopped green peppers

1 T. chopped onion
1 c. Bisquick
½ c. shredded Cheddar cheese
¼ c. cold water

Heat oven to 375°. Grease square baking dish, 8×8×2. Cook and stir ground beef until brown; drain. Mix sour cream, mayonnaise, cheese, and onion; reserve. Mix baking mix and water until soft dough forms. Pat in pan, pressing dough ½" up on sides. Layer beef, tomatoes, and green peppers in pan. Spoon sour cream mixture over top. Sprinkle with paprika if desired. Bake until edges of dough are light brown, 25-30 min.

Cheryl Troyer, (Cashier, Gift Shop)
Susanna Miller (Cook)
Laura Bontrager (Bakery)
Esther Hershberger

If in doubt about how much spice to use, remember Grandmother's rule and "season to taste."

DRIED BEEF CASSEROLE

1 c. chopped onions	pinch of salt and pepper
4 oz. dried beef (cut up)	2 c. corn
¼ c. butter	2 big potatoes
2 T. flour	2 c. milk

Saute onions and add beef. Stir in flour, add milk a little at a time. Pour this over potatoes and corn and bake 25-30 min. at 425°.

Ida Mae Schmucker (Pie Baker)

Soak mildew stains for several hours in a weak solution of chloride of lime—afterwards rinse in cold water.

DRIED BEEF CASSEROLE

2 cans cream of mushroom soup	2¾ c. milk
2 c. Velveeta cheese	1¾ c. uncooked macaroni
½ lb. dried beef (chopped)	2 sliced hard boiled eggs

Directions: Stir soup until creamy. Add milk, cheese, macaroni and diced beef. Fold in egg slices. Pour into buttered dish. Refrigerate 3-4 hours. Bake 1 hour uncovered in 350° oven.

Laura Anna Miller (Grill Worker)

EGG ROLLS

Fry:

1 lb. sausage
2-3 large cloves garlic, minced

1 onion

Add and heat briefly:

½ head cabbage, shredded
1 t. salt

1 handful bean thread
½ t. pepper

Wrap in egg roll wrappers, following directions on back of package. This makes approximately 2 dozen egg rolls.

Sauce: Saute 2 large cloves garlic, minced in 2 T. oil. Add 3 T. ketchup and 1 T. sugar.

Alice Golden (Waitress)

MOTHER: "Another bite like that, and you'll have to leave the table."
HUNGRY BOY: "Another bite like that, and I'll be through."

DUTCH COUNTRY CORN PUDDING

1 c. dried corn
3 c. milk
2 T. sugar

2 eggs
1 T. butter
½ t. salt

Grind the dried corn in a good chopper and pour on 2 c. of hot milk and let stand for an hour. Then add the eggs, well beaten, 1 c. of milk, the butter, sugar, and salt to taste and put into a buttered baking dish. Set the dish in a pan of hot water and bake for 2 hours in a moderate oven at 350°.

Leora Kauffman (Purchasing)

EGG AND HAM CASSEROLE

ham shavings
3 doz. eggs, beaten
6 cans mushrooms

1 can mushroom soup
1 can milk
salt and pepper to taste

Mix together and pour into greased baking dish. Top with Velveeta cheese and bake at 350° for 30 min.

Mary Esther Mast (Waitress)

EL PASO CASSEROLE

1¾ lbs. Velveeta cheese
2 lbs. cubed ham
1½ lb. wide noodles

Cook noodles in water and drain. Put noodles and ham in casserole. Add cheese to a white sauce made of ½ lb. butter, 1 c. flour and 2 quarts milk. Pour sauce over noodles and ham. Bake 30 min. at 350°. If you like, add bread crumbs on top before baking. Also good with potatoes instead of noodles.

Laura Anna Miller (Grill Worker)

FIRESIDE SUPPER

1 - 7¼ oz. pkg. macaroni
  and cheese
2 c. chopped cooked ham,
  turkey or chicken
1 - 10 oz. pkg. frozen peas,
  carrots, cooked, drained

1 c. dairy sour cream
¼ c. chopped onion
1 T. chopped parsley
¼ t. rosemary
dash pepper

Prepare macaroni as directed on package. Add remaining ingredients; mix well. Heat thoroughly, stirring occasionally. 6 servings.

Sue Miller (Manager)

FLUFFY OVEN EGGS AND BACON

½ lb. bacon (about 12 slices)
½ lb. chopped onions
3 eggs
¼ t. salt

½ c. Bisquick baking mix
1¼ c. milk
1/8 t. pepper
½ c. shredded Cheddar or
    Swiss cheese

Heat oven to 375°. Grease 1½ quart round casserole. Cut bacon slices into thirds. Cook and stir bacon in 10" skillet over medium heat until almost crisp. Add onions. Cook, stirring frequently, until bacon is crisp; drain. Spread bacon and onion in bottom of casserole.

Beat baking mix, eggs, milk, salt and pepper with hand beater until almost smooth. Slowly pour egg mixture over bacon, sprinkle with cheese. Bake uncovered until knife inserted in center comes out clean, about 35 min. Makes 4-6 servings. May substitute 1 c. fully cooked ham or bacon. Spread ham and onion in bottom of casserole. Continue as directed.

Polly Yoder (Bakery)

FRANKS'N CRESCENTS

8 frankfurters, partially split
sharp Cheddar cheese, cut in strips

1 - 8 oz. can refrigerated
crescent rolls

Fill each frankfurter with cheese strip. Separate crescent dough into eight triangles. Place frankfurter on wide end of each triangle; roll up. Place on greased cookie sheet, cheese side up. Bake at 375° for 15 min. or until rolls are golden brown. 8 servings.

Sue Miller (Manager)

You're not what you think you are; but what you THINK—you are!

FRIED RICE

1 pound ground beef
1 medium onion
2 T. soy sauce
4 T. oil

1½ c. mixed vegetables
1 c. minute rice
3 eggs
salt and pepper to taste

Brown hamburger and onion. Add oil and soy sauce. Mix in vegetables and cook until soft. Add cooked rice. Beat eggs and pour over mixture. Stir-fry until eggs are well done. Serves 4-6.

Denise Henke (Waitress)

GOULASH

4 c. macaroni
1 qt. tomato juice
1 pt. catsup

2 lb. hamburger fried with salt
  and pepper and a little onion
¼ c. brown sugar

Heat water to boil, add 1 t. salt. Cook macaroni over low heat till done, stirring occasionally. Put in a 4 quart casserole dish, add remaining ingredients. Mix and bake. Bake at 350° for ½ hour or till done. Optional: you may add stewed tomatoes if you like.

Lydia Ann Miller (Head Cook)

HAMBURGER TATER TOT CASSEROLE

1 or 2 lbs. hamburger
1 onion
Velveeta cheese

1 can cream of mushroom soup
milk

Brown hamburger and onion. Drain. Put in large casserole dish. Add slices of Velveeta cheese on top of all the hamburger. Add 1½ c. milk to can of mushroom soup and put over cheese. Cover with Tater Tots. Bake at 375° for 45 min.

Mary Miller (Waitress)
Beth Ann Yoder (Salad Girl)

HAMBURGER CASSEROLE

1½ lb. hamburger, fried with 1 onion
1 c. sour cream
1 can mushroom soup
1 can cream of chicken soup
1 quart corn
3 c. noodles (cooked). Mix all together and top with onion rings (frozen).
Bake at 350° for 45 min.

Ida Weaver (Cook)
Esther Nisley (Pie Baker)

HAM LOAF

1½ lb. hamburger
2 lb. pork
1 lb. ham
salt to taste

2 c. bread crumbs
3 eggs

Bake at 350° for 2 hours.

Ida Weaver (Cook)

HAM AND GREEN BEAN CASSEROLE

Sauce:

½ c. margarine
3 c. milk

½ c. flour
1½ c. grated cheese

Melt margarine, stir in flour, add milk. Stir over low heat till thickened.
Add cheese. Allow to melt.

3 med. potatoes, cooked and diced   1 qt. green beans
3 c. chopped ham

Arrange potatoes in greased casserole. Cover with green beans. Pour half of cheese sauce over beans. Cover with ham. Add remaining cheese sauce. Put bread crumbs on top. Bake at 350° for 30 min.

Katie Miller (Gift Shop Manager)

HAMBURGER AND RICE CASSEROLE

1 lb. ground hamburger
1½ c. celery, cut fine
2 cans water
1 c. rice, uncooked

2 small onions
1 can mushroom soup
¼ c. soy sauce

Put rice in bottom of casserole. Brown meat and onion, add the rest and pour over rice. Bake at 350° for ½ hr. Don't stir and don't season. Serves 8.

Edna Schrock (Cook)

The new hired hand spoke right up to his employer. "Your farming methods are terribly old-fashioned. I doubt if you'll get ten pounds of apples from that tree." "I doubt it, too," said the farmer, "it's a peach tree."

HAMBURGER SAUCE MIX

10 lb. ground beef
10 large onions, chopped
10 - 6 oz. cans tomato paste

6⅔ c. water
10 t. salt
2¼ t. pepper

Cook beef and onion till browned. Add remaining ingredients. Bring to a boil and simmer for 5 min. Put into jars and can in pressure cooker. (For pints: 10 lbs. pressure for 75 min. For quarts 10 lbs. pressure for 90 min.)

This is very handy to use whenever ground beef is an ingredient—chili soup, spaghetti sauce, pizza, etc.—and it's ready at a moment's notice.

Mary Ellen Yutzy

HAYSTACKS

The following is a favorite meal for Amish community gatherings. The ingredients vary from one occasion to another, but the basic concept remains the same:

½ lb. soda crackers, crushed
2 c. cooked rice
2 heads lettuce, chopped
2 pkg. corn chips
6-8 tomatoes, diced
chopped nuts

sliced olives
3 lb. hamburger, browned
   and drained
1 jar spaghetti sauce, heated
2 cans cheddar cheese soup,
      mixed with 1 soup-can of
      milk and heated

Layer all ingredients on each person's plate in the order given. Serves 12-14 people.

Edna Bontrager (Cook)
Rosa Borntrager (Gift Shop)

JULIE'S GREEN BEANS

1 qt. green beans
1 can cream of mushroom soup
2 eggs, hard-boiled and diced

2 c. cheese
½ c. milk
½ c. buttered bread crumbs

Mix all ingredients except bread crumbs. Put into baking dish and top with bread crumbs. Bake at 325° for 45 minutes.

Esther Nisley (Baker)

JEWISH MEATBALLS

1½ lb. ground beef
½ c. milk
1 t. salt
½ t. pepper

1 c. oatmeal
1 medium onion, finely chopped
1 can cream of mushroom soup,
      mixed w/ 1 c. milk

Mix ground beef with all other ingredients except soup and milk. Form into small balls. Brown the meatballs in margarine. Place in casserole dish and add the soup-and-milk mixture. Bake in 325° oven for 1 hour.

Laura Ann Miller (Grill Cook)

HOMINY

Shell and wash 4 ears of white or yellow, dried, field corn. Put in kettle and cover with water. Add 4 T. soda (1 T. for each ear of corn). Cook until the hulls come off and the corn is tender. Drain and wash 10-12 times, until there are no hulls left. Put back on the stove with a little water and continue cooking until done.

Ida Weaver (Cook)

LASAGNA

1 lb. ground beef
½ c. chopped onion
1 - 16 oz. can tomatoes
1 - 6 oz. can tomato paste
⅓ c. water
1 garlic clove, minced
1 t. oregano leaves
¼ t. pepper

8 oz. lasagna noodles, cooked, drained
2 - 6 oz. pkgs. mozzarella cheese slices
½ lb. Velveeta cheese spread, thinly sliced
½ lb. grated Parmesan cheese

Brown meat; drain. Add onion, cook until tender. Stir in tomatoes, tomato paste, water and seasonings. Cover; simmer 30 min. In 11¾"×4×7½" baking dish, layer half of noodles, meat sauce, Mozzarella cheese, cheese spread and Parmesan cheese; repeat layers. Bake at 350° for 30 min. Let stand 10 min. before serving. Serves 6 to 8.

Sue Miller (Manager)

Speak out for the Lord; remember, silence isn't always GOLDEN, on occasion it may be just plain YELLOW!

Lettuce will not rust so quickly if you line the bottom of the refrigerator vegetable drawer with paper towels—the paper absorbs the excess moisture, keeping vegetables and fruits fresher for a longer period of time.

MANHATTAN MEATBALLS

2 lbs. ground beef
2 c. soft bread crumbs
½ c. chopped onion
2 T. chopped parsley
2 eggs

2 t. salt
2 T. margarine
1 - 10 oz. jar apricot preserves
½ c. barbecue sauce

Combine meat, crumbs, onion, eggs, parsley and salt; mix lightly. Shape into 1 inch meatballs. Brown in margarine; drain. Place in 2 quart casserole. Combine preserves and barbecue sauce; pour over meatballs. Bake at 350° for 30 min. stirring occasionally. Approximately 4½ dozen.

To make ahead: Prepare recipe as directed, except for baking. Cover seal securely. Freeze. When ready to serve, place in refrigerator 6 to 8 hours. Uncover; bake at 350° for 1 hour, stirring occasionally.

Sue Miller (Manager)

Faults are thick where love is thin.

MEAT BALLS

1 lb. hamburger
½ c. bread crumbs
⅓ c. minced onion
¼ c. milk
1 egg

1 T. parsley
1 t. salt
1/8 t. pepper
½ t. Worcestershire sauce
½ c. brown sugar

Mix all ingredients together and form meat balls. Brown meat balls in little oil, then drain.

Mix together 12 oz. chili sauce and 10 oz. grape jelly. Heat, then add meatballs to sauce and simmer in sauce for ½ hour. Serve hot.

Barbara Bainter (Cleaning Service)

MEXICAN FOOD

Brown 1 lb. beef until tender

Add:

¼ c. soy sauce
2 c. celery
2 c. onions

2 green peppers
½ lb. mushrooms

Cook until boiling, then cook 5 min. more, stir constantly. Thicken with 1 large tablespoon flour. Cook 1 c. rice to eat with this.

Rosa Hochstetler (Cook)

The lazy man aims at nothing and usually hits it.

MOCK HAM LOAF

1 lb. hamburger
1 c. cracker crumbs
1 t. salt
½ glaze mix

½ lb. hot dogs (ground)
1 egg, beaten
pinch of pepper

Mix together well.

Glaze Mix:

½ c. brown sugar
1 T. vinegar

½ c. hot water

Mix and add ½ of glaze to hamburger mixture. Pour the other half over top of hamburger mixture. Bake at 350° for 1 hour.

Ruth Elaine Miller (Waitress)

MOCK TURKEY

2 lb. hamburger (browned in butter)
dash of salt and pepper
2 cans cream of chicken soup
4 c. milk
1 loaf bread toasted and cubed
1 can cream of mushroom soup

Mix together and put in pan. Bake at 350° for 45 min. till brown.

Rosa Hochstetler (Cook)

Any housewife, no matter how large her family, can always get some time to be alone by doing the dishes.

OVEN BARBECUED STEAKS

3 lbs. round steak, cut ¾" thick
2 T. vegetable oil
½ c. chopped onion
¾ c. catsup
½ c. vinegar
1/8 t. black pepper

¾ c. water
1 T. brown sugar
1 T. prepared mustard
1 T. Worcestershire sauce
½ t. salt

Pre-heat oven to 350°. Cut steak into ten equal portions. Pour oil into skillet, browning each piece of steak on both sides. Transfer steak to roasting pan. Add onion to oil in skillet and brown lightly. Add rest of ingredients to make barbecue sauce and simmer for 5 min. Pour sauce over steaks in pan. Cover. Bake 2 hours or until meat is tender.

Martha Miller (Cook)

PARTY CHICKEN-NOODLE CASSEROLE

1 lg. can Chinese noodles
1 can cream of mushroom soup
1 lg. can evaporated milk
8 chicken breasts or 1 #3 can
    chicken cooked and cut in pieces

1 sm. jar pimento
1 can cream of chicken soup
2 cans mushrooms
buttered crumbs

Mix ingredients together in 9×13 pan. Can use more or less chicken. Top with buttered crumbs. Bake at 350° for about 45 min.

Carol Wiggins (Cashier in Bakery)

PEPPER STEAK

1 lb. flank steak, cut in strips ¼"×2" long
1 T. cornstarch
¼ t. pepper
pinch of garlic

4 T. soy sauce
¼ t. ginger
1 T. sugar

Mix and let stand 15 min. Slice onions into rings, mushrooms and green peppers into long slices and stir-fry in hot oil, not more than 3 min. Remove from pan, and brown meat in oil. Mix everything together and serve over rice.

Carolyn Mast (Waitress)

PIZZA CASSEROLE

2 c. macaroni
2 lbs. hamburger
1 pint pizza sauce
1 can mushroom soup
2 c. mozzarella cheese
pepperoni

Cook macaroni. Brown hamburger with onion. Add all ingredients except cheese and mix well. Put ½ of mixture in baking dish, add 1 c. cheese and then repeat. Bake at 350° for 30 min. Serves 8-10.

Denise Henke (Waitress)
Doris Miller (Waitress)

Pour leftover tea into ice tray and freeze it. Use the cubes in iced tea the next day.

PIZZA BURGERS

2 lbs. hamburger, browned, drained and cooled.

Mix together:

¼ lb. pepperoni

1 lb. Velveeta cheese
may add 1 can mushrooms

Add:

1 pt. pizza sauce
1 T. sugar

1 t. salt
¼ t. pepper

Put on half of hamburger bun, English muffin or French bread and bake 15 min. at 350°.

Laura Bontrager (Bakery)
Edith Herschberger (Cashier)

PIZZABURGER PIE

1 lb. ground beef
1½ c. chopped onion
½ t. salt
¼ t. pepper
1½ c. milk

¾ c. Bisquick
3 eggs
1 can pizza sauce
1 c. shredded cheese

Heat oven to 400°. Grease pie plate (10"). Brown beef and onions, stir in salt and pepper. Spread in plate. Beat milk, Bisquick, and eggs until smooth. Pour over hamburger. Bake for 25 min. Top with pizza sauce and cheese. Bake 5-8 min. Cool for 5 min. and serve.

Amanda Troyer (Waitress)
Fannie Yoder (Cook)

PIZZA POTATOES

Half fill a large roaster with raw sliced potatoes. Add 3-4 lbs. browned hamburger and 2 large onions, chopped fine. Top with 2 quarts drained tomato chunks. Add salt and pepper to taste.

Bring to boil:

1 qt. tomato juice
1 T. oregano
1 can tomato soup

1 c. catsup
1 t. garlic powder (optional)

Thicken with 2½ T. cornstarch and ½ c. water. Pour over contents of roaster. Top with cheese (Velveeta is good). Bake at 325° for 1 hour.

Mary Ellen Yutzy

The great man is he who does not lose his child's heart.

PIZZA CASSEROLE

Fry together: 1 lb. hamburger, salt and pepper and onion.

Simmer for 5 minutes:

1 can mushroom soup
1 can tomato soup
¼ t. thyme

¼ t. oregano
¼ t. garlic powder
1 c. minute rice

Combine these 2 mixtures and pour into 2 quart baking dish. Top with grated mozzarella cheese. Bake for 20 min. at 350°.

Marlene Eash (Cook)

A person completely wrapped up in himself makes a small package.

PIZZA CASSEROLE

1 lb. hamburger   1 chopped onion

Brown together and season with salt and pepper.

Add:

2 - 16 oz. cans pizza sauce
1 - 10 oz. pkg. shredded mozzarella cheese
1 - 7 oz. pkg. elbow macaroni (cooked)
4 oz. sliced pepperoni
1 can mushrooms

Put in layers in greased casserole dish and bake at 350° for 45 min.

Ruth Elaine Miller (Waitress)

POKOGI (Korean)

2 lbs. round steak (freeze and slice thin)
1 T. sesame seeds   3 chopped scallions
3-4 cloves minced garlic   5 T. soy sauce
2 T. vegetable oil   ½ c. sugar
2 T. dry sherry (or orange juice)   ¼ t. accent (optional)
1/8 t. pepper

Mix meat with sugar. Mix other ingredients; pour over meat, stir well, cover and let stand overnight or longer in refrigerator. Stir occasionally. Fry (don't need extra oil). Serve over rice.

Alice Golden (Waitress)

POT PIE

2 qts. rich broth with water (beef or ham or chicken)
1 medium onion   1 egg
1 large potato   ¼ t. baking powder
2½ c. flour   dash of salt

In large pot bring to boil broth, onion and potato. Beat 1 egg, add water to make 1 c. Put egg in bowl, add dash of salt, ¼ t. baking powder, 2½ c. flour as mixing. It will be sticky if you don't add a little water. Flour table top, roll out dough. Don't make it too thin. Cut in squares. Pick up each piece and put in the boiling broth. It may start to boil over, turn heat down, continue cooking until tender. Serve it with meat.

Barbara Bainter (Cleaning Service)

POTATO CAKES

2 c. mashed potatoes   2 eggs
2 rounding T. flour   1 t. onions, chopped
sprinkle of parsley

Mix all together and fry in skillet over low heat with a little oleo. Frying over low heat gives them a chance to set.

Lydia Ann Miller (Cook)

POTATOES SUPREME

6 medium potatoes
2 c. shredded cheese
¼ t. pepper
2 c. sour cream

¼ c. melted margarine
1 t. salt
½ to 1 c. green onions, tops too

Boil potatoes in skins until just tender. Cool, peel and shred coarsely. Mix cheese with melted margarine and add potatoes and green onions. Season with salt and pepper, fold in sour cream. Put in baking dish. Sprinkle generously with paprika. Bake for 30 min. at 350°

Top with 2 c. crushed cornflakes mixed with ¼ c. melted butter (optional).

Leora Kauffman (Purchasing)
Wilma Weaver (Waitress)

QUICKY CASSEROLE

Grease a Pyrex dish with margarine and crush 4 c. soda crackers into it. Add a can of tuna and a can of peas, drained. Moisten with enough milk to soften crackers and bake until hot—delicious! A small child can complete this alone.

Edna Schrock (Cook)

QUICK AND EASY CASSEROLE

1 lb. hamburger
1 medium onion
1 pint peas or green beans
salt and pepper to taste

½ lb. noodles
1 can mushroom soup
  or tomato soup
1½ c. milk

Fry hamburger and onion. Cook noodles and peas. Mix together milk and mushroom soup. Mix altogether and bake at 350° for 1 hour. Put buttered crumbs or cheese on top if you like.

Meredith Mast (Dishwasher)
Wilma Weaver (Waitress)

QUICK PIZZA TREATS

1 - 8 oz. can tomato sauce
2 T. finely chopped green pepper
1 T. finely chopped onion
¼ t. oregano leaves, crushed

4 English muffins, split, toasted
4 Deluxe Choice process
  American cheese slices,
  cut in half

Combine tomato sauce, green pepper, onion and oregano. For each appetizer, spoon tomato mixture onto muffins; broil until hot. Top with cheese; continue broiling until melted. 8 servings.

Variation: Substitute Swiss cheese slices, shredded Mozzarella or grated Parmesan cheese.

Sue Miller (Manager)

ROAST BEEF

5 lbs. chuck roast (with bone) or
4 lbs. chuck roast (without bone)

Put in a 2½ quart baking dish. Sprinkle over top of beef:

½ t. salt
¼ t. pepper
1 T. beef base

Pour 1 c. tomato juice over top and add water to barely cover beef. Cover and bake at 350° for approximately 3 hours. Use the juice of baked beef and thicken for a gravy.

Lydia Ann Miller (Cook)

 Keep your face to the sunshine and you cannot see the shadow.

RANCH STYLE HASH

2 lbs. hamburger
2 c. macaroni
1 medium onion, chopped
¼ t. basil
½ lb. grated cheese

4 oz. chopped green chilies
14 oz. stewed tomatoes
2 c. water
1 t. salt and a dash of pepper

Brown meat, drain off any fat, add all other ingredients (except cheese). Cover, bring to a boil. Simmer for 25 min. Add cheese, when cheese is melted it's ready. This makes enough for 4 or 5 people.

Norine Borkholder (Cook)

Let us cherish and love old age; fot it is full of pleasure, if one knows how to use it.

SALMON LOAF

2 T. lemon juice
1 - 1 lb. can (2 c.) salmon, drained and flaked (save juice)
1 c. medium white sauce
½ c. milk
½ t. salt
2 beaten eggs
¾ c. dry bread crumbs

Add lemon juice to salmon; add white sauce, milk, salt, eggs and bread crumbs; mix well. Bake in greased baking dish in moderate oven (350°) till brown. Approximately 30 min.

White Sauce: Melt 2 T. butter or margarine in the upper part of a double boiler over low heat. Add 2 T. flour, blend together. Take the salmon juice and milk to make a cup; add to butter and flour mixture. Cook till thick and smooth, stirring constantly. (Water shouldn't touch top of pan.) Add ¼ t. salt, dash of white pepper.

Barbara Bontrager (Cashier)

SAUCE FOR GREEN BEANS

3 T. white sugar
2 T. Wesson oil
1 small onion, cut fine

3 T. vinegar
1 T. prepared mustard
salt and pepper

Mix together and beat well. Pour over 1 qt. cooked drained green beans.

Beth Ann Yoder (Salad Girl)

SAUCY SANDWICHES

1 lb. sliced hot dogs
1 onion
½ c. catsup
2 T. flour
½ c. water
1 c. diced cheese

½ t. dry mustard
½ t. Worcestershire sauce
1 c. chopped celery
pinch pepper
½ t. salt

Brown hot dogs and onion. Mix catsup, flour, water, dry mustard, Worcestershire sauce, salt and pepper, and the celery. Stir into hot dog mixture, cook and add the cheese. Spoon into rolls and wrap in foil. Can be served right away or put in oven for 10-15 min. before serving.

Betti Kauffman (Cashier-Hostess)

SAUSAGE GRAVY

4 lbs. fresh sausage, fried and chopped. Then add: 3 c. flour and brown (if sausage is dry, you may need to add some shortening when adding flour), 2 T. salt, ½ T. pepper. Stir well and add: 18 c. milk. Heat to boiling point and reduce heat and simmer a few minutes. Makes approximately 5 qts. of gravy.

Lydia Ann Miller (Head Cook)

SALAD MASTER CASSEROLE

Put hamburger, pressed in pan. Grate large onion and put on top. Add 2 or 3 large potatoes, grated. Also carrots and 1 can of soup (any kind). Add large amount of grated cheese. Bake at 350°.

Wilma Weaver (Waitress)

SIX LAYER DINNER

1 lb. ground beef
1 c. onion (sliced)
1 c. celery (sliced)

2 c. carrots (sliced)
2 c. potatoes (sliced)

Place meat in bottom of casserole. Add remaining ingredients in order given. Salt each layer. Top with 1 can cream of chicken or celery soup and about ½ can water. Cover casserole and bake 1½ hours at 350°.

Barbara Bainter (Cleaning Service)

SKILLET LASAGNA

1 lb. ground beef
1 envelope spaghetti sauce mix
1 lb. cream style cottage cheese
3 c. noodles (uncooked)
1 - #2½ can tomatoes (1 lb. 12 oz.)
1 c. water
8 oz. pkg. shredded mozzarella cheese

Lightly brown hamburger, sprinkle ½ of spaghetti mix over meat. Spread cottage cheese over meat. Next add noodles in layer. Sprinkle remaining spaghetti mix. Add tomatoes with liquid and water and continue cooking slowly for 30-35 min. Sprinkle cheese over top. Return cover and let stand 10-15 min. before serving.

Mary Esther Mast (Waitress)

SOUR CREAM POTATOES

1 pint sour cream
1 T. onion
1 can cream of chicken soup
2 t. melted butter
1 c. grated Cheddar cheese

salt
9 cooked potatoes, grated
2 T. melted butter
½ c. crushed corn flakes

Mix together first 6 ingredients, add potatoes. Mix 2 T. butter and corn-flakes, and put on top. Bake at 350° uncovered for 1 hour. You can substitute cottage cheese or yogurt for part of cream.

Ellen Miller (Cashier, Gift Shop)

To rid frying pans of fish odor, sprinkle salt in pan, add hot water and let stand awhile before rinsing.

STROMBOLI

Thaw one frozen bread dough. Roll out to fit pizza pan. Spread pizza sauce over dough. Cover with one layer each:

shaved ham
salami
pepperoni
(any meat or vegetable may be used)

Sprinkle on mozzarella cheese, Parmesan cheese, and oregano. Roll up like jelly roll. Stick toothpicks in on top to hold dough together as it bakes. Be sure both ends are tucked shut tight. Brush with 1 beaten egg. Sprinkle with Parmesan and oregano. Bake at 325° for 40-45 min.

Arlene Miller (Waitress)

To remove fish odor from hands, rub them with vinegar or salt.

SPINACH LASAGNA

2 pkgs. (10 oz. each) frozen chopped spinach	9 lasagna noodles
¼ t. basil	1 lb. cottage cheese
1 t. salt	1 egg, beaten
¼ t. oregano	dash of pepper and garlic
cream (sweet or sour)	10 oz. Monterey Jack cheese, shredded

Cook noodles and steam spinach until limp. Mix cottage cheese with egg and spices. Layer noodles, spinach, cottage cheese, and Monterey Jack cheese into buttered 2-qt. baking dish, starting with noodles and ending with cheese. Spread cream (sweet or sour) on top to keep moist. Bake at 350° for ½ hour covered and 15 minutes uncovered.

Julianna Bontrager (Waitress)

SPICY CHICKEN GUMBO

¼ c. vegetable oil	1½ T. Worcestershire sauce
2 cloves garlic, minced	½ t. chili powder
2 onions, diced	1 bay leaf
1 green pepper, diced	2 c. cooked okra or celery
2 T. flour	3 c. broth or stock
2½ c. cooked tomatoes	¼ t. pepper
⅔ c. tomato paste	⅛ t. ground cloves
1½ T. salt	pinch dried basil
2 c. rice	4 c. water
1-3 c. chicken, cooked, boned, and diced	parsley (garnish)

In a large kettle, sauté garlic, onions, and green peppers in vegetable oil. Blend in flour. Cook and stir over low heat until vegetables are tender, then add remaining vegetables and seasonings. Simmer 1 hour.

Sauté 2 c. rice (white or brown) 5-10 minutes in enough oil to coat kernels evenly. Add 4 cups water and simmer until tender and all the water is absorbed.

Add 2-3 cups cooked chicken to gumbo. Simmer briefly. Remove bay leaf. To serve, mound rice in center of soup bowls and top with gumbo. Sprinkle with parsley. Serves 8.

Carolyn Mast (Waitress)

SPANISH OMELET

1 (4 oz.) green chilies, chopped and drained
1 lb. Monterey Jack cheese, grated
1 lb. Cheddar cheese
4 egg whites
4 egg yolks
⅔ c. evaporated milk
1 T. flour
½ t. salt
1/8 t. pepper
2 medium tomatoes

In large bowl combine cheese and green chilies. Put into 2 qt. buttered casserole dish. Beat egg whites until stiff. Beat yolks slightly, and add milk, flour, salt, pepper. Mix well and gently fold in egg whites. Pour into casserole and stir thru with fork. Bake at 325°.

Rosa Borntrager (Dutch Country Gifts)

SPAGHETTI SUPREME

½ lb. spaghetti (cooked in salted water)
¾ c. chopped onion
¼ c. salad oil

Saute above ingredients. Add:

1 ¼ lb. ground beef, browned
½ c. chopped carrots
½ c. chopped celery

Boil vegetables in water. Combine all above ingredients. Add ½ lb. grated cheese (Velveeta), 1 qt. tomato juice, 1 (12 oz.) can tomato soup, 1 (12 oz.) can cream of mushroom soup, 1 T. salt. Bake at 300° for 2 hours or 325° for 1½ hours.

Kathryn Helmuth (Pie Baker)

Work is love made visible.

SPAMBURGERS

1 can of Spam
1 small onion
3 T. milk
2 T. pickle relish

½ lb. cheese
3 T. catsup
2 T. mayonnaise

Grind Spam, cheese, and onion through food chopper, mix thoroughly. Add catsup, milk, mayonnaise and pickle relish. Spread on buns, wrap in foil, and bake at 300° for about 20 min.

Laura Bontrager (Bakery)

This time, like all other times, is a very good one if we but know what to do with it.

SWEET POTATO SOUFFLE

3 c. mashed sweet potatoes
1 c. brown sugar
1 c. canned milk
½ stick margarine (melted)
2 eggs
1½ t. vanilla

½ t. cinnamon
Topping:
1 c. chopped nuts
1 c. brown sugar
½ c. flour
1 stick margarine

Put all 7 ingredients together in blender or mix well with mixer. Pour into baking dish. Top with topping mixture. Bake in 10" × 10" at 350° for 1 hour.

Sharon Boley (Head Waitress)

SWEET AND SOUR BEEF

Marinate 2 lbs. beef. Cover and refrigerate overnight or longer.

Meat Marinate:

½ c. vegetable oil
4 t. cornstarch
4 t. red wine

8 t. sugar
8 t. soy sauce

4 green peppers, cut in strips
4 stalks celery, coarsely chopped
⅔ c. onion, chopped

In covered skillet, over medium high heat, heat meat and marinate to boiling. Reduce heat and simmer 30 min. or until meat is fork tender, stirring occasionally. With slotted spoon, remove meat and set aside. To skillet, add peppers, celery and onion. Cover and cook over medium heat until tender and crisp.

Wilma Weaver (Waitress)

God has a thousand ways
Where I can see not one
When all my means have reached their end
Then His have just begun.

TACO PIE

1 unbaked pie shell
1 lb. hamburger
1 medium onion
½ pkg. taco seasoning
water

½ c. sour cream
4 oz. shredded yellow cheese
shredded lettuce
½ c. crushed taco chips

Brown hamburger with onion; drain grease. Add taco seasoning and enough water to moisten. Put mixture into crust. Top with sour cream and cheese. Bake at 375° for 20-25 min. Top with lettuce and taco chips and serve.

Elma Miller (Waitress)

ROSY CHEESE BAKE

3 eggs, beaten slightly
2 cans tomato sauce
1 c. milk
1 t. salt

¼ t. pepper
8 slices bread
½ lb. American cheese, grated

Mix eggs, tomato sauce, milk and seasonings. Arrange alternate layers of bread, cheese, and sauce in greased square pan. Place pan over hot water and bake in slow oven (325°) for 50 min. or until knife inserted in center comes out clean.

Ida Weaver (Cook)

The gem cannot be polished without friction, nor man perfected without trials.

TUNA NOODLE CASSEROLE

Sauce:

1 large onion, chopped fine
½ c. butter or oleo
¼ c. flour

5 (10 oz.) cans mushroom soup
1 qt. milk

Saute the onion in the butter. Stir in flour and add the soup and milk gradually.

In very large roaster layer:

1 lb. noodles or macaroni, cooked and salted
2 (10 oz.) pkgs. frozen peas, cooked
5 cans tuna, drained and flaked
Add sauce
1¼ lb. potato chips, crushed to about 12 cups

Bake at 350° until heated through—about 1 hour. Serves 40-50.

Mary Ellen Yutzy

TACO RICE SKILLET

1 lb. hamburger
onion
½ pkg. taco seasoning
1 c. shredded lettuce

1 c. rice
2½ c. tomatoes
1 c. shredded cheese
salt

Cook rice, tomato juice for 20 min. Brown hamburger and onions and salt, add to rice, also ½ pkg. taco seasoning. Put in oven. Then put shredded cheese on top about 15 min. before serving. Put lettuce on top of everything just before serving. Do not heat after lettuce is on top.

Mary Rose Yoder (Pie Baker)

TALARIMA

8 c. noodles = (1 lb. uncooked)
4 lbs. hamburger, browned
4 c. corn
4 cans tomato soup
4 c. cheese
2 pkgs. onion soup
4 T. oleo
4 c. water

Bake 45 min. at 350°. Serves approximately 30.

Melissa Hershberger (Bakery Cashier)

TOMATO OYSTERS

1½ c. tomato juice
½ t. salt
½ t. sugar

1 egg, beaten
1¼ c. cracker crumbs
¼ t. pepper

Mix well, then with a tablespoon, put in frying pan and shape like a patty. Fry in shortening on both sides till brown.

Amanda Troyer (Waitress)

QUICK, CANDIED YAMS

4 large yams   ½ c. dark corn syrup
3 T. butter or margarine   salt

Peel yams and slice crosswise in ¼" slices. Melt butter or margarine in skillet. Lightly brown sliced yams in hot fat. When browned, sprinkle with salt and pour corn syrup over slices. Cover tightly and cook slowly for 10 min.

Ida Weaver (Cook)

VEGETABLE SAUSAGE LOAF

1 large carrot   1 egg
4 medium potatoes   ½ lb. sausage
1 medium onion   ¼ c. crumbs
4 stalks celery   ¼ c. milk
¼ t. summer savory   ½ t. salt

Grind vegetables. Beat egg and add with remaining ingredients. Form loaf and bake at 350° for 1 hour. Serves 6.

Ida Mae Schmucker (Pie Baker)

You give but little when you give of your possessions. It is when you give of yourself that you truly give.

VEGGY PIZZA

2 c. Bisquick
½ c. water

Press in jelly roll pan (ungreased). Bake 10 min. at 450°. Cool 20 min.

Mix with mixer:

8 oz. cream cheese
2 t. horseradish
½ c. onion or 1 T. minced
1 small can of shrimp, (tuna, crab or chicken)
½ c. mayonnaise

Spread on crust. Top with raw vegetables and cheese. I use radishes, broccoli, cauliflower, sliced olives, carrots, celery and shredded cheese. Pat gently.

Janet Mast

There is no happiness in having or in getting, but only in giving.

WESTERN MEAT BALLS

Mix well:

1 lb. ground beef	1 t. salt
½ c. rolled oats	pinch of pepper
½ c. milk	

Shape in 8 balls. Roll each ball in a mixture of 2 T. flour, 1 t. paprika, ½ t. salt. Brown in hot fat in heavy skillet. Add ¼ c. finely cut onions. Cook 5 min. slowly. Stir in ¼ c. Bar-B-Que sauce and 1¼ c. water. Simmer covered for 45 min.

Laura Anna Miller (Grill Worker)

ZUCCHINI BISCUIT CASSEROLE

1½ c. Bisquick	1 t. oregano
4 T. butter or margarine, softened	1 t. garlic salt
4-5 c. sliced zucchini	2 t. Parmesan cheese
2 c. onions, diced	5 eggs
1½ c. mozzarella cheese, shredded	½ c. vegetable oil
1 t. salt	¼ t. pepper

In a large bowl, combine Bisquick and butter till it resembles corn meal. Add zucchini, onoins, Mozzarella cheese, salt, pepper, and spices. Mix thoroughly. Place in greased baking dish, 9×13. In blender put eggs and oil, whip until foamy. Pour over zucchini mixture. Do not stir the egg mixture into zucchini mixture; it will blend as it bakes. Sprinkle Parmesan cheese on top. Optional—top with tomato slices. Bake at 350° for 1 hour. Serves 5-6.

Lois Landis (Cook's Helper)

 Keep your fears to yourself, but share you courage with others.

SANDWICH SPREAD

6 onions	6 green tomatoes
6 peppers	6 cucumbers
6 carrots	6 sticks celery

Grind all ingredients, cover with salt water and let stand overnight. Next morning drain and place in large kettle. Add 2 pints vinegar, 4 c. sugar and 1 c. ground mustard. Boil for 25 min. Make a paste using ⅔ c. flour and 1 c. water. Stir in after it boils to thicken the mixture. Can be put in jars and covered with paraffin.

Alma Hershberger (Bakery)
Mary Ellen Yutzy

EGG SALAD SANDWICHES

1 doz. hard boiled eggs, chopped

Mix and add to eggs:

½ c. salad dressing
1 t. vinegar
½ t. salt
¼ t. celery salt

1 T. mustard
1 T. sugar
¼ t. onion salt

You may add ground hot dogs or ham (optional).

Ruth Elaine Miller (Waitress)

Cakes & Frostings

MATCH SCRATCHES ON WALLS—Some menfolk are careless in scratching matches at any handy place to light their pipes or cigars. To keep your walls or mantlepieces from being marked up, take a piece of 4 in. by 4 in. sandpaper, frame it neatly and hang on to the wall in a handy place.

Dedicated to the generation now and those to follow of Earl Franklin and Vesta Louise Miller.

Did you hear me say I love you when I whispered in your ear?
Yet I heard no answer in my fear.

Oh, how I hoped and cried and prayed.
But in a deep sleep you were to lay
Until the Lord would take you away.

On earth in my arms you'll never be,
Yet in my heart memories of you will always be.

Until one day, we'll meet in heaven to hold each other ever and ever.
Then I'll know you'll have heard me say,
I love you in my heart and in it we'll never part.

Elaine Cox (Dishwasher)

AFTER BREAKFAST PRAYER

Dear Father, now that my family
    has gone to work and to school,
    a sudden quiet falls on this disordered house.
Help me to face the work for this day
    with a singing heart—
    the dishes to wash, the beds to make,
    the clothes to launder, and the picking up
    which sometimes seems as futile as
    sweeping a forest floor in time of falling leaves.
I thank Thee: that I am needed
    that my job in these busy years
    is to create a home that will be a
    place of warmth and comfort and love.
Help me to see each task, not as a dull chore,
    but as a strand woven into a pattern of living.
Grant, I pray, that it may be a pattern to remember,
    a pattern of order, and beauty, and through
    it always may there gleam the golden thread
    of Christ's spirit.

—Amen.

Cakes & Frostings

APPLE CRUMB COFFEE CAKE

¼ c. warm water
½ c. butter or margarine
½ t. salt
3 eggs
2 or 3 large apples, cored and sliced

1 pkg. dry yeast
½ c. sugar
2½ c. flour
¼ c. milk

Measure warm water into small bowl. Sprinkle in yeast and stir until dissolved. In large mixer bowl, cream butter or margarine with sugar and salt. Add yeast mixture, eggs and milk. Beat at medium speed until well blended.

Gradually add flour, medium speed, blend well. Spread batter into a well greased 9×9×2 square pan. Arrange apple slices on top, and sprinkle crumb topping over. Cover and let bake at 375° oven for 35 to 40 min. Turn out of pan, and cool on wire rack.

Crumb Topping:

⅔ c. sugar
2 t. cinnamon

½ c. flour
6 T. butter or margarine

Combine all ingredients and mix until crumbly. Sprinkle over apples.

Barbara Bontrager (Cashier)

CHERRY FRUITCAKE

3 c. all-purpose flour
2 c. sugar
2 t. baking powder
2 t. salt
2 lbs. pitted dates

2 lbs. diced, candied pineapple
4 lbs. red maraschino cherries, drained
3 lbs. pecan halves
12 eggs
⅔ c. orange juice

Grease pans and line with foil, allowing a 2 inch overhang and grease again. Sift flour, sugar, baking powder and salt into a large mixing bowl. Add fruits and pecans and toss until coated. Beat eggs and orange juice together and pour over the fruit mixture. Toss until completely combined. Pour mixture into prepared loaf pans, pressing with spatula to pack tightly. Bake at 250° for 1½-1¾ hours or until toothpick inserted in center comes out clean. Allow cakes to cool in pans for 10 min. Remove from pans. Tear off foil and brush with white Karo while still warm. Cool thoroughly before serving or storing.

6 - 6 inch round cake pans.   Mary Esther Miller (Bakery Manager)

CHOCOLATE ANGEL FOOD CAKE

2 c. egg whites
2 t. cream of tartar
½ t. salt
2 c. sugar

2 t. vanilla
1 c. plus 5 T. cake flour
3 T. cocoa

Put egg whites, cream of tartar and salt in a large bowl and beat at medium speed until foamy. Add 1 c. sugar, 2 t. at a time into foamy egg whites while beating at medium speed. After last of sugar is in, beat on high until stiff. Fold in vanilla. Sift together remaining sugar, flour and cocoa. Fold into stiff egg whites in three parts, 25 whips of each addition. Bake at 375° for 45-50 min. Invert on bottle to cool.

Elmina Troyer (Waitress)

CHOCOLATE SPICE CAKE

2 c. flour
2 c. sugar
1 c. oleo
4 T. cocoa
1 c. cold water

2 eggs
½ t. cinnamon
1 t. soda
1 t. vanilla
½ c. sour milk

Preheat oven to 325°. Blend flour and sugar, set aside. Bring oleo, cocoa and water to boil.

Pour cocoa mixture over the flour, blend well. Add remaining ingredients and mix well. Pour into 10½×15½" pan and bake for 30 min.

Frosting:

1 stick oleo
4 T. cocoa

⅓ c. milk
3½-4 c. powdered sugar

Alma Swartzentruber

CHOCOLATE PUDDING CAKE

1 c. flour
¼ t. salt
¾ c. sugar

2 t. baking powder
1½ T. Hershey cocoa

Sift together, then add:

½ c. milk
1 t. vanilla

2 T. melted butter
½ c. chopped nuts

Mix well. Pour into 8"×8" greased pan. (Like brownie dough)

Mix following ingredients and pour over chocolate mixture in pan.

½ c. brown sugar
½ c. granulated sugar

¾ c. water

Bake at 325° for 1 hour. Cool and serve with whipped topping or plain.

Barb Weaver (Cashier - Bakery)

CHRISTMAS FRUIT LOAF

2 c. sugar   1 c. milk and cream

Boil together till soft ball stage. Then add:

1 t. butter
1 lb. dates
1 c. nuts, chopped fine

Simmer till thick, then take off heat and let cool. Then beat good and pour on damp cloth, roll until hard, then slice and roll in powdered sugar.

Barbara Bainter (Cleaning Service)

COTTAGE PUFFS

Mix all together and bake in well-oiled cupcake or muffin tin:

⅓ c. butter   1½ c. flour
½ c. sugar   1½ T. baking powder
1 egg   ⅓ t. salt
½ c. milk   1 t. vanilla

Bake at 350° for 20 min. Serve with cocoa sauce.

Cocoa Sauce:

1½ c. boiling water   1½ T. flour or cornstarch
½ c. sugar   ½ t. vanilla
3 t. cocoa   1 t. butter
½ t. salt

Cook until sauce coats spoon. Pour over puffs just before serving.

Susie Bontrager (Cook)

CREAM FILLED COFFEE CAKE

Scald 1 c. milk, add ½ c. sugar, 1 stick oleo, and 1 t. salt. Beat 2 eggs in a large bowl and add above mixture. Dissolve 1 pkg. yeast in ¼ c. warm water and add to mix 3½ c. flour and let rise. (May rise in refrigerator overnight). Work dough in 3 pans (bread pans) and spread crumbs on top and let rise. Bake at 325° for 15 min. or until done. Cool and split each cake and fill with filling.

Crumbs:

½ c. brown sugar
½ c. flour
¼ c. butter

Filling:

Cook 3 T. flour (heaping) and 1 c. milk. Cool. Cream 1 c. sugar and 1 c. Crisco, then add flour mixture and 1 t. vanilla. Cream well and add 2⅓ c. powdered sugar.

Ida Weaver (Cook)

CREAM FILLED SPONGE CAKE

Mix together:

1 box yellow cake mix
1 box instant vanilla pudding
1 c. water

4 eggs
½ c. Wesson oil

Bake in two flat cookie sheets.

Filling:

3 egg whites, beaten
1 c. Crisco
5 T. milk

3 t. vanilla
3 T. flour
3 c. powdered sugar (or as needed)

Mix all together and beat until smooth. Then put on 1 cake and put the other on top and cut into pieces the size you want.

Fannie Yoder (Cook)

CREAM FILLED SPONGE CAKE

Mix together:

1 yellow cake mix
1 c. water
4 eggs

1 box vanilla instant pudding
½ c. Crisco oil

Divide into 2 pans and bake for 15-20 min at 325°.

Filling:

Cook 5 T. flour and 1¼ c. milk, stirring occasionally. Set aside to cool. Must be cold before adding to other ingredients.

Mix:

1 c. sugar
½ c. butter
1 t. vanilla

½ c. Crisco
½ t. salt

Beat until fluffy, add cooked mixture and beat again until fluffy. Spread on 1 cake and place the other cake on top. Cut into serving size pieces.

Lou Anna Yoder (Bakery)
Ruth Ann Bontrager (Busser)
Luanna Gingerich (Bakery Salesroom)
Elsie Miller (Grill Cook)

INDIVIDUAL CHEESE CAKES

18 vanilla wafers
½ c. sugar
2 t. vanilla

2 eggs
2 pkgs. (8 oz.) cream cheese
1 can (22 oz.) pie filling
(cherry or blueberry)

Place 18 paper cupcake liners in muffin tins. Put 1 wafer in each. Mix eggs, sugar, cream cheese, and vanilla together at medium speed for 5 min. Spoon into liners until ¾ full. Bake for 12-15 min. Let cool, then spoon on pie filling. Bake at 375°. Serves 18.

Lynette Zimmerman (Grill Worker)

DATE CAKE

1 c. dates, cut up
1 ¼ c. sugar
1 T. butter
1 egg, beaten

1 ½ c. flour
1 t. baking powder
1 t. vanilla
½ c. nuts

Pour 1 c. boiling water with 1 t. soda over dates and allow to cool. Cake part: Mix sugar, butter and egg. Next add date mixture, followed by remaining ingredients. Bake at 350° for 35 min. Cool cake and cover with topping.

Topping:

1 c. sugar
1 T. flour
½ c. nuts

1 c. dates, cut up
1 c. water

Cook slowly until thickened. Cool partly and spread on cake.

Rosa Borntrager (Dutch Country Gifts)

DELICIOUS RASPBERRY CAKE

1 regular size box white cake mix
⅔ c. Wesson oil
4 eggs

1 (3 oz) box raspberry jello
1 (10 oz.) pkg. frozen red
    raspberries (thawed—also
    use juice)

Mix all ingredients together. Bake in 9×13 pan at 325° for 50 min.

Katie Miller (Dutch Country Gifts)

Live every day of your life as though you expected to live forever.

DOUBLE DELIGHT COFFEE CAKE

2 c. flour
2 t. baking powder
1 c. water
1 t. vanilla

4 eggs
1 c. sugar
1 t. salt
¾ c. cooking oil

2 (3½ oz.) pkgs. vanilla instant pudding or other flavor

Topping:

1 c. chopped nuts
1 c. brown sugar
2 t. cinnamon

Frosting: (optional)

1 c. powdered sugar
2 T. milk

Mix together all batter ingredients in separate bowl, mix topping ingredients. Pour ½ of batter in 9×13 pan. Sprinkle ½ of topping on batter, pour in remaining batter. Put remaining topping on top and bake for 40 min. at 350°. Mix powdered sugar and milk and drizzle over cooled cake.

Katie Miller (Dutch Country Gifts)
Edna Slabach (Cook)

FOUR DAY COCONUT CAKE

1½ c. sugar
1 pint sour cream

24 oz. coconut
2 (8") layer white or yellow cakes

Mix sugar, coconut, and sour cream. Store in tightly covered container for 24 hours in refrigerator. Bake cake mix in 2 (8") pans. Chill. Split to make 4 layers. Put coconut mixture between layers, sides and on top. Store tightly covered in refrigerator for 3 days before serving.

Sharon Boley (Waitress)

MOTTO: Keep your nose to the grindstone, your shoulder to the wheel, and your eye on the ball. Now, try to work in that position.

FRUIT COCKTAIL CAKE

Mix:

1 c. white sugar
1¼ c. flour
1 t. baking soda
1 can #303 fruit cocktail

1 t. vanilla
1 t. salt
1 egg

Pour batter into cake pan. Sprinkle over the top ¾ c. brown sugar and chopped nuts. Bake at 375° for 45 min. Serve with whipped cream or —

Topping: (optional)

Boil together for 5 minutes:

1 stick butter
¾ c. sugar

¾ c. canned milk
1 t. vanilla

Prick hot cake with fork and pour topping on cake.

Barbara Bainter (Cleaning Service)
Mary Smucker (Busser)

If you want really great meatballs, put them in the refrigerator for twenty minutes before frying and they won't fall apart.

HUMMINGBIRD CAKE

3 c. all-purpose flour
1 t. baking soda
1 t. cinnamon

Combine in large bowl:

1 c. vegetable oil
8 oz. can crushed pineapple,
   undrained

2 c. sugar
1 t. salt
3 eggs, beaten
1½ t. vanilla
1 c. chopped pecans
2 c. chopped bananas

Combine first 5 ingredients in a large mixing bowl; add eggs and oil, stirring until dry ingredients are moistened. Do not beat. Stir in vanilla, pineapple, pecans, and bananas. Spoon batter into 3 greased and floured 9" round cake pans. Bake at 350° for 25-30 min. or until wooden toothpick inserted in center comes out clean. Cool in pans for 10 min.; remove and cool completely. Spread frosting between layers, on top and sides. Sprinkle pecans on top.

Cream Cheese Frosting:

8 oz. pkg. cream cheese, softened
1 lb. powdered sugar, sifted

½ c. butter or margarine, softened
1 t. vanilla

Combine cream cheese and butter, beating until smooth. Add powdered sugar and vanilla; beat until light and fluffy. Makes enough frosting for one 3-layer cake.

Alma Hershberger (Bakery)
Joyce Schrock (Waitress)

LADY BALTIMORE CAKE

¾ c. shortening
2 c. sugar
3 c. cake flour
¾ t. salt
3 t. baking powder

½ c. milk
½ c. water (cold)
½ t. vanilla
½ t. lemon juice
1 c. egg whites

Cream together sugar and shortening. Add alternately flour, salt, baking powder, milk and water. Lemon flavoring may be substituted for lemon juice. Fold in stiffly beaten egg whites. Put in 9×13 greased pan or two 9 in. pans and bake for 35 min. at 350°.

Ella Bontrager (Cook)

LEMON CAKE

1 pkg. lemon cake mix
1 pkg. instant lemon pudding mix
½ c. salad oil

¾ c. water
4 eggs

Combine cake mix, pudding mix, salad oil and water at medium speed on mixer. Add eggs one at a time, beating after each addition. Pour batter in greased 9×13 pan and bake at 350° for 35 min.

Lemon Icing:

2 c. powdered sugar
2 T. butter

2 T. water
⅓ c. lemon juice
or use 6 oz. can frozen lemonade
and 2 c. powdered sugar

Make icing while cake is baking. Melt butter and add powdered sugar and water and lemon juice. Blend thoroughly. When cake is done, pierce all through with long cooking fork. Pour icing over hot cake and spread so that it is absorbed throughout. Serve from the pan after cooling.

Ida Weaver (Cook)
Lois Landis (Cook's Helper)

MAGIC CUPCAKES

Use your favorite chocolate cake recipe or mix. Fill cupcake liners as usual and add the following filling.

Cream Filling for Cupcakes:

1 (8 oz.) pkg. cream cheese, room temperature
½ c. sugar
1 egg

Mix until creamy, stir in:

½ c. nuts
1 c. chocolate bits

Put 1 t. chocolate bits on each cupcake and bake as usual.

Elsie Miller (Grill Cook)

I have only just a minute.
Only sixty seconds in it.
Didn't seek it, didn't choose it.
But it's up to me to use it.
I must suffer if I lose it.
Give account if I abuse it.
Just a tiny little minute.
But Eternity is in it.

MAPLE PECAN CHIFFON CAKE

2 c. flour
¾ c. brown sugar
¾ c. white sugar
¾ c. water
½ c. salad oil
4 eggs, separated

1 c. chopped nuts
3 t. baking powder
1 t. salt
½ t. cream of tartar
2 t. maple flavor

Put flour, baking powder and white sugar in sifter. Set aside. In a mixing bowl add the oil, egg yolks, water and maple flavor. Beat well. Sift in flour mixture. Sift brown sugar and add to mixture. Add nuts. Beat egg whites, salt, and cream of tartar for 5 min. Fold into flour mixture and mix thoroughly. Pour into angel food cake pan and bake at 325°.

Mary Yoder (Bakery)

A four-year-old was showing the family's new bathroom scale to a five-year-old.
"What is it?" asked the five-year-old.
"I don't know, but when Mommy and Daddy stand on it it makes them mad."

MAPLE COFFEE CAKE

2¾ c. to 3 c. flour
1 c. buttermilk
¼ t. baking soda
1 egg

1 envelope yeast
¼ c. sugar
¼ c. margarine
1 t. salt

Filling:

½ c. brown sugar, packed
2 T. flour
¼ c. margarine
½ t. maple flavoring

⅓ c. white sugar
½ t. cinnamon
¼ c. maple syrup
½ c. chopped walnuts

Combine 1½ c. flour, yeast and soda in large bowl. Heat and stir buttermilk, margarine, sugar and salt until margarine melts. Add to dry ingredients. Stir in egg. Beat at low speed ½ min. scraping bowl constantly. Beat 3 min. at high speed. Stir in enough remaining flour to make dough moderately stiff. Turn onto floured board and knead 5 min. Cover and let rest 10 min., meanwhile combine all ingredients for filling except nuts. Beat at medium speed 2 min. Stir in nuts. Divide dough in half and roll each half to a 14×6″ rectangle. Spread each half with filling. Fold dough in half to make 14×3″ rectangle. Cut in 1″ strips, twist each strip. Arrange in 9″ pie pan start in center or on greased baking sheet. Let rise 1 hour. Bake at 375° oven for 15 min. Cool. Frost with confectioner's icing if desired.

Millie Whetstone (Cook)

MOM'S ONE EGG CAKE

1 c. sugar
2 c. flour
2 t. baking powder
pinch of salt

1 c. milk
1 egg
butter size of an egg
any flavoring desired

Mix together and put in 8×8 greased pan. Bake at 375° for 25-30 min.

Martha Miller (Cook)

By the time you think you have the world on a string, someone shows up with a pair of scissors.

OATMEAL CHOCOLATE CHIP CAKE

1¾ c. boiling water
1 c. lightly packed brown sugar
½ c. butter
1¾ c. unsifted flour
½ t. salt
1 pkg. (12 oz.) chocolate chips

1 c. uncooked oatmeal
   (quick or regular)
1 c. white sugar
2 extra large eggs
1 t. baking soda
1 heaping T. cocoa
¾ c. walnuts

In large bowl, pour boiling water over oatmeal. Let stand for 10 min. Add brown sugar, white sugar, and butter. Stir till butter melts. Add eggs, mix well. Add dry ingredients, mix well. Add ½ pkg. chocolate chips, mix and pour into greased pan. Top with nuts and rest of chocolate chips. Bake at 350° for 40-50 min.

Beth Ann Yoder (Busser)

Always remember to forget the things that made you sad. But never forget to remember the things that made you glad.

ORANGE SLICE CAKE OR FRUIT CAKE

1 c. butter
4 eggs

2 c. sugar
3 c. flour

Mix above in order given.

2 c. pecans
1 t. grated orange rind
1 lb. orange slices (cut in pieces)

½ lb. chopped dates
4 oz. coconut

Mix above with ½ c. flour

Combine both mixtures in a cake batter. Bake in a well greased angel food cake pan at 275° for 2 hours and 15 min. Poke holes in cake and pour hot orange juice glaze over top. Let cool completely.

Orange Juice Glaze:

1 c. orange juice
½ c. sugar
½ t. cornstarch

Boil for 5 min.

Anne Yoder (Evening Manager)
Elsie Miller (Grill Cook)

PARTY WHITE CAKE

1½ c. sugar
⅔ c. Crisco
2½ c. flour
2 t. salt

4½ t. baking powder
1 c. sweet milk
1 t. vanilla
4 beaten egg whites

Cream the sugar and shortening. Add the milk and dry ingredients alternately with the milk. Add the egg whites last. Bake in a 350° oven in 2 - 8 in. round greased pans until toothpick inserted in center comes out clean.

Ida Troyer (Baker)

Nature is an outstretched finger pointing toward God!

PEACH CUSTARD CAKE

Put into a 1½ qt. bowl 1½ c. flour, ½ t. salt and ½ c. soft butter or margarine. Mix with a pastry blender until mixture looks like coarse meal.

With back of spoon, press mixture firmly on bottom and half way up sides of buttered 8″ pan.

Drain well, 1 lb. 14 oz. can sliced peaches, saving ½ c. syrup. Arrange drained peaches on crust in pan. Sprinkle over peaches a mixture of ½ c. sugar and ½ t. cinnamon. Bake in 375° oven for 20 min.

Mix the ½ c. peach syrup, 1 egg, slightly beaten and 1 c. Pet evaporated milk. Pour over peaches. Bake for 30 min. more, or until custard is firm except in center. Center becomes firm on standing. Serve warm or cold. Serves 9.

Millie Yoder (Cashier, Country Cupboard)

The motto above the kitchen sink of a family of nine.
Eat it up,
Wear it out.
Make it do,
or do without.

PUMPKIN SPICE CAKE

2 c. flour
2 c. sugar
2 t. baking powder
2 t. soda
½ t. salt

2 t. cinnamon
2 c. pumpkin
4 eggs
1 c. salad oil
1 c. nuts

Sift flour with sugar, baking powder, soda, salt and cinnamon. Add remaining ingredients except nuts. Beat until smooth. Add nuts. Pour into 9 × 13 pan. Bake at 350° for 45 min. Can be baked in bundt or angel food cake pan.

Frosting:

1 stick butter or margarine
1 (8 oz.) pkg. cream cheese
1 t. vanilla
1 box powdered sugar

Cream butter and cream cheese. Add vanilla and powdered sugar. Mix until smooth. Or can be glazed with powdered sugar and water glaze.

Fanny Yutzy (Bakery)
Julianna Bontrager (Waitress)

Well digging is the only job left where you start at the top.

PINEAPPLE CAKE

2 c. sugar
2 eggs
1 #2 can crushed pineapple

2 c. sifted flour
2 t. soda
1 c. nuts (optional)

Beat eggs, add sugar, flour, soda, etc. Bake at 350° for 25-30 min. Bake in 9×13 ungreased pan.

Frosting:

1 (8 oz.) pkg. cream cheese
2 c. powdered sugar

½ stick oleo
1 t. vanilla

Fannie Yutzy (Pie Baker)
Julianna Bontrager (Waitress)
Edna Fern Schmucker (Bakery)

 Swallow your pride occasionally. It's not fattening.

PUMPKIN DELIGHT

1 large can pumpkin
3 eggs, slightly beaten
1 c. white sugar
1 c. brown sugar
1 c. evaporated milk
1 t. cinnamon

¾ t. nutmeg
½ t. cloves
1 t. salt
1 pkg. yellow cake mix
1 c. chopped nuts
1 stick margarine, melted

Combine first five ingredients and all spices. Mix well. Pour into greased 9×13 inch pan. Sprinkle cake mix on top and cut mix through batter. Sprinkle nuts on top. Drizzle melted margarine over top. Bake at 350° for 45-60 min. Good warm or cold and also with whipped topping.

Barb Weaver (Cashier - Bakery)

PUMPKIN CAKE

2¾ c. sugar
3 eggs
½ t. salt
1 t. vanilla
1 t. cinnamon
¼ t. allspice

1 c. salad oil
½ c. pumpkin
1 t. soda
2¾ c. flour
¼ t. cloves

Sift dry ingredients together. Beat sugar, eggs, oil and add pumpkin mix with dry ingredients. Add vanilla.

Can be baked in angel food pan or oblong cake pan. Bake for 1 hour at 350°. Serve with whipped topping.

Rosalie Bontrager (Essenhaus Country Inn Manager)

RUM COCONUT CAKE

1 box yellow or white cake mix
1¼ c. water
¼ c. oil
1 (3 oz.) box coconut cream instant pudding
1 t. rum flavoring
2 eggs

Frosting:

8 oz. can crushed pineapple
1 (3 oz.) box instand vanilla pudding
1 t. rum flavoring
9 oz. carton Cool Whip
1 c. coconut

Mix together in large mixing bowl the cake mix, water, oil, pudding, flavoring and eggs until well blended. Pour on greased sheet cake pan. Bake at 350° for 20-25 min. Cool completely before icing. To make frosting, beat the pineapple and pudding together. Add flavoring and fold in Cool Whip. Spread on cake. Sprinkle with coconut.

Sharon Boley (Waitress)

SAUCE TOPPING FOR CAKE

1 c. sugar
1 c. water
1 heaping T. flour

1 T. butter
1 t. vanilla
1 t. vinegar

Combine ingredients and cook in saucepan until thick, stirring frequently. Serve warm or cold over squares of cake. Best on white or yellow cake.

Mary Ellen Yutzy

MIRACLE WHIP® CAKE

3 c. cake flour
3 t. baking soda
1½ c. warm water
1½ t. vanilla

6 T. cocoa
1½ c. sugar
1½ c. Miracle Whip®

Sift together the flour, cocoa, sugar, and baking soda. Combine the other ingredients in another bowl, then add the sifted dry ingredients. Pour batter into a 9"x13" greased pan. Bake at 375° for 30 minutes or until done.

Rose Schrock (Baker)

My praise shall be of thee in the great congregation: I will pay my vows before them that fear him.

The meek shall eat and be satisfied: they shall praise the LORD that seek him: your heart shall live for ever....

The LORD knoweth the days of the upright: and their inheritance shall be for ever.

They shall not be ashamed in the evil time: and in the days of famine they shall be satisfied.

Psa. 22:25-26; 37:18-19

STREUSEL CAKE

1 c. sugar
2 eggs
1 t. baking powder
½ t. salt
1 c. sour cream or
1 c. sweet milk with 1 T. vinegar

½ c. butter
2 c. flour
1 t. soda
1 t. vanilla

Topping:

¼ c. sugar
1 c. nuts
2 T. butter

⅓ c. brown sugar
2 t. cinnamon

Combine all topping ingredients and set aside. Cream butter, sugar and eggs. Sift dry ingredients and add, alternating with sour cream. Add vanilla. Mix and pour ½ of batter into pan which has been greased. Sprinkle ½ of topping over batter. Repeat process. Bake at 350° for 30 min. Use 8×8 in. greased pan.

Mary Esther Miller (Bakery)
Roberta Lantz (Bakery Cashier)

SUNSHINE CAKE

12 eggs, separated
2 t. vanilla
2 t. cream of tartar

1¼ c. sugar
1 c. flour, sifted
½ t. salt

Beat egg yolks. Add ½ of the sugar and vanilla. Beat egg whites till frothy. Add cream of tartar. Beat till stiff. Fold yolk mixture into whites. Fold flour, salt and remaining sugar into mixture. Bake at 325° for 45-60 min. in tube pan.

Lillian Miller (Cashier-Hostess)

SWEDISH APPLE CAKE

1¾ c. flour
1 t. soda
1 t. cinnamon
½ t. nutmeg

1 c. sugar
½ c. shortening
2 eggs, beaten
1 t. vanilla

Cream sugar and shortening, add eggs and vanilla. Sift and stir in remaining dry ingredients. Add 3 c. chopped apples and ½ c. chopped nuts. Bake 25 min. at 350°. Remove, spread on topping. Bake another 25-30 min. Serve with whipped cream. Use 8×8 in. greased pan.

Topping:

6 T. melted butter
2 T. cream or milk

1 c. brown sugar

Julianna Bontrager (Waitress)

SPONGE CAKE (Good for Strawberry Shortcake)

Beat until very light:
4 eggs
2 c. sugar

Beat in:
2 t. salt
2 t. flavoring

Add:
2 T. melted butter
1 c. hot milk

Sift together and beat in:
2 c. sifted flour
2 t. baking powder

Grease and flour 9×13 pan. Bake at 350° for 25-30 min.

Edna Slabach (Cook)

SPICE CAKE

½ c. butter
1½ c. brown sugar
1 egg, beaten
1 c. raisins
¼ t. salt
1 t. cinnamon

1 t. cloves
3 c. cake flour, sifted
1 c. sour milk
½ t. nutmeg
1 t. soda

Cream butter and sugar. Add salt and egg, raisins and spices. Add flour alternately with milk. Bake at 350° for 20-30 min.

Rose Schrock (Baker)

If there is anger—Forgive!
If there is resentment—Forgive!
If there is bitterness—Forgive!

TURTLE CAKE

1 pkg. German Chocolate cake mix
6 oz. chopped pecans
7 oz. Eagle Brand Milk

14 oz. caramels
¼ lb. butter
6 oz. semi-sweet chocolate chips

Mix cake as on package. Bake half of the mix in greased and floured 9×13 pan at 350° for 15 min. In top of double boiler, melt butter, caramels and milk. Remove top of double boiler from heat. Cool mixture slightly and pour over baked half of cake. Pour on remaining cake batter. Sprinkle with pecans and chocolate chips. Bake at 350° for 25 min.

Mary Ann Schlabach (Waitress)

WARM CHOCOLATE CAKE

¾ c. white sugar
1 ¼ c. flour
2 t. baking powder
¼ t. salt
2 T. butter

½ c. milk
1 egg, beaten
1 t. vanilla
½ c. nuts
2 T. cocoa

Mix together and put on top:

½ c. white sugar
½ c. brown sugar
2 T. cocoa

Pour 1 c. boiling water on top of batter. Bake at 350° for 30-35 min.
30-35 min.

Fannie Yoder (Cook)

ZUCCHINI CAKE

3 c. zucchini, grated
⅔ c. vegetable oil
2 t. baking powder
4 eggs, separated

3 c. sugar
1 ½ t. cinnamon
1 t. baking soda
3 c. flour

Sift all dry ingredients. Make a well and add zucchini, oil and egg yolks. Mix well. Beat egg whites stiff and add to mixture. Bake at 300° for 1 hour.

Rose Schrock (Baker)

CHOCOLATE FROSTING

2 c. powdered sugar
2 T. cocoa
½ t. vanilla

pinch of salt
3 T. butter or shortening
3 T. boiling water

Beat together till smooth.

Betty Miller (Pie Baker)

SEVEN MINUTE ICING

2 egg whites   3 t. light corn syrup
⅔ c. sugar   1/8 t. cream of tartar

Mix in double boiler and place over boiling water. Stir 6 min. to about
150 strokes. Remove from heat. Beat with rotary beater until icing will
hold its shape. Fold in 1½ t. vanilla.

Betty Miller (Pie Baker)

QUICK CHOCOLATE FROSTING

⅓ c. cocoa   pinch of salt
¾ c. sugar   1 c. milk
1 T. cornstarch

Mix dry ingredients. Add milk gradually, stirring until smooth. Cook
over medium heat until thick, stirring constantly. Add 1 t. vanilla and
1 T. butter. Cool slightly and spread over cake.

Mary Ellen Yutzy

Cookies, Snacks & Candies

DEFINITIONS:

AMISS—A women who is not married.

ADULT—One who stopped growing except in the middle.

ANT—A small insect, always working, but still finds time to go on picnics.

BABY-SITTER—Someone you pay to watch your television and eat your food.

BACHELOR—Footloose and fiancé free.

BUS DRIVER—One who only thought he liked children.

BUDGETING—Orderly way to get into debt.

BRAT—A child who acts like your own but belongs to someone else.

DIET—What you keep putting off while you keep putting on.

FRECKLES—A nice suntan if you could just get them together.

FLIRT—The girl who got the boy you wanted.

JUNK—Something you keep for years and throw away just days before you need it.

LIFE INSURANCE—The thing that keeps you poor all your life so you can die rich.

PEDESTRIAN—The wife who counted on her husband to fill the car up with gas.

SUCCESS—When other people envy you.

SWEATER—What a child must wear when his mother is cold.

ULCER—Something you get when you mountain climb over mole hills.

VACATION—A time when people find out where to stay away from next year.

WILLPOWER—Ability to eat just one piece of chocolate.

He who thinks by the inch and talks by the yard, ought to be moved by the foot.

Cookies, Snacks & Candies

BLONDE BROWNIES

⅔ c. margarine
2 eggs
2 c. flour
1 t. salt
1 c. raisins or chocolate chips

2 c. brown sugar
2 t. vanilla
1 t. baking powder
½ t. soda
½ c. nuts

Melt margarine in 2 quart sauce pan. Add brown sugar and stir. Add eggs and vanilla and stir. Sift dry ingredients and add to butter mixtures. Add raisins or chocolate chips and nuts. Bake at 350° for 30 min. (Check after 25 min.) Use 8×8 in. greased pan.

Amanda Troyer (Waitress)

BROWN SUGAR DROPS

2 c. brown sugar
1 c. lard
1 c. sour milk
2 eggs

1 t. baking powder
2 t. soda
4 c. flour
1 t. vanilla

Mix together. Drop on baking sheet. Bake at 350°.

Alma Hershberger (Bakery)

BROWNIES

¾ c. flour
1 c. sugar
5 T. cocoa
½ t. salt

½ c. shortening
2 eggs
1 t. vanilla

Cream sugar with shortening, add eggs, beat well, add dry ingredients. Mix well, add vanilla. Bake at 350° for 30 min.

Meredith Mast (Dishwasher)

To keep beets red, cook them whole with two inches of stem. Don't peel until cooked. Also add a few tablespoons of vinegar to the cooking water to prevent fading.

BROWNIES

1 c. butter, softened
1 t. vanilla
¾ c. white sugar
1 t. soda
2 c. chocolate chips

2 eggs
¾ c. brown sugar
1 t. salt
2¼ c. sifted flour
1 c. pecans

Combine flour, soda, salt, set aside. In large bowl, combine butter, sugars and vanilla. Beat until creamy. Beat eggs. Gradually add flour mixture. Mix well. Stir in chips and nuts. Spread into greased 15×10×11 baking pan. Bake for 20-25 min. in 325° oven. Cool. Cut into 2" squares.

Fannie Yoder (Cook)

BROWN-EYED SUSANS

1 c. margarine
¼ c. sugar
½ t. almond extract
whole almonds

2 c. flour
½ t. salt
chocolate frosting

Cream margarine and sugar until light and fluffy. Blend in extract. Add flour and salt; mix well. Shape rounded teaspoonfuls of dough into balls. Place on ungreased cookie sheet; flatten slightly. Bake at 350° 10-12 min. Cool. Frost with Chocolate Frosting; top with almonds. Approximately 5 dozen.

Chocolate Frosting: Combine 1 c. sifted confectioners' sugar and 2 T. cocoa. Add 1 T. hot water and ½ t. vanilla; mix well.

Sue Miller (Manager)

BUSHEL COOKIES

	¼ batch	½ batch
5 lbs. brown sugar	1 ¼ lbs.	2½ lbs.
2½ lbs. lard	scant ¾ lb.	1 ¼ lbs.
12 eggs	3	6
1 c. maple syrup	¼ c.	½ c.
2 oz. soda	½ oz.	1 oz.
2 oz. baking powder	½ oz.	1 oz.
1 qt. milk	¼ qt.	½ qt.
6 lbs. flour	1½ lbs.	3 lbs.
2 lbs. quick oatmeal	½ lb.	1 lb.
2 lbs. raisins & chocolate chips, mixed	½ lb.	1 lb.
1 lb. ground salted peanuts	¼ lb.	½ lb.

Cream together sugar and lard. Add beaten eggs and maple syrup. Mix soda and baking powder with flour and add alternately with milk and quick oatmeal to above mixture. Add raisin/chocolate chip mixture and ground salted peanuts. Mix well. Drop by spoonful on greased cookie sheets and bake at 350° for 10-12 min.

Sylvia Slabaugh (Cook)

BUTTERMILK COOKIES

2 c. brown sugar
2 eggs
3¾ c. flour
1 c. Crisco

1 c. buttermilk
2 t. baking powder
1 t. vanilla
2 t. soda

Cream together sugar and Crisco, add vanilla and eggs, mix well. Add the soda to the buttermilk, then add to other ingredients. Sift together baking powder and flour. Add to mixture a little at a time. Mix well. Bake at 350°. Cool and ice.

Frosting:

6 T. butter
2 c. sifted confectioner's sugar

3 T. hot water
1 t. vanilla

Heat butter in saucepan over low heat until brown. Remove from heat. Add remaining ingredients. Beat until smooth.

Sylvia Arlene Slabaugh (Cook)

BUTTERMILK SUGAR COOKIES

2 c. Wesson oil
3 c. sugar
4 eggs
2 t. vanilla
1 t. lemon

2 c. buttermilk
2 t. soda
6 t. baking powder
6 c. Robin Hood flour

Mix first 5 ingredients. Add soda to buttermilk. Alternately add flour mixture and buttermilk to sugar batter; stirring by hand. Sprinkle dropped cookies with sugar. Bake at 350° for 12 min. Optional: add 2 (12 oz.) pkgs. chocolate chips before baking.

Lillian Miller (Cashier-Hostess)

APPLE SURPRISE

½ c. butter
   or ¼ c. butter and ¼ c. oleo
1 egg, beaten
1 c. flour
½ c. nuts, if desired
1 t. soda
½ t. salt
½ t. cinnamon
½ c. sugar

Cook and serve on Apple Surprise:
Caramel Sauce
¼ c. butter
1 c. brown sugar
1 T. flour
1 c. cold water
1 t. vanilla

4 medium cooking apples, peeled and sliced. Mix first eight ingredients and add to apples. Bake for 30 min. at 350°.

Wilma Weaver (Waitress)

CARROT COOKIES

1 c. shortening
1 c. cooked carrots (mashed)
1 egg, unbeaten
2 c. flour

¾ c. sugar
1 t. vanilla
2 t. baking powder
½ t. salt

Cream shortening and sugar. Add cooked carrots, egg, and vanilla. Sift flour, baking powder and salt. Mix well. Put on greased sheet. Bake for 20 min. at 350°. Cool and ice.

Frosting for Carrot Cookies:

Put 1 t. butter into 1½ c. powdered sugar. Add juice of one orange. Beat until smooth.

Wilma Weaver (Waitress)

 When looking for faults, use a mirror, not a telescope.

CHOCOLATE BIT COOKIES

2 c. brown sugar
1 c. white sugar
1 c. shortening
1 c. margarine
6 eggs
1 T. vanilla

2 t. salt
4 t. soda
4 t. Cream of Tartar
7 c. sifted flour
1 pkg. chocolate bits
chopped nuts if you wish

Cream sugar, oleo and shortening. Add eggs and vanilla beating well. Add dry ingredients mixing well. Add chocolate bits and nuts. Drop on cookie sheet and bake at 350° for 10-12 min.

Erma Bontrager (Manager of Country Cupboard)
Rosalie Bontrager (Manager Essenhaus Country Inn)

CHOCOLATE CHIP BARS

¾ c. brown sugar
¾ c. white sugar
½ c. shortening
½ c. butter
2 eggs
½ t. water

2½ c. flour, unsifted
1 t. salt
1 t. vanilla
1 c. chocolate chips
1 c. nuts

Mix thoroughly. Press ½" thick into baking pan. Bake at 375° for 20 min.

Wilma Schlabach (Dessert Counter)

CHOCOLATE CHIP PUDDING COOKIES

2¼ c. flour, unsifted
1 t. baking soda
1 c. butter or margarine, softened
¼ c. sugar
¾ c. light brown sugar,
  firmly packed

1 pkg. (4 serving size) Jello
  choc. or vanilla instant pudding
1 t. vanilla
2 eggs
1 pkg. (12 oz.) chocolate chips
1 c. nuts, optional

Mix flour with baking soda. Combine butter, sugar, brown sugar, pudding mix and vanilla in large bowl. Beat until smooth and creamy. Add eggs. Gradually add flour mixture. Stir in chocolate chips and nuts. Batter will be stiff. Drop by rounded measuring teaspoon on ungreased cookie sheets. Bake at 375° for 8-10 min. Makes 7 dozen.

Wilma Schlabach (Dessert Counter)

CHEWY OATMEAL COOKIES

1½ c. oleo or Crisco
2 c. flour
1 t. salt
½ t. nutmeg
2 t. vanilla

2 t. cinnamon
4 eggs
3 c. brown sugar
1½ t. soda
4 c. quick oats

Drop and bake at 350° for 10-12 min.

Filling:

1 beaten egg white
2 c. powdered sugar

1 t. vanilla
1½ T. Crisco

Mix until creamy. Fill between 2 cookies.

Bertha Miller (Dutch Country Gifts)
Laura Anna Miller (Grill Worker)
Arlene Miller (Country Cupboard)

Life isn't fair, but God is!

CRUNCHY CRISPY COOKIES

1 c. salad oil
1 c. margarine
1 c. white sugar
1 c. brown sugar
1 egg
1 T. sour milk
3½ c. flour
1 t. salt

1 t. cream of tartar
1 t. soda
½ c. coconut
1 c. corn flakes
1 c. oatmeal
1 c. chopped nuts
1 t. vanilla

Cream sugar, oleo, oil and egg. Add remaining ingredients. Bake at 350° for 10-12 min. Yields 5 to 7 dozen cookies.

Sarah Yutzy

COOKIES

Mix thoroughly:

8 c. brown sugar
8 eggs, beaten

1 c. white sugar
5 c. lard, melted

Add:

4 c. cream
8 t. soda (dissolved in a little
　vinegar)
salt to flavor

4 c. milk or buttermilk
8 t. baking powder
8-9 c. flour

Bake 10-12 min. at 375°. Makes a big lard can full.

Ida Weaver (Cook)

Sometimes bending a child over has a strange way of straightening him out.

DATE FILLED COOKIES

2 c. brown sugar
⅔ c. shortening
3 eggs, beaten

4½ c. flour
½ t. salt
1 t. soda (dissolved in a little
　warm water)

Cream together sugar and shortening. Add eggs, flour, salt and soda. Mix well. Roll as thin as possible and cut with a cookie cutter. Put 1 t. filling on each cookie and cover with another cookies. Press edges together and bake at 350° until done.

Filling:

1 c. brown sugar
⅔ c. nuts, chopped
2 T. flour

1 c. chopped dates
1 c. water

Mix together and boil for 1 min. or so. Cool.

Susie Bontrager (Cook)

DANISH APPLE BARS

3 c. sifted flour
1 t. salt
1 c. shortening
1 egg yolk (beaten)
milk
1 c. crushed cornflakes
8 large apples, pared and
   sliced (8 cups)

1 c. sugar
1 t. cinnamon
1 egg white (beaten stiff)
1 c. powdered sugar
1 t. vanilla
3 T. water

Sift flour and salt into bowl. Cut in shortening until crumbly. Add enough milk to egg yolk to make ½ cup. Add to flour mixture. Mix until moistened. Divide dough almost in half. Roll out larger half, place in jelly roll pan. Press up on sides of pan. Sprinkle with cornflakes. Arrange apple slices over cornflakes. Combine sugar and cinnamon and sprinkle over apples. Roll out other half of dough to fit top. Make vents in top. Moisten edges of dough with water; seal. Spread egg whites over crust. Bake in 375° oven for 1 hour or until golden brown. Combine powdered sugar, water, and vanilla. Spread on bars while still warm.

Lizzie Ann Bontrager (Cook)

DATE BROWNIES

1 c. graham cracker crumbs
   (about 14 squares)
½ t. salt
1½ t. baking powder
1 t. vanilla

3 eggs, well beaten
1 lb. pkg. dates, cut up
1 c. walnuts or pecans, chopped
1 c. brown sugar

Combine graham cracker crumbs, salt, baking powder, dates and nuts. Beat vanilla into eggs and add brown sugar gradually. Beat until mixture is smooth. Beat into crumb mixture. Pour into greased 9 × 12 inch pan. Bake at 375° for 25 min. Cut in 1¼" squares while warm. Roll in confectioners sugar or place pecan halves on dough before baking.

Esther Nisley (Bakery)

DROP COOKIES

2 c. brown sugar
1 t. soda
1 c. cold water
4 c. flour
1 bag chocolate chips

3 t. baking powder
3 eggs
1 c. lard
1 t. vanilla

Mix in order given, drop by teaspoonfuls on cookie sheet and bake at 350° until light brown.

Doretta Mast (Dishwasher)

DROP COOKIES

1 c. white sugar
1 c. brown sugar
½ c. shortening
½ c. butter
2 eggs
1 c. coconut

1 t. salt
1 t. soda
1/8 t. baking powder
2½ c. flour
2 c. cornflakes

Mix and drop on cookie sheet. Bake at 375° 8-10 min.

Maurice Berkey (Controller)

Two little boys came bursting into the house, shouting to their mother that the youngest brother had fallen into the lake.
"We tried giving him artificial respiration," one of them gulped, "but he kept getting up and running away."

ELEPHANT EARS

1½ c. milk
6 T. shortening
1 t. salt
oil for frying

2 T. sugar
2 pkgs. dry yeast
4 c. flour

Sugar mixture: ½ c. sugar, 1 t. cinnamon.

In a saucepan combine milk, sugar, salt and shortening; heat until shortening is melted. Do not let mixture boil. Cool mixture to luke-warm. Add yeast and stir until dissolved; stir in flour two cups at a time. Beat after each addition until smooth. Put in a greased bowl, cover with a damp cloth and let rise until double, about 20 min. Dust hands with flour, pinch off pieces of dough about the size of a golf ball. Stretch each piece into a thin 6 to 8 inch circle. Fry, one a time in oil 350° until dough rises to the surface. Turn and fry on other side until light brown. Drain on absorbent paper and sprinkle with the sugar mixture.

Laura Anna Miller (Grill Worker)

FILLED OATMEAL COOKIES

2½ c. sifted flour
1 t. salt
1 c. soft shortening
2½ c. Quaker Oats (quick
    or old-fashioned uncooked)

1 t. soda
1 c. brown sugar
½ c. water
½ c. jelly or jam

Sift together flour, soda, and salt into a bowl. Add sugar, shortening and water. Beat until smooth, about 2 min. Fold in oats.

Sprinkle a bread board generously with confectioners sugar. Roll dough very thin, cut with cookie cutter. Place plain cookies on lightly greased cookie sheet. Top with ½ t. jelly and cover with another cookie with a hole cut out of the center. Press edges together lightly. Bake in moderate oven at 350° for 10-12 min. Makes approximately 2 dozen cookies.

Lydia Ann Miller

GINGER SNAPS

⅓ c. vegetable shortening
1 c. light brown sugar
1½ c. molasses
⅔ c. water
6 c. flour

2 t. baking soda
1 t. salt
½ t. cinnamon
¼ t. nutmeg
¼ t. ginger

Beat shortening, brown sugar and molasses until creamy. Add water. Sift together dry ingredients and add to batter, ⅓ at a time. Beat thoroughly. If dough is sticky, add a little more flour. Roll out to ¼ inch thick with a rolling pin. Mold into holiday shapes with hands or use cookie cutters. Bake on lightly greased cookie sheets at 350° for about 10 min.

Wilma Schlabach (Dessert Counter)

GRAHAM CRACKERS

1 c. shortening
2 c. brown sugar
1 c. white sugar
2 c. flour
4 c. graham flour

1 t. soda
2 t. baking powder
½ t. salt
1 c. sweet or sour milk
1 t. vanilla

Cream shortening and sugar. Add vanilla. Sift flour. Add salt, soda and baking powder. Sift again. Add sifted ingredients to creamed mixture alternately with milk. Chill dough in refrigerator overnight. Turn out on floured board and roll as thin as possible. Cut into squares and poke with fork several times. Bake at 350°. A sugar/cinnamon mixture sprinkled on top makes them tastier.

Ida Fern Mast (Busser)

Think of your future. You're going to spend the rest of your life there.

INDOOR S'MORES

⅔ c. Karo, light
1 pkg. (11½ oz.) chocolate morsels
3 T. margarine or butter
1 t. vanilla
8 c. Golden Grahams cereal
3 c. miniature marshmallows

Butter baking pan 13x9x2. Heat corn syrup, margarine and real milk chocolate morsels just to boiling in 3 quart sauce pan, stirring constantly; remove from heat. Stir in vanilla. Pour over Golden Grahams cereal which has been measured in large bowl; toss quickly until completely coated with chocolate. Fold in marshmallows 1 c. at a time. Press mixture evenly in pan with buttered back of spoon. Let stand until firm at least 1 hour. Cut in 1½" squares. Makes 48 squares.

Fannie Yoder (Cook)

The trouble with doing nothing is that it's too difficult to tell when you're finished.

MATRIMONY DATE BARS

1 c. oatmeal
1 c. brown sugar
¾ c. shortening
1 t. soda
1 c. flour
¼ t. salt

Mix all ingredients, forming a crumbly mixture. Put about ⅔ in pan. Spread and pack evenly.

Filling:

1 c. chopped nuts
¼ c. sugar
1 c. boiling water
1 c. chopped dates

Put ingredients in a saucepan and simmer until thick. Cool. Spread on crumb mixture. Sprinkle the remaining crumbs on top. Bake at 350° for 35 min.

Sharon Boley (Head Waitress)

CHOCOLATE CARAMEL NUT BARS

1 (14 oz.) bag caramels
1 (2-layer) German choc. cake mix
1½ c. nuts, chopped

⅔ c. evaporated milk
½ c. margarine, melted
1 (6 oz.) pkg. semi-sweet
    chocolate pieces

Melt caramels with ⅓ c. milk over low heat, stirring until smooth. Combine remaining milk, mix, and margarine, mix well. Press half of cake mixture into bottom of greased 13×9 baking pan. Bake at 350° for 6 min. Sprinkle 1 c. walnuts and chocolate pieces over crust; top with caramel mixture spreading to edges of pan. Top with teaspoonfuls of remaining cake mixture. Press gently into caramel mixture. Sprinkle with remaining walnuts. Press lightly into top. Bake at 350° for 20 min. Cool slightly, refrigerate. Cut into bars to serve.

Norine Borkholder (Cook)

MASTER MIX COOKIES

9 c. flour
3 c. shortening
2 t. soda
6 c. brown sugar

1 t. salt
7½ c. oatmeal
2 t. baking powder

Sift flour, salt, baking powder, and soda into a large bowl. Add sugar, put in shortening until mixture is crumbly. Stir in oatmeal.

How to use the mix:

6 c. mix
2 eggs, beaten

½ c. milk
2 t. vanilla

Note: Add more milk to make a moister cookie. Also co-co drops can be added. Makes 27 cups. Bake 350° for 10-12 min.

Mary Rose Yoder (Pie Baker)

MAGIC COOKIE BARS

½ c. butter or oleo
1½ c. graham cracker crumbs
1 (14 oz.) pkg. semi-sweet chocolate morsels
1 (3½ oz.) can flaked coconut
1 c. chopped nuts

Preheat oven to 350° (325° for glass dish). In 13×9 baking pan melt butter. Sprinkle crumbs over butter, pour sweetened condensed milk evenly over crumbs. Top evenly with remaining ingredients, press down gently. Bake 25-30 min. or until lightly browned. Cool thoroughly before cutting. Store loosely covered, at room temperature.

Ruth Schlabach (Busser)

Greet the dawn with enthusiasm and you may expect satisfaction at sunset.

Lydia Ann Miller (Cook)

MEXICAN WAFERS

½ lb. butter
2 c. flour
1 t. vanilla

4 T. powdered sugar
¾ c. nuts

Mix and pat into roll and chill. Cut in thin slices, bake at 350°. When they start to turn brown, remove and cool. When cool roll in powdered sugar.

Mary Esther Miller (Bakery)

MOLASSES CRINKLE COOKIES

1 c. brown sugar
¾ c. shortening
1 egg
4 T. molasses
2¼ c. flour

½ t. salt
2 t. soda
1 t. cinnamon
1 t. ginger
½ t. cloves

Cream shortening and sugar, add egg and molasses and beat well. Add flour and all other dry ingredients to creamed mixture. Chill dough in refrigerator for at least 1 hour. Shape into balls 1" in diameter. Roll in sugar and place on cookie sheet 2" apart. Bake at 350° for 12-15 min.

Mary Esther Miller (Bakery Manager)
Ginger Yoder (Waitress)
Wilma Weaver (Waitress)

MOLASSES BARS

4 c. white sugar
1 t. salt
3 T. soda
1 pint Brer Rabbit Molasses (½ c. green label, add Karo to make one pint)

1 lb. oleo
5 eggs
½ c. boiling water
14 c. all-purpose flour
2 c. chocolate chips

Cream together sugar and oleo, add eggs, beaten, then add soda (dissolved in boiling water), Karo, flour and chips. Mix well. Take a handful of dough, roll in a rope about 1" thick. Place 3 rolls on a cookie sheet lengthwise. Brush tops with beaten egg for a nice glaze. Bake at 375° for 13 min. Do not bake too dark and they will remain soft and chewy. Take spatula and cut in bars soon after removing from oven.

Sharon Miller (Cook)

MUD COOKIES

2 c. sugar
¼ c. margarine

4 T. cocoa
½ c. milk

Boil for one minute. Then add:

3 c. oatmeal (instant)
½ c. peanut butter
1 t. vanilla

Drop on cookie sheet and put in refrigerator until set.

Rhoda Troyer (Typist)

NO BAKE BARS

Bring to full boil ½ c. white sugar, ½ c. light Karo syrup. Remove from heat and stir in ¾ c. peanut butter, 1 t. vanilla. Then stir in 3 c. Special K or 4 c. Rice Krispies. Pour in buttered 13×9×2 pan. Melt in pan (over boiling water) 1 pkg. each of butterscotch bits and chocolate bits. Pour over mixture and chill. Cut in squares to serve.

Mary Esther Lehman (Busser)

NO BAKE PEANUT BUTTER COOKIES

¼ c. brown sugar
½ c. light corn syrup
1 t. vanilla

¼ c. white sugar
¾ c. peanut butter
2 c. rice cereal

In a 2 quart pan stir together sugars and syrup. Bring to boil, remove from heat and stir in remaining items, mix well. Drop from teaspoon onto wax paper.

Bonnie Schrock (Gift Shop)

OVERNIGHT COOKIES

3 c. brown sugar
1 c. white sugar
1¼ c. Crisco
4 eggs
6 c. flour

¼ c. milk
1 T. soda
¾ t. salt
1 T. baking powder
1 T. vanilla

Cream shortening and sugar. Add eggs and vanilla. Heat milk and add soda, adding to first mixture, alternately with dry ingredients. Mix well and drop on cookie sheet and bake at 350° 10-12 min.

Fannie Yoder (Cook)

PARTY COOKIES

1 c. brown sugar, packed
½ c. granulated sugar
1 c. shortening
2 eggs
1½ t. vanilla

2¼ c. flour
1 t. soda
1 t. salt
1½ c. M & M's plain chocolate
    candies

Cream sugars and shortening. Add eggs and vanilla. Mix dry ingredients and add to creamed mixture. Mix well. Add ½ c. M & M's. Reserve the remaining M & M's to put on top. Drop by spoonful on greased cookie sheets. Put 2 or 3 M & M's on each cookie. Bake at 375° for 10-12 min. Makes 5-6 dozen cookies.

Sylvia Slabaugh (Cook)

PINEAPPLE COOKIES

2 c. sifted flour
1½ t. baking powder
½ t. soda
1 t. salt
⅔ c. shortening

1¼ c. brown sugar
2 eggs
¾ c. crushed pineapple, drained
1 t. vanilla

Mix all together and drop from teaspoon on ungreased baking sheet. Oven at 400° for about 10 min.

Ida Troyer (Baker)

PRUNE COOKIES

2 c. brown sugar
2 eggs
½ c. sweet milk
1½ c. chopped prunes
1 t. baking powder
½ t. salt

⅔ c. butter
1 t. vanilla
1 t. soda
2½ c. flour
1 t. cinnamon
1 c. chopped nuts

Cream the butter and brown sugar. Add the eggs, vanilla, milk, soda and prunes. Add the dry ingredients and last the nuts. Drop by teaspoon on cookie sheet and bake at 350° 12-15 min.

Leora Kauffman (Purchasing)

Don't use a painted plate for serving salad with vinegar dressing. Vinegar corrodes the paint on the plate.

PUMPKIN COOKIES

1 c. shortening
1 c. pumpkin
2 c. flour
1 t. cinnamon

1 c. white sugar
1 egg
1 t. soda
½ t. salt

Cream together sugar and shortening; add pumpkin and beaten egg. Add remaining ingredients. Bake at 400° for 8-10 min. Frost when cool.

Frosting: (optional)

3 T. butter, melted
½ c. brown sugar
¾ t. vanilla

4 t. milk
1 c. powdered sugar

Mix together and spread on cookies.

Edna E. Bontrager (Cook)
Ida Weaver (Cook)

PUMPKIN OATMEAL DROPS

¾ c. butter
2 eggs
1 t. vanilla
2 t. baking powder
1 t. cinnamon
1/8 t. cloves
½ c. coconut
½ t. baking soda

1½ c. sugar
1 c. pumpkin
1½ c. flour
½ t. salt
½ t. nutmeg
1½ c. oats (uncooked)
½ c. nuts

Cream butter and sugar together. Beat in eggs. Add pumpkin and vanilla. Sift dry ingredients. Stir into creamed mixture. Add rest of ingredients. Drop on cookie sheet and bake at 350° for 12 min.

Sharon Boley (Head Waitress)

RHUBARB DREAM BARS

Crust:

2 c. flour
¾ c. confectioners sugar
1 c. butter

Combine flour and sugar; cut in butter until crumbs form. Press onto bottom of 15×10×1 jelly roll pan. Bake at 350° for 15 min. While crust is baking prepare filling.

Filling:

4 eggs
2 c. sugar
½ c. flour

½ t. salt
4 c. diced rhubarb

Blend eggs, sugar, flour, and salt until smooth. Fold in rhubarb, spread over hot crust. Bake 40-45 min. at 350° until filling is lightly browned. Cool, cut into squares or bars.

Cheryl Troyer (Cashier, Gift Shop)

SOFT CHOCOLATE CHIP COOKIES

4 c. brown sugar
4 eggs
4 T. hot water

2 c. Crisco
1½ T. vanilla

Beat with mixer for 10 min. or more.
Stir in by hand:

6½ c. flour
3 t. soda
½ t. salt

2 (12 oz.) chocolate chips
2 c. nuts (optional)
coconut (optional)

Bake at 375° for 10 min.

Lillian Miller (Cashier)
Edna Nissley (Waitress)

"HE SHOULD KNOW"

Doctor: "The pains in your right leg are due to old age."
Grandpa: "Old age nothing. The other leg's the same age, and it's okay."

SOUR CREAM COOKIES

3 c. sugar
4 eggs
1 c. sour milk
2 t. baking soda
1 t. salt
1 t. lemon flavoring

1¾ c. shortening
1 c. sour cream
6 c. flour
4 t. baking powder
1 T. vanilla

Mix together shortening and sugar. Add eggs and mix well. Add rest of ingredients, mix well. Roll out, cut and sprinkle tops with sugar. Also good frosted. Bake in 350° oven till done. The more sour the cream, the better the cookie.

Gayle Kauffman (Waitress)

TEEN-TIME CHOCOLATE NUT BARS

1 c. brown sugar (packed)
½ c. milk
1 t. salt
½ t. soda
1 c. (6 oz.) semi-sweet
   chocolate pieces

½ c. butter or margarine
1¼ c. all-purpose flour
1 t. baking powder
2 eggs
1 c. coarsely chopped nuts

Heat oven to 350°. Blend sugar, butter and milk in saucepan. Bring just to a boil, stirring constantly. Cool for 5 min. Measure flour by dipping method or by sifting. Blend flour, salt, baking powder, and soda. Beat eggs into butter mixture. Add flour mixture, mix thoroughly. Stir in chocolate pieces and nuts. Spread in greased and floured oblong pan, 13×9. Bake for 25 min. Cool, cut in bars. Makes about 4 dozen bars.

Patty Kauffman (Grill Worker)

TREASURE BARS

1 c. sifted flour
2 c. brown sugar
½ c. butter
1 c. brown sugar
2 slightly beaten eggs
1 t. vanilla

½ t. baking powder
¼ t. salt
1 c. chopped walnuts
1 c. shredded coconut
½ c. chocolate chips
1 T. flour

Combine flour and ½ c. brown sugar. Cut in butter. Press into greased 13x9x2 inch baking pan. Bake at 350° for 12 min. For topping, gradually add 1½ c. brown sugar to eggs, beating till light and fluffy. Blend in vanilla. Add sifted dry ingredients. Stir in nuts, coconut and chocolate chips. Spread over baked crust. Bake for 25 min. or more. Cool, cut in bars.

Julianna Bontrager (Waitress)

ZUCCHINI BARS

Cream together:

¾ c. oleo
½ c. white sugar

½ c. brown sugar
1 t. vanilla

Add:

1¾ c. flour
2 c. grated zucchini
¾ c. nuts

1½ t. baking powder
1 c. coconut

Spread in greased cookie sheet. Bake at 350° for 40 min.

Frosting:

1 c. powdered sugar
1 t. vanilla
½ t. cinnamon

2½ T. milk
1½ T. oleo, melted

Spread on cake while still slightly warm.

Rosa Borntrager (Dutch Country Gifts)

WORLD'S BEST SUGAR COOKIES

1 c. powdered sugar
1 c. white sugar
1 c. margarine
2 eggs
1 t. cream of tartar

1 t. salt
1 T. soda
5 c. New Rinkle flour
2 t. vanilla

Cream sugar and margarine until light and fluffy. Then beat in eggs. Sift dry ingredients together. Add the first mixture to the second mixture and mix well. Roll into balls, and press with a glass dipped in sugar. Bake at 350° for 15-20 min. on an ungreased cookie sheet.

Lizzie Ann Bontrager (Cook)

BUTTER CARAMELS

2 c. sugar
1 c. whipping cream

1 c. light corn syrup
1 c. butter (do not use margarine)

Cook ingredients to just past the soft ball stage, stirring constantly. Pour ¼" thick into buttered pans. Refrigerate several hours. Cut into squares and wrap in waxed paper.

Ruth Schlabach (Busser)

BUCKEYES

1 stick butter, softened
1 lb. powdered sugar

2 c. crunchy peanut butter
3 c. rice krispies

Cream butter, sugar and peanut butter until smooth. Add rice krispies and form into balls. Melt 12 oz. chocolate chips in double boiler. Dip balls into chocolate and place on waxed paper.

Ida Mae Schmucker (Bakery)
Denise Bontrager (Waitress)

CALICO FUDGE

1½ c. sugar
⅔ c. milk
4 T. peanut butter

¾ c. brown sugar
2 T. butter
12 marshmallows

Cook milk, sugar to soft ball stage. Remove from heat and add butter and peanut butter. Beat at once till creamy. Pour over marshmallows on buttered pan, cut when cool.

Barbara Bainter (Cleaning Service)

CHOCOLATE CARAMEL CREATURES

1 c. pecan halves
3 (1.45 oz.) milk chocolate
   candy bars

1 (14 oz.) bag Kraft caramels
1 T. milk

Cut candy bars into twelfths. Arrange clusters of five pecans on greased wax paper. Melt caramels with milk in heavy saucepan over low heat, stir frequently until smooth. Let stand at room temperature 3 to 5 min. or until thickened. Drop heaping teaspoonfuls of caramel mixture onto each pecan arrangement. Top with chocolate. Spread chocolate evenly over caramel. Cool. Store in refrigerator. Yields about 2 dozen.

Laura Anna Miller (Grill Worker)

CHOCOLATE COVERED CHERRIES

8 T. butter, melted
6 T. corn syrup

1 can Eagle Brand milk
1 t. vanilla

Blend together and add 3 pounds powdered sugar. Knead and form in balls. Put a maraschino cherry inside each ball and set in freezer for 1 hour. Melt 1 square paraffin. Add 1 large bag chocolate chips and melt in top of double boiler. Dip cold cherries in chocolate and drop on waxed paper. Makes about 125 cherries.

Carolyn Hershberger (Bakery)
Sue Bontrager (Grill Cook)

Tablecloths and sheets should be folded crosswise occasionally. It will make them last longer.

To bleach handkerchiefs, towels, etc., soak overnight in a solution of ½ t. cream of tartar to each quart of water.

CHOCOLATE YUMMIES

No baking—just melt chocolate and marshmallows; stir, drop, and chill.

1 (6 oz.) pkg. semi-sweet chocolate pieces
⅓ c. butter or margarine
16 large marshmallows
½ t. vanilla
1 c. flaked or shredded coconut
2 c. rolled oats (quick or old-fashioned)

Melt chocolate pieces, butter and marshmallows in double boiler; stir until smooth. Remove from heat. (Chocolate, butter, marshmallow mixture may separate but will hold together when rest of ingredients are added). Stir in vanilla, coconut and oats. Mix thoroughly. Drop by teaspoonfuls on waxed paper. Refrigerate. Makes 3 dozen.

Patty Kauffman (Grill Worker)

Remove gum from hair by rubbing on a dab of peanut butter. Massage the gum and peanut butter between your fingers until the gum is loosened. Remove it gently with a comb, then shampoo hair.

COCONUT CHEWS

Bottom Layer:

½ c. brown sugar, firmly packed
½ c. shortening (half butter)
1 c. all-purpose flour sifted

Second Layer:

2 eggs, well beaten
½ c. brown sugar, firmly packed
½ c. Karo syrup
1 t. vanilla
2 T. flour
1 t. baking powder
½ t. salt
1 c. shredded coconut
1 c. coarsely chopped walnuts

Blend sugar and shortening. Stir in flour. Pat out mixture onto bottom of an ungreased pan 9×9×2. Bake in moderate oven 325° for 10 min. Meanwhile, blend eggs, brown sugar. Stir in Karo and vanilla. Add flour, baking powder and salt, mixing well. Stir in coconut and nuts and spread over bottom layer. Return to oven and bake 25 min. longer or until golden brown. Cool. Cut into bars. Makes 24 bars.

Lydie Ann Miller

CRUNCHY

1 pkg. chocolate bits
1 pkg. butterscotch bits
nuts (optional)

1 pkg. caramel bits
1 large can chow mein noodles

Melt bits in double boiler. Remove from heat. Stir in nuts and noodles. Drop by teaspoonfuls on waxed paper. Keep in refrigerator.

Bertha Bontrager (Pie Baker)

CREAM CARAMELS

(This is used in our bakery)

2 c. white sugar
few grains of salt
2 c. cream

2 c. white corn syrup
1 stick butter (½ c.)
1 t. vanilla

Boil sugar, corn syrup, and salt rapidly to 245°. Add butter and cream gradually so that the mixture does not stop boiling at any time. Cook rapidly to firm ball stage (245°). Stir constantly because the mixture sticks easily at the last. Add flavoring and pour into buttered pan. Cut in squares and wrap in waxed paper.

Laura Anna Miller (Grill Worker)
Edna Borntrager (Cook)

CINNAMON CANDY

2 c. sugar
¾ c. water
½ t. cake coloring

1 c. white Karo
½ t. cinnamon oil

Boil sugar, water, Karo, to 310° and let stand 3 min. Add cinnamon oil and coloring. Pour in buttered pan and cut in pieces.

You can use any flavoring and coloring. If you want to you can use as much flavoring and coloring as you wish to have.

Kathy Sue Yoder (Busser)

CORNFLAKE CANDY

1 c. sugar
1 c. light corn syrup
4 c. cornflakes

½ c. cream
1 c. coconut
1 c. chopped nuts

Boil sugar, syrup and cream until it reaches the soft ball stage. Stir in the remaining ingredients. Drop by spoonfuls on waxed paper and let cool.

Alma Hershberger (Bakery)

DATE CANDY

1½ lb. pitted dates
1 pint white Karo
5 c. granulated sugar

1 lb. walnuts
1½ pint cream

Boil sugar, syrup and cream until thick. Add dates. Stir until sugar dissolves. Add nuts. Pour into buttered pan. Cut when cool. Makes 5 pounds.

Ida Mae Schmucker (Bakery)

ENGLISH TOFFEE

2 c. finely chopped walnuts
1 c. butter
1¼ c. sugar

2 T. water
2 T. light corn syrup
6 oz. chocolate chips

Spread 1 c. chopped nuts in a cookie sheet. Melt butter. Add sugar, corn syrup and water. Cook to hard crack stage. Pour over the nuts. Spread chocolate chips over the top. When chips are melted, spread and cover with remaining nuts. When cool break into pieces.

Mary Rose Yoder (Cook)

OUT OF THIS WORLD FUDGE

1 lb. oleo
1 lb. Velveeta cheese
1 c. cocoa

4 c. confectioners' sugar
2 t. vanilla
1 c. nuts

Carefully melt oleo and cheese together. Add remaining ingredients and mix well. Makes 5 pounds.

Mary Jane Bontrager (Cook)

FUDGE

3 c. sugar
⅓ c. butter or margarine
1 c. Milnot
1 (6 oz. or 8 oz.) jar
  marshmallow creme

2 (8 oz.) pkgs. chocolate chips (2 c.)
1 c. nuts
1 t. vanilla

Combine sugar, butter, Milnot, and marshmallow creme in a saucepan. Heat slowly to a boil, stirring frequently. When mixture boils vigorously, boil for 4 min, stirring constantly. Remove from heat. Stir in chocolate chips until melted. Add nuts and vanilla. Pour into buttered 9" × 9" pan. Cool. Makes approximately 3 pounds. Butterscotch or caramel may be substituted for chocolate.

Alma Hershberger (Bakery)

If parsley is washed with hot water instead of cold it retains its flavor and is easier to chop.

FUDGE

2 c. sugar
12 regular marshmallows
½ c. butter or margarine
1 (6 oz.) pkg. (1 c.) Semi-Sweet
  Chocolate Chips

⅔ c. evaporated milk
1 c. cut-up nuts
1 t. vanilla

Mix in heavy 2 qt. saucepan: sugar, milk, marshmallows and butter. Cook, stirring constantly, over medium heat to a boil (mixture will be bubbling all over top). Boil and stir 5 min. more. Take off heat. Stir in until completely melted, chocolate chips, then stir in vanilla and nuts. Spread in a buttered 8" square pan. Cool and cut into 30 pieces.

Barbara Bainter (Cleaning Service)

WHITE FUDGE

3 c. sugar
1 T. corn syrup
1 c. cream or milk

chopped nuts
flavoring
2 T. butter

Mix together sugar, corn syrup, and milk. Cook to soft ball. When almost there, add butter. Set in water to cool. Beat until it shows signs of hardening. Then add nuts and flavoring. Pour into pan. Cool and cut into squares.

Rose Schrock (Baker)

FIVE MINUTE FUDGE

⅔ c. undiluted evaporated milk
1⅔ c. sugar
1½ c. diced marshmallows

½ c. chopped nuts
1½ c. semi-sweet chocolate bits
1 t. vanilla

Combine evaporated milk with sugar in a saucepan. Heat to boiling and cook for 5 min., stirring constantly. Remove from heat. Add remaining ingredients. Stir until marshmallows are melted. Pour into buttered 8" or 9" square pan.

Martha Miller (Cook)

GLASS CANDY

3¾ c. sugar
1½ c. light Karo

1 c. water

Mix in pan and cook to hard crack stage (290°). Remove from heat. Add desired food coloring and 1½ t. desired flavoring. Pour onto greased cookie sheet and allow to cool. Break into pieces.

Becky Schmucker (Busser)

GOOP BARS

Combine and set aside:

2 c. bite size Corn Chex
2½ c. thin pretzel sticks, broken
    in half

1½ c. M & M's, plain or with peanuts
¾ c. raisins (optional)

Melt in double boiler and stir until smooth:

½ c. margarine
⅓ c. peanut butter

5 c. miniature marshmallows

Pour immediately over cereal mixture and mix well. Press into a lightly buttered 9" × 13" baking pan. Let stand until firm and cut into bars.

Ginger Yoder (Waitress)

HEDGE HOUNDS

1 lb. dates, chopped
1 c. walnuts, chopped

1 c. sugar
2 eggs, slightly beaten

Shape and roll in ½ c. coconut. Bake for 12-15 min. in 350° oven.

Mabel Hershberger (Cashier)

HOT BUTTERED O'S

¼ c. butter
4 c. Cheerios (cereal)
salt

Melt butter in 10" skillet over low heat. Add cereal. Cook and stir until well coated and hot (2-3 min.). Sprinkle with salt. Serve warm or cool for snack.

Ruby Yoder (Grill Cook)

MAPLE CREAM CANDY

1 c. maple syrup
1 c. sugar

½ c. cream
1 T. butter

Cook to soft ball stage. Remove from fire and beat until cool and creamy. Pour into buttered pan and cut into squares. Nuts may be added while beating if desired.

Mary Jane Bontrager (Cook)

MOCHA PECAN BALLS

½ c. butter or margarine
2¾ c. confectioners' sugar
1 T. instant coffee powder
¼ c. boiling water

¼ t. salt
2 c. Quaker oats (quick or old-fashioned), uncooked
1 (6 oz.) pkg. (1 c.) semi-sweet chocolate pieces, chopped
1 c. pecans, finely chopped

Beat together butter and sugar until light and fluffy. Dissolve coffee powder in water. Blend coffee and salt into butter mixture. Stir in oats, chocolate pieces and ½ c. chopped pecans. Chill about 30 min. Shape to form one inch balls. Roll in remaining pecans. Chill several hours or overnight. Store in refrigerator. Makes 4 dozen balls. Can be frozen after making.

Becky Schmucker (Busser)

NUT CARAMELS

2 c. brown sugar
1/8 t. salt

½ c. molasses or white Karo
¼ c. cream

Cook until the mixture forms a fine thread when allowed to run from the spoon. Add another ¼ c. cream very slowly. Add 5 T. butter. Cook until the mixture forms a soft ball in cold water, stirring constantly. Remove from heat. Add 1 t. vanilla and pour into a buttered pan. Let cool. Cut into squares and top each square with a walnut half (optional).

Mary Rose Yoder (Cook)

OATMEAL CANDY

2 c. sugar
½ c. milk
¼ c. cocoa
1 t. vanilla

¼ lb. butter
3 c. oatmeal
½ c. peanut butter

Cook sugar, butter, and milk one minute. Then add oatmeal, cocoa, peanut butter, and vanilla. Mix together and drop by spoonfuls on waxed paper. Cool-N-eat.

Ruby Yoder (Grill Cook)

O'HENRY BARS

Combine:

4 c. oatmeal (scant)
½ c. melted butter
2 t. vanilla
½ c. white Karo

1 c. brown sugar
⅔ c. peanut butter
1 (6 oz.) pkg. chocolate chips

Combine the first 5 ingredients and bake on greased cookie sheet for 12 min. at 350°. Melt the peanut butter and chocolate chips together and spread on baked mixture while hot.

Edna Nissley (Waitress)

OPERA CREAMS

1½ c. sugar
½ c. cream

2 T. butter
2 T. chocolate

Cook together and boil to soft ball stage. Remove from fire and add 1 t. vanilla. Let cool without stirring. When cool, beat until light-colored and drop on waxed paper.

Ada A. Schrock (Bakery)

MICROWAVE CARAMEL CORN

1 c. brown sugar
¼ c. corn syrup

½ c. margarine
½ t. salt

Put in 3 quart bowl. Bring to boil on full power. Boil for 2 min. Stir while adding ½ t. baking soda. Stir, pour over 4 quarts popped corn in paper bag.

Fold top of paper bag down. Cook on full power for 4½ min. Stop and stir or shake every 45 seconds. Pour out on table and let dry.

Sharon Boley (Waitress)

PARTY O'S

4 c. Cheerios
1 c. mixed nuts
1 T. Worcestershire sauce
½ t. garlic salt

2 c. pretzel sticks
¼ c. margarine or butter
1 t. paprika

Heat oven to 275°. Combine cereal, pretzel sticks and nuts in ungreased oblong pan. Heat margarine in saucepan until melted. Remove from heat. Stir in Worcestershire sauce, paprika and garlic salt. Pour over cereal mixture, tossing until well coated. Bake stirring occasionally for 30 min. About 7½ c. snack.

Edna Fern Schmucker (Bakery)

PEANUT BUTTER FUDGE

2 c. sugar
½ c. evaporated milk

½ stick butter
pinch of salt

Bring to a rolling boil and boil for 5 min. on low heat. Remove from heat.

Add:

2 T. peanut butter
2 T. marshmallow creme

1 t. vanilla

Mix thoroughly. Pour into buttered dish. Let cool and cut into squares.

Joyce Schrock (Waitress)

PEANUT BUTTER PATTIES

2 lbs. powdered sugar
6 c. Rice Krispies
4 c. peanut butter

pinch of salt
2 sticks melted oleo

Mix all ingredients together. Melt chocolate chips or coating chocolate. Form candy mixture into small patties and dip in chocolate. Let set until dry.

Martha Miller (Cook)

PEANUT CREAMS

1 c. crunchy peanut butter
2 c. sugar

1 (7½ oz.) jar marshmallow creme
⅔ c. cream

Place peanut butter and marshmallow creme in bowl. Cook sugar and milk to soft ball stage (238°). Remove from heat and pour over peanut butter and marshmallow creme. Beat vigorously until smooth. Pour into greased pan.

Bertha Bontrager (Pie Baker)

PEANUT BUTTER BALLS

12 oz. chocolate chips
½ bar parrafin
1 stick margarine (soft)

1 box powdered sugar
2 c. peanut butter
3 c. Rice Krispies

Mix everything together except paraffin and chocolate chips. Roll into balls and place on waxed paper. Melt paraffin in double boiler, add chocolate chips. Dip balls in chocolate mixture and place on waxed paper.

Rosie Eash (Waitress)

PEANUT CLUSTER CANDY

1 (3 oz.) box regular chocolate
   pudding
1 c. sugar
1 T. butter

½ c. cream
1 c. salted peanuts
1 t. vanilla

Put first 4 ingredients in a saucepan and cook, stirring constantly, until mixture boils. Reduce heat. Boil 3 min., stirring all the while. Remove from heat. Let cool slightly. Add peanuts and vanilla. Stir until thick. Drop by spoonfuls onto waxed paper. Let cool completely.

Ada A. Schrock (Bakery)

PECAN PICK UPS

3 oz. Philadelphia cream cheese
1 stick oleo

1 c. flour

Mix until smooth. Form into 24 small balls and chill. Place in small size muffin pans and press firmly around the sides and bottom to form a pastry-like shell.

Filling:

¾ c. brown sugar
1 T. butter, melted
1 egg

1 t. vanilla
½ c. pecans, chopped

Mix well. Put 1 t. filling in each shell and bake at 350° for 25-30 min. Serves 24.

Wilma Schlabach (Dessert Counter)

ROCKY ROAD CANDY

½ c. butter
1 c. powdered sugar

1 pkg. butterscotch chips
1 egg, beaten

Heat ingredients in double boiler until melted. Stir in 2 c. miniature marshmallows. Pour into 8" x 8" pan lined with graham crackers.

Ada A. Schrock (Bakery)

PEANUT BUTTER FINGERS

Cream well:

½ c. butter or oleo
½ c. sugar
1 c. quick rolled oats

½ c. brown sugar (firmly packed)
½ t. vanilla

Blend in:

1 egg, unbeaten
½ t. soda

⅓ c. peanut butter

Stir in: 1 c. flour. Spread this mixture in greased 9×13 pan. Bake at 350° for 20-25 min. Then sprinkle 1 (6 oz.) pkg. chocolate chips on top. Let stand 5 min., then spread chocolate bits evenly across pan.

Combine:

½ c. powdered sugar
¼ c. peanut butter

2-4 T. evaporated milk

Mix this well, then drizzle across pan. Cool and cut into bars.

Betti Kauffman (Cashier-Hostess)

ROCKY ROAD SQUARES

1 (12 oz.) pkg. semi-sweet chocolate morsels
1 (14 oz.) can Eagle Brand Sweetened Condensed milk
2 T. butter or margarine
2 c. dry roasted peanuts
1 (10½ oz.) pkg. miniature white marshmallows

In top of double boiler, melt chocolate morsels with Eagle Brand milk and butter. Remove from heat. In large bowl, combine nuts and marshmallows. Fold in chocolate mixture. Spread in waxed-paper-lined 9"×13" pan. Chill 2 hours or until firm. Remove from pan. Peel off waxed paper and cut into squares. Cover and store at room temperature. Makes about 40 squares.

Lou Anna Yoder (Bakery)

RICE KRISPIE MARSHMALLOW TREATS

¼ c. regular margarine or butter
½ t. vanilla flavoring, if desired

1 (6 oz.-10 oz.) pkg. marshmallows
5 c. Kelloggs Rice Krispie cereal

Melt margarine in 3 quart saucepan. Add marshmallows and cook over low heat, stirring constantly until marshmallows are melted and mixture is very syrupy. Remove from heat and stir in vanilla. Add Rice Krispies and stir until well coated. Press warm mixture into 13×9×2 pan. Cut into squares when cool. Crushed Kellogg corn flakes can be used instead of Rice Krispies.

Alice Weaver (Waitress)

SUPERKREME CARAMELS

Boil rapidly for 2 minutes:

2½ c. sugar
2 c. cream

1¼ c. corn syrup
½ c. butter

Add slowly as not to stop boiling 2 c. cream. Boil rapidly again for 2 min. Add 1 can Eagle Brand milk and cook to 238° or desired firmness. Stir constantly after adding Eagle Brand milk. Can be cut in squares and some dipped in chocolate.

Laura Anna Miller (Grill Worker)

SUGAR COATED NUTS

Put nuts on dry cookie sheet. 2 c. pecans or almonds, 2 c. walnuts. Bake 15 min. in 325° oven. Beat 2 egg whites very stiff, then add: ¾ c. white sugar, dash of salt. Beat until peaks form; then add warm nuts and mix in a bowl. Put 1 stick oleo on cookie sheet and melt. Then spread nut mixture on sheet with oleo. Bake at 325° for 30 min., stirring every 10 min.

Lydia Ann Miller (Head cook)

SWEET SCRAMBLE

5 c. Wheat Chex
5 c. Rice Chex
5 c. Corn Chex

(or any 3 unsweetened cereals)

2 c. nuts
4 c. pretzels

Melt and heat to boiling:

2 c. brown sugar
½ lb. butter
1 t. salt

Heat cereal on cookie sheet at 200° until hot, 15-20 min. Then pour boiling syrup over and stir until cereal is covered.

Barbara Bontrager (Cashier)
Lizzie Ann Bontrager (Cook)

"Floating" church members make for a sinking church!

SWEDISH ROSETTES

2 eggs	1 T. sugar
¼ t. salt	1 t. vanilla
1 c. milk	1 c. flour

Mix together eggs, sugar, salt. Beat well, add remaining ingredients, and beat till smooth. Dip iron in hot oil until iron is well heated, then in batter half ways, then in hot oil till golden brown. Rosette iron will be needed.

Laura Bontrager (Bakery Department)

WALNUT CANDY

1½ c. sugar
½ c. rich milk
½ c. chopped walnuts

1 c. light Karo
1 T. butter
½ t. vanilla

Boil sugar and milk, Karo, to soft ball stage, when tested in cold water. Then put in butter and vanilla. Then nuts, cool and shape into balls.

Wilma Weaver (Waitress)

WALNUT CRUNCH

1¼ c. sugar
¾ c. butter or margarine
1½ t. salt
¼ c. water
1½ c. coarsely chopped walnuts

½ t. baking soda
⅓ c. semi-sweet chocolate bits, melted
½ c. finely chopped walnuts

Butter 15" × 10" jelly roll pan. In 2 quart saucepan over medium heat, bring to boil sugar, butter, salt and water, stirring often. Set candy thermometer in place and continue cooking, stirring frequently, until temperature reaches 290° or until a small amount of mixture dropped into very cold water separates into threads which are hard but not brittle. Remove from heat. Stir in coarsely chopped walnuts and soda. Pour at once into pan. Spread mixture with chocolate and sprinkle with finely chopped walnuts. Cool. Break or cut into small pieces. Makes 1½ pounds. Prepare 3½ hours ahead.

Sherry Bell (Waitress)

CHOCOLATE POPCORN BALLS

1½ c. sugar
⅓ c. corn syrup
⅔ c. water
⅓ c. molasses

3 T. butter
3 squares chocolate
1 t. vanilla
4 qt. popcorn, well salted

Boil to hard crack stage. Pour over popped corn. Work fast to make balls with buttered hands.

Martha Miller (Cook)

PRETZELS

Grease shallow baking pans and sprinkle with salt.

Boil:

3 c. water
3 t. baking soda

Mix:

⅓ c. brown sugar   1½ c. warm water
1 pkg. yeast

Set aside for 5 min. Add 5 c. flour. Stir until the dough no longer sticks to bowl. Turn out onto floured surface and knead until elastic. Pull off golf ball size pieces and form into pretzel shapes. Drop into boiling water. Cook until they rise to the top. Remove from water, place on greased pan and sprinkle with salt. Bake at 475° for 8 min.

Ginger Yoder (Waitress)

BIG SOFT PRETZELS

1 T. active dry yeast   3-4 c. Hot Roll mix
¾ c. lukewarm water   1 egg, beaten
1 egg, beaten   2 t. coarse salt
¼ c. vegetable oil or melted
    margarine

Lightly grease 2 large baking sheets. In a large bowl, dissolve yeast in lukewarm water. Blend in 1 egg and oil or margarine. Add 3 c. Hot Roll mix. Stir well. Add additional Hot Roll mix to make a soft, but not too sticky dough. Knead about 5 min. until dough is smooth. Roll pieces of dough into ropes about ½ inch in diameter and 18-24 inches long. Form into pretzel shapes. For pretzel sticks, cut dough into 5-6 inch long ropes. Place on prepared baking sheets. Preheat oven to 425°. Brush tops of pretzels with beaten egg and sprinkle with coarse salt. Bake immediately for 12-15 min., until brown and crisp. Makes 12-15 large pretzels.

Becky Schmucker (Busser)

SOFT PRETZELS

1 pkg. yeast
⅓ c. brown sugar
coarse kosher salt

1½ c. water
5 c. flour (may use ½ whole wheat)
baking soda

Grease 2 large cookie sheets and sprinkle with kosher salt. Put about 1½ inches of water in a medium sized pan. For each cup of water, add 1 t. baking soda. Bring to a gentle boil. Heat oven to 475°.

In a small bowl mix brown sugar with warm water. Sprinkle yeast on mixture and let rest about 5 min. Measure flour into a large bowl, add liquid all at once and stir until dough no longer sticks to sides. Knead on a lightly floured surface until stretchy. Pinch off golf ball sized pieces and roll into ropes. Twist ropes into pretzels. (May be frozen at this point, do not thaw, just drop in water.) Immerse in water until they float. Place on cookie sheets. Sprinkle with kosher salt. Bake for 8 min. Serve hot with mustard, peanut butter, cheese or whatever pleases you.

Sue Miller (Manager)
Mary Jane Bontrager (Cook)

PARTY MIX

⅔ c. margarine
1 t. Worcestershire sauce
½ t. garlic salt
2 c. toasted oat cereal
¼ t. onion salt (optional)

2 c. bite-size crispy wheat squares
2 c. bite-size crispy rice squares
2 c. pretzel sticks
2 c. mixed nuts
¼ t. celery salt (optional)

Combine margarine, Worcestershire sauce and garlic salt. Pour over combined remaining ingredients; mix lightly. Spread on ungreased 15½ × 10½ jelly roll pan. Bake at 250° for 1 hour, stirring occasionally. Approximately 10 cups.

Variation: Raisins and peanuts can be substituted for the oat cereal and mixed nuts. Party mix can be prepared in advance and stored in a tightly covered container. Reheat briefly at 350°.

Sue Miller (Manager)
Mary Jane Bontrager (Cook)

Pies

DOWN THE LINE

Before I married Maggie dear,
I was her pumpkin pie,
Then precious peach, her honey lamb,
The apple of her eye.
But after years of married life
This thought I pause to utter
Those fancy names are gone, and now,
I'm just her bread and butter.

Have I done the best I could
To be to others kind and good
Or have I failed to do my part
And caused someone a broken heart?
Lord, if I have, please do forgive
And a better life I'll try to live.

A HOLIDAY RECIPE

4 c. of Love
2 c. of Loyalty
3 c. of Forgiveness
1 c. of Friendship
5 spoons of Hope
2 spoons of Tenderness
4 quarts of Faith
1 barrel of Laughter

Take love and loyalty, mix it thoroughly with faith.
Blend it with tenderness, kindness and understanding.
Sprinkle abundantly with laughter. Bake it with sunshine.
Serve daily with generous helpings.

Doretta Mast (Dishwasher)

"A pound of patience is worth more than a bushel of brains."

𝒫ies

NEVER FAIL PIE CRUST

Sift 4 c. flour, 1 t. sugar, 1 t. salt and 1 t. baking powder. Mix with 1¾ c. Crisco or 1½ c. lard. Now add 1 egg, well beaten with 1 t. vinegar and ½ c. cold water. Mix well. Makes a flaky crust and keeps in refrigerator for a long time if desired.

Rose Schrock (Baker)

NEVER FAIL PIE CRUST

1½ c. shortening
3 c. flour
1 t. salt

1 egg
1 t. vinegar
5 T. cold water

Mix together shortening, flour and salt. Beat together egg, vinegar and water. Add last a little at a time. Makes 3 pies.

Betty Miller (Pie Baker)

Why can't life's problems hit us when we're eighteen and know all the answers?

APPLE PIE

Fill unbaked pie shell with chopped apples and 1 T. butter or margarine.

Mix:

½ c. sugar   sprinkle of cinnamon
1 T. flour

Add enough cream to make a thick paste. Pour over apples. Top with crust and bake at 350° for 45 min. or until apples are done.

Tip: The sugar varies according to the tartness of the apples.

Esther Nisley (Bakery)

APPLE CREAM PIE

⅔ c. sugar   1/8 t. salt
1 egg, slightly beaten   2 T. flour
1 c. sour cream   1 t. vanilla
2 c. finely chopped apples

Topping:

⅓ c. flour   1 t. cinnamon
⅓ c. sugar   ¼ c. butter

Combine sugar, flour and salt. Add cream, egg, vanilla and beat until smooth. Add chopped apples and pour into unbaked pie shell. For topping combine flour, sugar, cinnamon and cut in butter. Sprinkle over top of pie. Bake at 425° for 25 min.

Norine Borkholder (Cook)

APPLE CRUMB PIE

4 c. sliced apples
1½ c. water
2 T. Clear-Jel
1 c. sugar
1 t. cinnamon

pinch salt
½ c. brown sugar
¾ c. flour
2 T. butter

Put apples, sugar, cinnamon, 1 c. water and salt in saucepan. Cook until apples are half cooked. Combine Clear-Jel with ½ c. water and stir into apple mixture. Cook just long enough to cook Clear-Jel. Pour into unbaked pie shell. Combine remaining ingredients and put on top of pie. Bake at 425° until nice and brown.

Lou Anna Yoder (Bakery)

DIFFERENT APPLE PIE

4 c. apples, shredded
1 c. sugar
1 stick oleo, softened

2 eggs, beaten
1 t. lemon juice
1 t. vanilla

Mix together and pour into deep 10″ unbaked pie shell. Sprinkle with sugar and cinnamon. Bake at 350° for 45-60 min.

Sharon Boley (Head Waitress)

MOCK APPLE PIE

Boil together 1½ c. sugar, 1½ c. water, 1½ t. cream of tartar, 2 or 3 min. Cool. Break 8 or 10 soda crackers into an unbaked pie crust. Sprinkle cinnamon, and put 4 T. butter on crackers. Pour cooled syrup over and put on a top crust. Bake at 350° for 40-45 min.

Ida Troyer (Baker)

BANANA MALLOW PARTY PIE

1 (3½ oz.) pkg. vanilla pudding
  and pie filling mix
1½ c. miniature marshmallows

1 c. heavy cream, whipped
2 bananas
1 (9") baked vanilla wafer crust,
  chilled

Prepare mix as directed for pie filling on package, except using 1¾ c. milk. Cover surface of pie filling with waxed paper or transparent wrap; chill. Mix until well blended; fold in marshmallows and whipped cream. Slice bananas into crust. Pour filling over bananas. Chill several hours or overnight.

Sue Miller (Manager)

BUTTERSCOTCH PECAN PIE

Cook together until bubbly:

½ c. butter
½ c. brown sugar

½ c. pecans

Pour into partly baked pie crust and bake another 5 min. Let cool. Mix 1 box instant butterscotch pie filling according to package directions and pour into pie shell. Top with whipped cream and serve.

Sylvia Slabaugh (Cook)

BUTTERNUT SQUASH PIE

¾ c. brown sugar
½ t. salt
½ t. allspice
3 large eggs
1 c. milk

1 T. flour
¼ t. ginger
¾ t. lemon juice
1½ c. cooked, mashed squash

Pour in unbaked pastry and bake in preheated 400° oven for 40-50 min.

Beth Ann Yoder (Salad Girl)

CARAMEL PIE

Mix together until crumbly and put in unbaked pie shell:

1 c. brown sugar
1 t. melted butter

Mix and pour over crumbs:

1½ c. rich milk   2 T. flour
2 eggs   pinch of salt
2T. sugar

Bake at 350° for 40 min.

Bertha Bontrager (Pie Baker)

CARAMEL PECAN PIE

Mix all together and pour in unbaked pie shell:

3 eggs, beaten   1 c. brown sugar
¾ c. light Karo   1 T. melted butter
pinch of salt   1 c. pecans
½ c. water

Makes 1 (9") pie. Bake in slow oven at 325° till set.

Susanna Miller (Cook)

COCONUT PIE

½ c. sugar   ½ c. cream
2 eggs, separated   1 t. vanilla
1½ c. milk   ⅓ c. coconut

Combine sugar, egg yolks (beaten), milk, cream, vanilla and coconut. Mix well. Beat egg whites and fold into mixture. Pour into unbaked pie shell and bake at 400° for 10 min. Reduce heat to 350° and continue baking until set.

Mary Jane Bontrager (Cook)

CHOCOLATE CHIP PIE

24 marshmallows
½ c. milk
1 c. whipping cream

½ t. vanilla
1 (6 oz.) pkg. chocolate chips, grated
graham cracker crust

Heat marshmallows and milk until melted. Cool. Fold in remaining ingredients and let stand a few minutes. Pour into graham cracker crust. Chill.

Wilma Schlabach (Dessert Counter)

CRANBERRY APPLE PIE

2 c. sugar
4 T. cornstarch
½ t. cinnamon
5 c. sliced, peeled apples

2 c. fresh cranberries
¼ t. lemon, finely chopped
10" unbaked pie shell, double crust

Combine all ingredients. Mix until apples and cranberries are coated. Spoon into pie shell and dot with butter. Place top crust over mixture. Brush lightly with 1 T. milk and sprinkle with sugar. Bake until bubbly and brown on top—approximately 1 hour. Bake at 350°.

Sharon Boley (Head Waitress)

CRANBERRY CRUMB PIE

1 (9") unbaked pie shell
1 (14 oz.) can sweetened
   condensed milk
¼ c. brown sugar (divided)
1 (16 oz.) can whole cranberry
   sauce
⅓ c. flour

1 (8 oz.) cream cheese, softened
¼ lemon juice
2 T. cornstarch or Clear-Jel
¼ c. oleo or butter
¾ c. chopped nuts (optional)

Bake shell 8 min. at 425°, remove and reduce temperature to 375°. Beat cream cheese and milk until smooth, add lemon juice. In small bowl mix 2 T. sugar and cornstarch, mix well, stir in cranberry sauce, spoon over cheese mixture, cut oleo into flour and remainder sugar until crumbly. Sprinkle over cranberry sauce and bake for 45-50 min. or until bubbly or golden brown.

Ida Anna Miller (Cook)

CRUSTLESS CUSTARD PIE

4 eggs	1 t. vanilla
½ c. sugar	nutmeg
2 c. milk	4 level T. flour

Beat eggs with sugar until light and fluffy; add flour, milk and vanilla. Pour into lightly greased pie pan; sprinkle with nutmeg. Bake 1 hour at 350°, or until knife inserted in center comes out clean. During baking, the flour settles to the bottom and forms a very light crust, which enables this to be cut and served as pie.

Ida Anna Miller (Cook)

Home is where a fellow goes when he is tired of being nice to people.

MOM'S CUSTARD PIE

4 medium eggs	1 c. brown sugar
4 T. (rounded) flour	4 C. milk

Beat 3 egg whites, not stiff. Then beat 1 egg white and 4 yolks. Add brown sugar, flour, and egg whites. Add milk last. Pour in unbaked pie shells. Makes 2 pies. Bake at 450° till brown, then lower to 425°.

Amanda Troyer (Waitress)

TACT—The ability to make your guests feel at home when you wish they were.

The safest way to knock the chip off a fellow's shoulder is by patting him on the back.

CHERRY PIE (Won National Pie Baking Contest)

2 c. canned tart red cherries
1 c. sugar
3 T. flour
1/8 t. almond flavoring

1 c. cherry juice
¼ t. salt
¼ t. red food coloring
1 T. flour

Mix thoroughly in a saucepan, the sugar, salt and flour. Add cherry juice, red coloring and almond extract. Stir until well blended. Carefully mix the cherries into the mixture. Let stand while making pastry.

Crust:

2 c. sifted flour
1 T. sugar
about ⅓ c. cold milk

1 t. salt
⅔ c. shortening
1 T. melted butter

Sift into a mixing bowl the flour, salt and sugar. Add shortening. Cut it into the flour with a pastry blender until the mixture is in even bits no larger than peas. Sprinkle milk, one T. at a time on a small area of the flour mixture.

Toss the mixture lightly with a fork after each spoonful of milk is added. Continue this procedure, adding only enough milk to make the pastry mixture moist enough to form a ball when patted lightly together. Roll out half of dough with quick light strokes. Fit into pie pan. Trim off surplus pastry. Brush this crust with melted butter. Roll out the other ball of dough for top of pie. Put cherry filling into pastry lined pan and dot with T. of butter. Bake on top rack of oven at 450° for 5 min., then place on bottom rack and reduce heat to 375°. Bake 35 min. longer.

Wilma Weaver (Waitress)

CHERRY CREAM PIE

¼ c. sugar
¼ c. flour
¼ t. salt

3 egg yolks, slightly beaten
2 t. vanilla
2 c. milk

Bake a 9″ pie shell. Combine sugar, flour, salt in top of double boiler. Add milk and egg yolks, mixing well. Cook over rapidly boiling water 10 min., stirring constantly. Remove from heat, add vanilla, pour into pie shell. Cool.

Cherry Glaze:

2 c. tart cherries, drained
1 c. sugar

1¼ c. cherry juice
¼ c. cornstarch

Heat juice to boiling point. Combine sugar, cornstarch and enough cold water to make a paste. Pour into boiling juice. Cook until mixture thickens (about 3 min.). Stir constantly. Add cherries and allow to cool slightly. Pour this mixture over cream filling in pie shell. Top with meringue and brown. If preferred, it may be topped with whipped cream.

Barbara Bontrager (Cashier)

Your vocabulary may not be filled with ''Baloney,'' but what you say does make a difference. Like it or not, you are judged by your conversation.

The way you listen.
The words you choose.
The interest you express in others.
And the emotion you express.

Yes, you are immediately given the ''thumbs up'' or ''thumbs down'' treatment because of both your spoken and unspoken words.

CREAM CHEESE PECAN PIE

1 (8 oz.) cream cheese, softened
1 egg, beaten
1 t. vanilla
1¼ c. chopped pecans

½ c. sugar
½ t. salt
1 (10") unbaked pie shell

Topping:

3 eggs
½ t. vanilla

1 c. light corn syrup

Cream together softened cheese, sugar, beaten egg, salt and vanilla. Spread over bottom of unbaked pie shell. Sprinkle pecans evenly over cream cheese layer. Combine all topping ingredients and beat till smooth. Pour over pecan layer. Bake for 35-45 min. at 375° until pecan layer is golden brown. Serve slightly warm with whipped cream if desired. Yields 12 servings.

Ellen Miller (Cashier-Gift Shop)

CHOCOLATE PIE

2 T. butter

3 c. milk

Put in saucepan, after it reaches boiling point add:

1 c. sugar
2 T. flour

2 T. cocoa
1 t. vanilla

Mix above four ingredients with 1 c. milk. Bring to boil. Cool before putting in baked pie shell.

Elsie Miller (Grill Cook)

Nothing is all wrong. Even a clock that has stopped running is right twice a day.

DUTCH CREAM PIE

1 c. brown sugar
3 T. flour or cornstarch
1 egg, beaten

1 t. vanilla
enough milk or cream (about
2½ c.) to make one pie

Pour into unbaked pie shell and top with butter and nutmeg. Bake at 400° for 10 min. Reduce heat to 325° and continue baking for 30 min.

Sylvia Slabaugh (Cook)

EASY CHERRY CHEESE PIE

8 oz. pkg. cream cheese, softened
14 oz. can Eagle Brand sweetened
    condensed milk

1 t. vanilla
cherry pie filling, chilled
⅓ c. lemon juice

In medium bowl, beat cheese until light and fluffy. Add condensed milk, blend thoroughly. Stir in lemon juice and vanilla. Pour into baked pie crust and chill for 2 hours or until set. Top with desired amount of pie filling before serving.

Tip: Any of your favorite pie fillings may be used instead of cherry.

Esther Nisley (Bakery)

ELDERBERRY PIE

2 serving spoonfuls flour
½ c. sugar
elderberries

Enough cream to make a thick pancake-like batter consistency. Cover the bottom of an unbaked pie shell with ½" elderberries (more or less as desired). Make a thick batter of the flour, sugar and cream. Pour over berries and bake at 400° for 10 min. Reduce heat to 350° and bake 30 min.

Ida Anna Miller (Cook)

EASY PEACH PIE

1 large can sliced peaches
1 c. sugar
1 stick margarine
1 c. flour

1½ t. baking powder
¼ t. salt
½ c. milk

Heat peaches and juice and set aside. Melt margarine. Pour into bottom of Pyrex dish. Make batter of sugar, flour, baking powder, salt and milk. Pour over melted margarine. Do not stir. Place peaches and juice on top of batter. Do not stir. Bake at 350° for 25-30 min. Serve while warm.

Sharon Boley (Head Waitress)

ELDERBERRY PIE

1 c. Milnot
3 T. flour
1 c. elderberries

1 c. sugar
1 t. vanilla

Bake at 425° for 10 min., then reduce heat to 350° till done.

Rosa Borntrager (Dutch Country Gifts)

ELDERBERRY PIE

1 recipe plain pastry
½ c. sugar
2 T. flour

2½ c. stemmed elderberries
pinch of salt
3 T. lemon juice

Line a pie pan with pastry. Fill with elderberries. Mix the sugar, salt, and flour. Sprinkle over the berries. Add lemon juice. Cover with top crust. Bake in 450° oven for 10 min., then reduce heat to 350° and bake for 30 min. more.

Leora Kauffman (Purchasing)

FRUIT PIE WITH 7-UP®

1½ c. 7-Up®
1 c. sugar
2 T. Sure-Jel®
9″ baked pie shell

1 box Jell-O®
(pick flavor to match fruit)
choice of fruit

Boil 7-Up®, sugar, and Sure-Jel® together. Add Jell-O®. When nearly set, add fruit. Pour into baked pie shell and top with whipped cream.

Wilma Schlabach
(Dessert Counter)

FRESH PEACH PIE

3 ripe peaches, peeled and
crushed
⅛ t. cinnamon
4 peaches, peeled and sliced

1 c. sugar
3 T. cornstarch
½ c. water
9″ baked pie shell

Combined crushed 3 peaches, sugar, cornstarch, cinnamon, and water. Cook until thick and clear. Place the sliced peaches into a 9″ baked pie shell. Pour the cooled fruit mixture over fresh peach slices and chill. Cover with whipped topping and serve.

Ida Anna Miller (Cook)

FRESH PEACH PIE

1 baked pie crust
1 can Eagle Brand® milk
1 ripe peach, peeled and crushed
¼ c. water
3 firm peaches, peeled and sliced

1 pkg. (8 oz.) cream cheese
½ T. lemon juice
1 T. cornstarch
1 T. sugar
whipped topping

Whip milk, cream cheese, and lemon juice together and put in pie crust. Chill in refrigerator.

Combine crushed peach, sugar, cornstarch, and water. Cook in a saucepan until this becomes a thick glaze. Put peach slices on top of the chilled cream pie, then glaze. Top with whipped topping.

Millie Whetstone (Cook)

GRAPE PIE

1½ c. grape pulp
1 c. sugar
½ c. Milnot

1 T. Minute Tapioca
2 T. cornstarch

Mix together and put in unbaked crust and top with crumbs: 3 T. flour, 3 T. sugar, 2 T. butter. Bake at 425° for 10 min. and reduce heat to 325° until finished, about 40 min.

Rosa Borntrager (Dutch Country Gifts)

GERMAN SWEET CHOCOLATE PIE

1 (4 oz.) pkg. sweet chocolate
1⅔ c. thin cream or milk
1 c. coconut
1 t. vanilla
½ t. salt
1 unbaked pie shell

2 T. butter
1⅓ c. sugar
2 eggs
3 T. cornstarch
½ c. chopped pecans

Melt chocolate with butter; stir until blended. Remove from heat and blend in cream. Mix sugar, cornstarch and salt thoroughly. Beat in eggs and vanilla. Gradually blend in chocolate mixture. Pour into pie shell. Combine coconut and nuts; sprinkle over top of filling. Bake at 375° for 45 min. Cool at least 4 hours. Filling will set while cooling.

Esther Hershberger

GROUND CHERRY PIE

3 c. ground cherries
2 T. lemon juice
pastry shell

2 c. sugar
3½ T. Minute Tapioca

Mix together cherries, lemon juice, sugar and tapioca and pour into pie shell. Cover with top crust and bake at 400° for 10 min., then reduce heat to 350° for about 45 min.

Ida Anna Miller (Cook)

HEAVENLY PIE

Crust:

16 graham crackers, crushed   ¼ c. butter
¼ c. sugar

Mix well and press into a 9" pie pan. Bake at 350° for 10 min.

Filling:

½ c. milk   ½ t. vanilla
30 marshmallows   2 squares sweet chocolate, grated
1 c. whipping cream, whipped

Heat milk in double boiler. Add marshmallows and stir until melted. Let cool. Add whipping cream, vanilla and chocolate. Pour into crust. Chill until firm. Top with whipped cream and serve.

Sylvia Slabaugh (Cook)

ICE CREAM PIE

½ c. peanut butter   vanilla ice cream (approx. ½ gallon)
½ c. light Karo   ¼ c. ground peanuts
2½ c. Rice Krispies

Mix peanut butter and Karo. Blend in Rice Krispies. Pat mixture into a pie pan. Chill. Fill with ice cream. Top with peanuts and freeze. Strawberries on top are also good.

Mary Rose Yoder (Cook)

Let raw potatoes stand in cold water for at least half an hour before frying to improve the crispness of french fried potatoes.

JELLO PUDDING PECAN PIE

1 (3¼ oz.) pkg. Jello vanilla pudding
1 c. light corn syrup
¾ c. evaporated milk

1 egg, slightly beaten
1 c. pecans, chopped

Blend pudding mix with corn syrup. Gradually add evaporated milk and egg, stirring to blend. Add pecans. Pour into unbaked pie shell. Bake at 375° until top is firm and just begins to crack (about 40 min.). Cool at least 3 hours.

Doris Yoder (Dishwasher)

LEMON PIE

1 c. sugar
1 T. butter
6 T. lemon juice (fresh squeezed)
1 t. lemon peel

1¼ c. water
¼ c. cornstarch
3 egg yolks
2 T. milk

Combine sugar, water and butter, heat until sugar dissolves. Add cornstarch, blended with a little water. Cook slowly until clear (about 8 min.). Add lemon juice and peel. Cook 2 min. Slowly add egg yolks beaten with milk. Bring to boil. Cool. Pour in cooled 8" baked pie shell.

Elsie Miller (Grill Cook)

LEMON FLUFF PIE

Mix together in saucepan 3 egg yolks, ½ c. sugar, 3 T. water, 3 T. lemon juice, 2 t. grated lemon rind. Cook until boiling, stirring constantly. Remove from heat. Immediately fold into a meringue made of 3 egg whites, ¼ t. cream of tartar, ½ c. sugar. Pour into a baked shell and chill for several hours.

Edith Herschberger (Cashier)

FAMOUS LEMON PIE

3 T. cornstarch
¼ c. lemon juice
3 eggs, separated
1 (9") baked pie shell

1¼ c. sugar
1 T. grated rind (optional)
1½ c. boiling water
6 T. sugar

Combine cornstarch, sugar, lemon juice and rind. Beat egg yolks; add to cornstarch mixture. Gradually add boiling water. Heat to boiling over direct heat and then boil gently 4 min., stirring constantly. Pour into pie shell. Beat egg whites until stiff, but not dry. Gradually beat in 6 T. sugar. Spread over filling. Brown in oven 4 to 5 min. at 425°.

Alma Hershberger (Bakery)

MAPLE SYRUP PIE

Pastry for 1-crust 9" pie

2 T. butter or margarine
3 eggs, well beaten
¼ t. salt

1 t. vanilla extract
1 c. maple syrup
½ c. or more of hickory or
black walnuts

Cream butter. Add syrup slowly, then stir in all of remaining ingredients. Pour into pie shell. Additional large pieces of nutmeats may be put on top if desired. Bake at 375° until a knife inserted near the center comes out clean.

Beth Ann Yoder (Salad Girl)

MILLIONAIRE PIE

1½ c. sugar
2 T. vinegar
1 heaping t. flour
1 c. nuts

2 eggs
2 T. water
1 t. allspice
1 c. raisins

Mix and put into unbaked crust and bake at 400° for 10 min. Reduce to 350° and bake for 40 min.

Edith Herschberger (Cashier)

MINCEMEAT PUMPKIN PIE

1½ c. prepared mincemeat
½ t. cinnamon
¼ t. cloves
¼ t. nutmeg

¼ t. salt
½ c. sugar
2 eggs
1 c. pumpkin

Mix mincemeat, spices and salt. Add sugar and eggs to the pumpkin then blend all together and pour into unbaked pie shell. Bake at 450° for 10 min. Reduce heat to 375° and bake an additional 30 min.

Leora Kauffman (Purchasing)

Meat loaf will not stick to the pan if you place a strip or two of bacon at the bottom of the pan before packing the meat mixture in.

MINCEMEAT

6 lb. beef, cooked with lid on pan on low heat. Reserve liquid and use in mincemeat with chopped meat.

10 c. apples, diced
1½ c. vinegar
3 or 4 c. raisins
2 lb. brown sugar
2 c. white sugar
2 t. salt
1 t. pepper

1 bottle of dark Karo
1 lb. butter or chopped suet (or use butter and leave fat on roast)
8 t. cinnamon
4 t. cloves
4 t. nutmeg

Mix all the above ingredients together with 1½ c. wine and keep covered and stored in cool place. Any kind of wine is O.K. If you have Mogan David, that's O.K. Note the meat is the only ingredient that is cooked. It can be sealed in jars and kept from one year to the next. Apple and raisins can always be added to this recipe when the mincemeat is to be used. It's very good.

Millie Whetstone (Cook)

OLD-FASHIONED SUGAR PIE

1 c. sugar
¼ t. salt
2 t. vanilla

3 T. flour
1½ c. cream or ½ cream and ½ milk
1 unbaked pastry shell

Combine sugar, flour, salt. Add cream and vanilla. Pour in 9" pastry, sprinkle with cinnamon. Bake at 425°.

Ida Anna Miller (Cook)

OUT OF THIS WORLD PIE

1 can cherry pie filling
¾ c. sugar
1 large can pineapple with juice
1 T. cornstarch
1 t. red food coloring

1 (3 oz.) box cherry flavored
gelatin or jello
4 small bananas
2 baked pie shells or graham
cracker crusts
whipped topping

Combine cherry pie filling, sugar, pineapple with juice, cornstarch, and food coloring. Cook until thick. Remove from heat and add jello. Allow to cool. Add sliced bananas and pour into crusts. Top with whipped topping.

Karen Yoder (Busser)

OLD-FASHIONED CREAM PIE

2 c. cream
1 c. brown sugar

2 T. flour, rounded
½ c. melted butter

Beat together and pour into unbaked pie shell. Bake at 400° for 40 min.

Sue Miller (Manager)

OATMEAL PIE

6 eggs, beaten
1½ c. brown sugar
½ c. white sugar
1 c. Karo
1 c. water

4 T. oleo
1 c. coconut
1 c. oatmeal
2 t. vanilla
½ t. salt

Blend all ingredients and pour into unbaked pie crust. Bake at 350° for 30-35 min. Makes 2 pies.

Rosalie Bontrager (Essenhaus Country Inn Manager)

OLD-FASHIONED CREAM PIE

Heat to boiling point:

1 pint whipping cream

1 c. cold milk

Mix together well:

1½ c. brown sugar
½ c. white sugar
½ c. flour

pinch of salt
vanilla
¼ c. butter

Pour boiling cream mixture over this and mix well. Then add 3 c. cold milk. Pour into 4 unbaked pie shells. Bake in 425° oven for ½ hour or until done.

Ida Anna Miller (Cook)

Just when you're successful enough to sleep late, you're so old you always wake up early.

PUMPKIN CHIFFON PIE

3 eggs, separated
⅔ c. sugar
1½ c. canned pumpkin
⅓ c. milk
½ t. salt

½ t. ginger
½ t. cinnamon
½ t. nutmeg
1 envelope unflavored gelatin
¼ c. cold water

Beat egg yolks. Add ⅓ c. sugar, pumpkin, milk, salt and spices. Heat in double boiler, stirring constantly. Dissolve gelatin in cold water and add to hot mixture. Chill until slightly thickened. Beat egg whites until stiff. Add remaining ⅓ c. sugar to egg whites gradually. Fold into pumpkin mixture. Pour into baked pie shell. Chill until firm.

Martha Miller (Cook)

OLD AGE: When the gleam in your eye is just the sun on your bifocals.

PARADISE PUMPKIN PIE

1 (8 oz.) pkg. cream cheese
¼ c. sugar
½ t. vanilla
1 egg
1 (9") unbaked pastry shell
maple syrup

1¼ c. canned pumpkin

1 c. evaporated milk
½ c. sugar
2 eggs, slightly beaten
1 t. cinnamon
¼ t. ginger
¼ t. nutmeg
dash of salt

Combine softened cream cheese, sugar and vanilla, mixing until well blended. Add egg; mix well. Spread onto bottom of pastry shell.

Combine remaining ingredients except syrup; mix well. Carefully pour over cream cheese mixture. Bake at 350°, 1 hour and 5 min. Cool. Brush with syrup.

Sue Miller (Manager)

PEANUT BUTTER FROZEN PIES

Graham cracker crust:

1¾-2 sticks butter, melted
1½ T. sugar

2 pkgs. graham crackers, crushed

Mix well and press into pie pan.

Filling:

8 oz. cream cheese
2 c. powdered sugar
⅔ c. peanut butter

1 c. milk
9 oz. Cool Whip

Beat cream cheese and powdered sugar until smooth. Add remaining ingredients and pour into shell. Freeze. Makes 2 pies.

Lou Anna Yoder (Bakery)

PEANUT BUTTER PIE

½ c. white sugar
½ c. brown sugar
⅔ c. flour
3 eggs, beaten
4 c. milk
¼ t. salt
¼ t. vanilla
2 T. butter

Crumbs:

1½ c. powdered sugar
⅔ c. peanut butter

Mix sugar, flour, eggs, salt and ¾ c. cold milk. Pour into scalded 3¼ c. milk. Stir constantly until thick. Remove from heat and cool. Makes 2 pies.

Mix powdered sugar and peanut butter to form small crumbs. Line baked pie shell with crumbs and add pudding. Top with whipped cream and sprinkle a few crumbs on top.

Ella Bontrager (Cook)

PECAN PIE

3 beaten eggs
½ c. sugar
1 T. flour
pinch of salt
1 c. white Karo

¼ c. water
2 T. melted butter
1 t. vanilla
1 c. pecans

Beat eggs, add rest of ingredients except nuts. Put nuts in unbaked pie shell. Pour mixture over nuts. Bake at 350° for 50-60 min.

Lillian Miller (Cashier-Hostess)

PUMPKIN PIE

1½ c. pumpkin
1 c. brown sugar
3 eggs
½ t. salt
1 T. cornstarch

¼ t. ginger
¼ t. cloves
1 t. cinnamon
1 can Milnot

Mix together first ingredients. Add milk last. Pour in unbaked pie shell. Bake at 425° for 10 min., then 350° for 30 min. or till done.

Lillian Miller (Cashier-Hostess)

PUMPKIN PIE

1 c. pumpkin
1 c. sugar
1 c. brown sugar
3 T. flour
3 eggs, separated
1 t. salt

½ t. nutmeg
½ t. cinnamon
3 c. milk
½ t. lemon
1 t. vanilla

Mix pumpkin, flour, sugar, spices and salt. Add egg yolks, milk, lemon, and vanilla. Beat egg whites and fold into mixture. Bake at 350° until firm. Makes 2 pies.

Ada A. Schrock (Bakery)

PUMPKIN PIE

2½ c. milk
6 eggs
2 c. sugar
1 T. flour
¼ t. nutmeg

¼ t. cloves
¼ t. allspice
⅓ t. salt
½ t. cinnamon
2 c. pumpkin

Heat milk. Set aside. In bowl beat the eggs. Add remaining ingredients. Beat well. Add ½ can Carnation milk, then heated milk. Mix thoroughly. Bake at 300° for 10 min. Reduce heat and bake at 250° until set. Makes 2 (9") pies.

Mary Esther Miller (Bakery Manager)

PUMPKIN ICE CREAM PIE

Bottom of pie:

20 graham crackers
¼ c. sugar
¼ c. melted butter

Filling:

1 c. pumpkin
½ t. salt
¼ t. ginger
1 quart vanilla ice cream

½ c. sugar
½ t. cinnamon
¼ t. nutmeg

Put graham crackers in bottom of pan. Pour pumpkin ice cream mixture on top and put in freezer. When frozen hard, cut in squares and serve.

Amanda Troyer (Waitress)

PECAN PIE

3 eggs
1 c. pecans
½ t. salt

½ c. sugar
1 c. dark corn syrup
3 T. butter

Beat eggs, add rest of ingredients and bake in pie shell. Bake at 425° for 15 min., then 350° for 30 min.

Melissa Hershberger (Bakery Cashier)

Never beat egg whites in an aluminum pan, it is sure to darken them.

PINEAPPLE-COCONUT PIE

Mix together:

1½ c. sugar
1 can Angel Flake coconut
3 eggs

½ c. butter or margarine
3 T. flour
1 small can crushed pineapple

After mixing thoroughly, bake in unbaked pie shell at 350°. Do not overbake.

Edith Herschberger (Cashier)

When bread is baking, a small dish of water in the oven will help to keep the crust from getting too hard.

RASPBERRY CREAM PIE

This recipe is for 2 pies.

¾ c. water   ½ c. sugar

Heat together; and while this is boiling, mix together the four following ingredients and add:

1 heaping T. Jell starch, or   ¼ c. water
   or 1 level T. cornstarch   ¼ t. lemon juice
pinch salt

Boil together until mixture is clear. Add: 4 oz. raspberry jello

Stir until the jello is well dissolved. Cool and add 2 c. fresh red raspberries.

In bottom of a baked 9" pie crust, put 2 cups of cooled vanilla pie filling. Place 1 cup raspberry pudding on top of the vanilla pie filling and top with whipped cream.

Mary Esther Miller (Bakery)

 To thicken soup, add instant rice or mashed potatoes.

RHUBARB PIE

2 eggs   1 T. (heaping) flour
1¼ c. sugar   ½ c. water
⅔ c. cream   2 c. rhubarb, cut

Beat eggs, sugar, cream and flour. Add ½ c. water. Beat again. Place rhubarb in unbaked pie shell and pour filling over rhubarb. Bake at 325° until set. Makes 1 pie.

Mary Esther Miller (Bakery Manager)

RHUBARB PIE

2 eggs (whites beaten and add last)
1¼ c. milk
¼ t. salt
¼ t. cinnamon
1 c. diced rhubarb
1¾ c. sugar
2 T. flour
2 T. butter

Note: Pineapple can also be used instead of rhubarb. Bake 325° till set.

Fannie Yoder (Cook)

RHUBARB CREAM PIE

2 T. butter or oleo
2 c. diced rhubarb
1 c. sugar

Cook slowly till tender. Combine:

¼ c. sugar
2 egg yolks, well beaten
1/8 t. salt

2 T. cornstarch
¼ c. light cream

Add to rhubarb, cook till thick. Cool. Pour in baked pie shell. Top with beaten egg whites and brown lightly if desired. Bake 325° till set.

Fannie Yutzy (Pie Baker)

RHUBARB PIE

2 c. rhubarb
1½ c. sugar
2 T. flour

pinch of salt
2 egg yolks
water to moisten

Mix all ingredients and pour into unbaked pie shell. Bake at 425° for 15 min. Reduce heat to 350° and bake until done. Whip 2 egg whites until stiff and spread over pie. Bake until browned.

Mary Ellen Campbell (Waitress)

SOUR CREAM APPLE PIE

3 c. shoestring apples
¾ c. sugar
½ c. sour cream
1 egg, beaten
1 unbaked pie shell

3 T. flour
½ t. vanilla
½ c. applesauce
¼ t. salt

Mix flour and sugar; add vanilla, sour cream, applesauce and eggs. Beat until smooth. Stir in apples and salt. Pour into pie shell. Bake at 450° for 15 min., reduce heat to 325°. Bake about 20 min. longer. Remove from oven; sprinkle with topping crumbs. Return to oven and bake 10 min. more.

Esther Hershberger

SOUR CREAM PIE

1 c. sour cream
½ c. seedless raisins
1 c. sugar
3 egg yolks

½ t. cinnamon
¼ t. cloves
pinch nutmeg
2 egg whites

Mix all ingredients together and bake until set (like custard). When done, beat 2 egg whites until stiff. Add 1 T. sugar to egg whites and spread over top of pie. Return to oven and continue baking until egg whites are brown.

Ida Mae Schmucker (Bakery)

VINEGAR PIE

1 c. sugar
⅓ c. flour
¼ c. vinegar

1¼ c. water
½ t. salt

Mix together sugar, flour, vinegar, water and salt. Pour into unbaked pie shell. Sprinkle with nutmeg and dot with butter. Bake at 350° until mixture is bubbly and crust is brown (about 1 hour).

Martha Miller (Cook)

CRUMB TOPPING FOR PIES

4 c. flour
2 c. sugar
2⅓ c. oleo (softened)

2 c. oatmeal
2 c. brown sugar
1 c. coconut

Mix flour, oatmeal, sugars and coconut. Cut in oleo. Store in airtight container. Will keep quite awhile. Delicious on any fruit pie. Will cover approximately 6 pies.

Ruth Elaine Miller (Waitress)

NEVER FAIL PIE MERINGUE

6 T. white sugar
1 T. cornstarch
½ c. water

3 egg whites
dash of salt

Mix cornstarch, sugar, water and salt. Cook until clear. Cool slightly. Beat egg whites until frothy. Continue beating while slowly pouring cooked mixture in. Beat 5 min. Cover cooled pie sealing edges to crust. Bake at 450° for 5-7 min. or until golden.

Rosa Borntrager (Dutch Country Gifts)

MERINGUE SHELLS

3 egg whites
1 t. vanilla
1 c. sugar

½ t. cream of tartar
dash of salt

Let egg whites stand 1 hour to become room temperature. Add vanilla, cream of tartar, and salt, beat to soft peak. Gradually add sugar beating until stiff. Cover baking sheet with brown paper and draw 3" circles. Spread meringue on circles. Bake 1 hour at 275°, turn off oven and allow to dry 1 extra hour. Peel off paper. To store, place in plastic bag.

Ida Anna Miller (Cook)
Rosa Borntrager (Dutch Country Gifts)

FRESH BLUEBERRY GLAZE

2½ c. water
2 c. sugar
½ c. fresh blueberries
½ c. sugar

¾ c. Clear-Jel
1 t. lemon juice
½ t. salt
¾ c. water

Mix first three ingredients together in a saucepan and bring to a boil. Mix remaining ingredients and add to boiling mixture. Cook until clear. Add 1 c. canned blueberry pie filling when mixture is cold. Add 6⅔ c. fresh blueberries and pour into baked pie shell. Top with whipped topping. Makes 3 pies.

Mary Esther Miller (Bakery Manager)

PEACH GLAZE

4 c. water
2 c. sugar
¼ c. Clear-Jel
1 t. lemon juice

¼ t. almond extract
¼ c. sugar
½ c. water

Mix first two ingredients together in a saucepan and boil until sugar is dissolved. Add remaining ingredients. Cook until thick. Add 8 oz. peach jello. Mix well. Cool. Add sliced, fresh peaches and pour into baked pie shell. Top with whipped cream.

Mary Esther Miller (Bakery Manager)

Desserts, Ice Cream & Beverages

THE INGREDIENTS

The sugar we use, the taste to please
Shortening is needed, the toughness to ease
The flour, we add to make it firm
Also the eggs, under the same term.

Milk is required for some that we make
While this all depends on the quality of cake.
A dash of salt, the taste to improve
Flavoring as desired, then may be used.

The leavening is added to make it light
But recipes are required to do it right.
You prefer a nice cake, then you may trust,
That accurate measurements are also a must.

Selected

TO CLEAN LOOKING GLASSES—First wash the glass all over with luke-warm soapsuds and a sponge. When dry, rub it bright with a buckskin and a little prepared chalk finely powdered.

CHARCOAL—All sorts of glass vessels and other utensils may be purified from long-retained smells of every kind, in the easiest and most perfect manner, by rinsing them out well with charcoal powder, after the grosser impurities have been scoured off with sand and potash.

TO CLEAN VARNISHED WOODWORK—Try just plain ordinary tea, cold tea. There are many more elaborate ways of doing this work, but none do it more effectively.

TO PREVENT GLASS, EARTHEN, POTTER'S, AND IRON WARE FROM BEING EASILY BROKEN—Put dishes, tumblers, and other glass articles into a kettle; cover them entirely with cold water, and put the kettle to boil. When it has boiled a few minutes, set it aside, tightly covered. When the water is cold, remove the glassware.

Treat new earthen ware in the same way. When potter's ware is boiled, a hand-ful or two of bran should be thrown into the water, and the glazing will resist damage by acids or salt.

If wax candles become discolored or soiled, they may be restored by rubbing them with a clean flannel slightly dipped in alcohol.

TO PREVENT LAMPS FROM SMOKING—Soak the wick in vinegar and dry it well before you use it; the lamp will then burn both sweet and brightly and give much satisfaction for the small trouble you took in preparing it.

Desserts, Ice Cream & Beverages

APPLE CRISP

1 c. flour
1 c. sugar
1 t. baking powder
¾ t. salt
1 t. cinnamon

½ t. nutmeg
1 egg
⅓ c. oleo, melted
½ c. pecans, chopped
4 c. sliced apples

Line buttered 8" × 8" × 2" pan with apples. Put dry ingredients together and work in egg. Add nuts. Crumble over apples. Drizzle melted margarine over crumbs. Bake at 375° for 45 min.

Esther Nisley (Bakery)

APPLE CRUMB BAKE

2 c. flour
1 c. brown sugar

¾ c. soft oleo
½ c. rolled oats

Work the above ingredients with hands as pie crust crumbs. Put half of the crumbs in a large pie pan. In a saucepan combine 1 c. brown sugar, 3 T. cornstarch, ¼ t. salt and 1 c. water. Stir well and cook until thick. Remove from heat and add 1 t. vanilla and 6 apples sliced thin. Spread the apple mixture on crumbs and put remaining crumbs on top. Bake at 350° for 50-55 min. or until done.

Laura Anna Miller (Grill Worker)

APPLE PUDDING

Melt ½ c. butter in a 2 quart casserole dish and set aside.

Sift together:

1 c. flour
2 t. baking powder
¼ t. cinnamon

1 c. sugar
¼ t. salt

Add:

1 c. milk

1 t. vanilla

Mix until blended and pour into melted butter. Don't stir, pour 2 c. applesauce in center of batter. Bake at 375° for 35-40 min.

Rosie Eash (Waitress)

BUTTERSCOTCH TORTE

6 eggs, separated
1½ c. sugar
1 t. baking powder

2 t. vanilla
2 c. graham cracker crumbs
1 c. pecans

Beat egg yolks well. Add sugar, baking powder and vanilla, mix well. Beat egg whites until real stiff. Fold in crumbs, nuts and egg whites. Bake at 350° for 25-30 min. until medium brown. After cooled, put 2 pkgs. Dream Whip, prepared on top, then dribble syrup over top, will cover almost completely.

Syrup:

¼ c. melted butter
1 c. brown sugar
1 egg, well beaten

1 T. flour
1 t. vanilla
¼ c. water

Cook until thickened, cool.

Marlene Eash (Cook)

BREAD PUDDING

Use approximately 10-12 rolls (day old) or rolls and bread enough to fill a 9×13 pan. Cut up rolls and bread, put in pan; meanwhile heat 5 c. milk, remove from heat and add:

2 c. sugar
10 eggs, beaten
1 T. vanilla

Mix and add this to rolls, pouring mixture over top. Sprinkle cinnamon or nutmeg over top and bake, uncovered at 350° until set and browned. Serve hot with lemon sauce over top.

Lemon Sauce:

Heat ¼ c. Real Lemon, approximately ½ c. sugar, 1 qt. hot water, pinch of salt, and a few drops of yellow food coloring. Thicken sugar and lemon to suit your taste.

Lydia Ann Miller (Head Cook)

BLUEBERRY COBBLER

Bring to boil:
6 c. fruit
9 c. water
3 c. sugar
3 T. Real Lemon
3 T. cinnamon
1 c. Clear-Jel, dissolve
in water. Boil a few minutes.
Put in two 9×13 pans

Mix dry ingredients:
3 c. sugar
4½ c. flour
1½ t. salt
6 t. baking powder
Add:
3 eggs
¾ c. shortening
1 c. milk
Drop by T. on thickened fruit

Bake at 350° for approximately 40 min.

Lydia Ann Miller (Head Cook)

BERRY TAPIOCA

½ c. tapioca
¼ t. salt
3 c. boiling water
2 c. berries, crushed & sweetened

1 t. lemon juice
½ c. sugar
1 t. butter

Cook tapioca and salt in water for 15 min. or until tapioca is clear, stirring frequently. Add sugar and butter. Remove from heat. Add berries and lemon juice. Chill. Serve with whipped cream.

Rose Schrock (Baker)

Dishes that have become brown from baking may have that stain removed by soaking in strong borax and water.

BANANA SPLIT DESSERT

Mix, then put in bottom of pan and chill:

1 stick oleo, melted

2 c. graham cracker crumbs

Beat together:

2 eggs
2 sticks oleo

2 c. powdered sugar
1 t. vanilla

Put on top of graham crackers. Split 6 bananas (dip in pineapple juice). Lay on top of 2nd mixture, add drained crushed pineapple. Next add drained strawberries. Add a 9 oz. tub of Cool Whip and nuts on top of that.

Edna Nissley (Waitress)

BUSTER BAR DESSERT

1 pkg. Oreo cookies (dark)
1 gallon ice cream
1 large container Cool Whip
2 c. peanuts
chocolate syrup

Crush Oreo cookies; not too fine. Put about ½ of crumbs in 9 × 13 pan, or larger if you have one. Slice ⅓ ice cream for next layer. Dribble chocolate syrup on top. For 3rd layer, crush peanuts or leave whole and sprinkle ½ on top. Spread on ½ of the Cool Whip.

Repeat layers, reserving ½ c. cookie crumbs for the top. Freeze and serve.

Mary Esther Mast (Waitress)

BUSTER BARS

Crush 15 oz. of Oreo cookies, mix with ½ c. butter. Press to form a crust. Spread ½ gallon of softened French vanilla ice cream.

Sprinkle 1-1½ c. of Spanish peanuts (best results if this is made day before and frozen).

Bring to a boil: 2 c. powdered sugar, ½ c. margarine, 6 oz. chocolate chips, large can Pet Milk (12 oz.). Boil for 8 min., stirring constantly. Cool and spread over the first 3 layers and freeze immediately.

Arlene Miller (Waitress)

When making soup, remember the maxim: *Soup boiled is soup spoiled.* The soup should be cooked gently and evenly.

BUTTERFINGER DESSERT

2 c. graham crackers, crushed   ½ c. butter or margarine, melted
1 c. soda crackers, crushed

Mix together and put ½ of mixture into 9" × 13" pan.

2 pkgs. vanilla instant pudding   1 qt. vanilla ice cream,
2 c. milk   softened slightly

Mix together with beater and pour over crumb crust. Cover with Cool
Whip and add rest of crumbs. Crush 3 large Butterfingers and sprinkle
over top. Refrigerate or freeze.

Ginger Yoder (Waitress)
Edna Borntrager (Head Cook, evening)

To avoid lumps in batter, add a pinch of salt to the flour before it is wet.

BAKED RHUBARB CRUNCH

3 c. diced rhubarb   ½ c. white sugar
1 T. flour   ½ t. nutmeg
1 c. brown sugar   ¾ c. flour
1 c. quick oats   ½ t. salt
¾ c. butter

In bottom of greased pan, place thoroughly mixed rhubarb, white
sugar, 1 T. flour and nutmeg. Combine brown sugar, remaining flour,
oats and salt, cut in butter as you would for pastry and sprinkle on top
of rhubarb mixture. Bake 30-40 min. at 375° or until crisp and nicely
browned.

Katie Miller (Dutch Country Gifts)
Laura Anna Miller (Grill Worker)

CREAMY BAKED CHEESECAKE

¼ c. margarine or butter, melted
1 c. graham cracker crumbs
¼ c. sugar
2 (8 oz.) pkgs. cream cheese
1 (8 oz.) container sour cream

1 (14 oz.) can Eagle Brand
  Condensed Milk
3 eggs
¼ t. salt
¼ c. Real Lemon reconstituted
  lemon juice

Preheat oven to 300°. Combine margarine, crumbs and sugar, pat firmly on bottom of buttered 9" springform pan. In large mixer bowl, beat cheese until fluffy. Beat in Eagle Brand, eggs and salt until smooth. Stir in Real Lemon. Pour into prepared pan. Bake 50-55 min. or until cake springs back when lightly touched. Cool to room temperature; chill. Spread sour cream on cheesecake. Garnish as desired. Refrigerate leftovers.

Rhoda Troyer (Typist)

CHERRY DELIGHT

2 c. graham cracker crumbs
¼ lb. melted margarine

Make above for bottom crust.

2 envelopes Dream Whip, make according to directions. Add 1½ c. powdered sugar and 1 t. vanilla.

Beat in an 8 oz. pkg. Philadelphia cream cheese. Spread on crust. Then top with 1 quart of cherry pie filling or any fresh fruit filling. Raspberries are also delicious if seeds are removed and thickened with minute tapioca.

Sylvia Arlene Slabaugh (Cook)

When cream will not whip, add the white of an egg to your cream. Chill it and it will whip.

CHOCOLATE COCONUT DESSERT

1 (6 oz.) pkg. chocolate chips
1 (13 oz.) can evaporated milk
1 (10½ oz.) pkg. miniature marshmallows
1⅓ c. flaked coconut
6 T. margarine
2 c. crispy rice cereal, crushed
1 c. nuts, chopped
½ gal. vanilla ice cream

In saucepan melt chocolate in milk. Bring to boiling, boil for 4 min. or till thickened, stirring constantly. Add marshmallows and stir till melted. In skillet, cook and stir coconut in margarine till lightly browned. Stir in cereal and nuts. Spread 3 c. of cereal mixture in bottom of 9×13 cake pan. Cut ice cream in half lengthwise and then horizontally into 12 slices, making a total of 24 slices. Arrange half the ice cream over cereal. Spread half the chocolate mixture. Repeat layers. Top with remaining cereal mixture. Cover and freeze till firm. Makes 16 servings (You may want to make 1½ batches of the coconut mixture instead of only one).

Sharon Boley (Waitress)

CHOCOLATE DESSERT

1 stick butter   1 c. flour
½ c. chopped nuts

Blend and press in 9×13 pan. Bake at 350° for 10 min. and cool.

Mix:

1 (8 oz.) pkg. Philadelphia cream   1 c. powdered sugar
   cheese   1 c. Cool Whip

Blend and spread on cool crust. Add:

3 c. milk   1 box milk chocolate pudding
1 box chocolate fudge pudding

Cook only to boil stage. Cool, spread on cheese filling. Top with Cool Whip and nuts.

Bonnie Schrock (Gift Shop)

To keep cauliflower a bright white, add a little milk during cooking.

CREAM CHEESE TURNOVERS

4 oz. cream cheese
1 c. flour

½ c. butter

Combine cheese and butter. Add flour and work with pastry blender or fingers until smooth. Chill well, about 2 hours. Roll dough to 1/8" thickness on floured surface. Cut into rounds with a 3" cutter, place a teaspoonful of filling on each and fold over. Crimp edges with a fork. Prick top with a fork. Place on ungreased cookie sheet and bake at 450° for 10-15 min. or until lightly browned. Serve warm. Yields about 3 dozen.

Filling:

1 onion, finely chopped
½ lb. fresh mushrooms, finely
   chopped
¼ t. thyme
pinch of pepper

3 T. butter
½ t. salt
2 T. flour
¼ c. cream

Saute onions in butter; add mushrooms, stirring constantly for about 5 min. Add seasoning, sprinkle with flour, stir in cream, stir until thickened. This is a great hors d'oeuvre for holiday parties.

Carolyn Mast (Waitress)

Don't discard celery leaves; dry them, then rub leaves through a sieve for powder that can be used to flavor soups, stews and salad dressings.

CREAM STICKS

2 pkg. dry yeast soaked in 1 c. warm water
1 c. milk (scalded)   2 eggs, well beaten
½ c. butter or oleo   1 t. salt
⅔ c. sugar   6 c. flour

Put butter, sugar, eggs, and salt into scalding milk. Let cool, then add yeast then flour and let rise once. Roll out and cut in strips. Fry in deep fat. Make a slit in side and fill with filling while still warm.

Filling: Mix and set aside.

2⅓ c. powdered sugar   ¼ t. salt
1 egg white, beaten

Boil 1 Minute:

2 T. water   ½ c. white sugar

Add to first mixture. Then add 1 t. vanilla and ½ c. Crisco.

Elmina Troyer (Waitress)

DELICIOUS DELIGHT

Mix together:

2 c. brown sugar   ½ c. margarine
1 c. flour (save 1 c. of crumbs)

Beat together and add to crumb mixture:

1 egg, beaten   1 t. soda
1 t. salt   1 t. vanilla
1 c. milk

Place this mixture in a greased 9×13 pan. Sprinkle ½ c. chocolate chips, then ⅓ c. nuts on top. Then sprinkle on remaining crumbs. Bake at 350° for 20-25 min. Serve with whipped topping or ice cream.

Edna Borntrager (Head Cook, evening)

DESSERT IN A MINUTE

1 large can fruit cocktail   1 large can pineapple chunks
2 pkgs. instant vanilla pudding

Mix these 3 items together and stir well. Then fold in 1 container Cool Whip. Ready to serve.

Beth Ann Yoder (Busser)

DELICIOUS PINEAPPLE RINGO

1 can pineapple rings   1 can Bordens Eagle Brand milk
1 c. whipping cream

Set unopened can of Eagle Brand milk into pan of water. Bring to a boil and boil for 2 hours. Remove milk and refrigerate till cold. When cold, remove both ends of can and slice. Place one pineapple ring on each slice of milk. Top with whipped cream and maraschino cherries.

Edna Ferm Schmucker

DANISH DESSERT

Bring to boil 2 c. fruit juice or water.

Combine:

1 (3 oz.) box gelatin (match flavor to fruit)
⅔ c. sugar
3 T. cornstarch
pinch of salt

Make a paste with 1 c. juice or water. Stir into boiling liquid. Cook until thick and clear (about 1 min.).

Mary Ellen Yutzy

ELDERBERRY POTPIE

Mix: 2½ c. flour, 1 t. salt, 2 t. baking powder. Cut in 1 c. shortening adding enough milk to make dough you can roll out. Roll out ½ of dough and place in greased 9×12 pan.

Mix: 1 c. sugar, ½ c. flour with a little water to make paste and add 1 c. elderberries. Pour on top of dough. Roll out remaining dough and cut in small squares. Arrange ½ of squares on top of elderberries. Next sprinkle on 1 c. elderberries and 1 c. sugar. Top with remaining dough squares. Bake at 425° for 10 min. Reduce heat to 350° and bake 30-40 min.

Rosa Borntrager (Dutch Country Gifts)

EASY CHERRY DELIGHT

1 large can cherry pie filling
1 (8 oz.) container Cool Whip
1 (16 oz.) can crushed pineapple, drained
1 (14 oz.) can Eagle Brand

Mix everything together and stir well until blended.

Diane Robinson (Waitress)

DIRTY DISHES

Thank God for dirty dishes,
  They have a tale to tell;
While others may go hungry,
  We're eating very well.
With Home, Health, and Happiness,
  I shouldn't want to fuss;
By the stack of evidence
  God's been very good to us.

FROZEN PUDDING DESSERT

1½ c. crushed Rice Chex
¾ c. coconut
¾ c. brown sugar
⅓ c. chopped nuts
½ c. melted butter

Mix all of the above ingredients together and press into the bottom of a 9×13 pan.

2 small boxes instant pudding (any flavor)
2 c. milk
1 quart vanilla ice cream
⅔ c. peanut butter

Mix together and pour over crust and freeze.

Cheryl Troyer (Cashier, Gift Shop)

FRUIT PIZZA

1 tube of Pillsbury sugar cookie dough. Slice thin and press on a pizza pan. Bake 10-12 min. Cool.

2nd Layer:

8 oz. pkg. cream cheese   1 medium Cool Whip

Mix together (if it's too stiff add a little pineapple juice to make it creamy). Spread on top of cookie dough.

3rd Layer:

Fruits: pineapple chunks, banana, strawberries, peaches sliced, mandarin oranges, cherries, blueberries and arrange any way you like on top of pizza.

Rosalie Bontrager
Essenhaus Country Inn (Manager)

FRUIT PIZZA

Cream together:

½ c. melted butter   ¾ c. sugar
1 egg   1⅜ c. flour

Then add:

1 t. cream of tartar   ½ t. baking soda
¼ t. salt

Bake at 350° for 8-10 min.

Take:

8 oz. cream cheese   ½ c. sugar
2 t. pineapple juice

Mix and spread on cooled crust. Add any fruit you want on top of cream cheese. Mix fruit juice and water to make 1 c. Add 3 T. cornstarch. Cook until thickened. Pour over apples, cherries, strawberries, blueberries, grapes, bananas, etc.).

Janet Mast (Assistant Decorator)

FROZEN PUMPKIN PARFAIT SQUARES

1½ c. graham cracker crumbs   1½ c. canned pumpkin
¼ c. melted butter   ½ c. brown sugar
¼ c. sugar   ½ t. salt
½ c. chopped pecans   1 t. cinnamon
1 quart vanilla ice cream   1/8 t. cloves
¼ t. ginger

Combine crumbs, butter, sugar and nuts. Press mixture firmly against sides and bottom of a 9" square pan. Bake at 375° for 8 min. Cool. Soften ice cream to custard consistency. Stir in pumpkin, brown sugar and spices. Pile into cooled crumb crust. Freeze until hard. Remove from freezer 5-10 min. before serving. Cut into squares. Garnish with whipped cream and nuts.

Laura Anna Miller (Grill Worker)

FROZEN MOCHA CHEESECAKE

1 ¼ c. chocolate wafer cookie crumbs (about 24 cookies)
¼ c. sugar   ¼ c. margarine or butter, melted

1 (8 oz.) pkg. cream cheese, softened
1 (14 oz.) can Eagle Brand sweetened condensed milk
⅔ c. chocolate flavored syrup
2 T. instant coffee
1 t. hot water
1 c. whipping cream (whipped)

In small bowl, combine cookie crumbs, sugar and margarine. Pat crumbs in a 9×13 pan (sides and bottom). Chill. In large bowl, beat cream cheese until fluffy, add Eagle Brand milk and chocolate syrup. In small bowl dissolve coffee in hot water, add to cream cheese mixture, mix well. Fold in whipped cream. Pour in prepared pan, cover. Freeze for 6 hours or until firm. Garnish with additional chocolate crumbs if desired. Return leftover to freezer.

Katie Miller (Dutch Country Gifts)

To reduce odor while cooking cabbage, place a small cup of vinegar on the range or add a wedge of lemon to the pot.

GLAZED FRUIT

Drain canned fruit (peaches, pears or fruit cocktail). Measure juice and heat in saucepan.

Meanwhile, dissolve Clear-Jel in a little water. (Using 1 rounding T. Clear-Jel to 1 c. fruit juice). Add dissolved Clear-Jel to hot juice and cook till clear. Add a few drops of yellow food coloring. Cool and pour back over fruit.

Lydia Ann Miller (Cook)

HEAVENLY HASH

2 c. miniature marshmallows
2 c. cooked rice, chilled
1 (8¼ oz.) can crushed pineapple, drained

¼ c. slivered almonds
1 c. heavy cream
¼ c. sugar
½ c. maraschino cherry halves

Combine marshmallows, rice, fruit and nuts. Whip cream, gradually adding sugar and vanilla; fold into rice mixture. Chill. 8 servings.

Sue Miller (Manager)

One of the mysteries of life is how the boy who wasn't good enough to marry your daughter can be the father of the smartest grandchild in the world.

HEATH BAR DESSERT

2 (3 oz.) pkgs. vanilla instant pudding
2 pints vanilla ice cream, softened
2 c. milk

Mix pudding and milk together until thick. Add soft ice cream.

Crust:

2 c. Ritz crackers, crushed
1 T. sugar

½ c. butter, melted

Mix and press tightly into a 13" × 9" × 2" pan. Pour ice cream mixture on top of crust. Top with whipping cream and 1 crushed Heath bar. Store in refrigerator, Add some crushed Heath bar to filling, if desired (takes about 3 Heath bars for entire recipe).

Denise Bontrager (Waitress)

HEATH BAR PUDDING

¼ lb. butter
3½ c. milk
3 T. brown sugar
whipped topping

1½ c. sugar
⅓ c. cornstarch
¼ c. milk
3 Heath bars

Brown butter, then add sugar and milk. Combine cornstarch, brown sugar and ¼ c. milk and blend together with butter mixture. Cook until thick. Cool, then add whipped topping and crushed bars.

Sharon Boley (Waitress)

HOT FUDGE PUDDING

Sift together into bowl:

1 c. sifted flour
¼ t. salt
2 T. cocoa

2 t. baking powder
¾ c. sugar

Stir in:

½ c. milk
2 T. shortening, melted

Blend in: 1 c. nuts

Spread in 9″ square pan. Sprinkle with mixture of:

1 c. brown sugar
4 T. cocoa

Pour over entire batter: 1¾ c. hot water. Bake at 350° for 45 min. During baking, cake mixture rises to top and chocolate sauce settles to bottom. Invert square of pudding on dessert plates. Dip sauce from pan over each square. Or the entire pudding can be inverted in a deep serving platter. Serve warm with whipped cream or ice cream.

Mary Esther Mast (Waitress)

ICE CREAM DESSERT

1 (12 oz.) vanilla wafers (crushed)
½ c. butter or margarine, melted

Mix together, put in loaf cake pan and set aside.

Melt in a saucepan:

¾ c. oleo   4 squares German sweet chocolate

Take off heat and add:

3 c. powdered sugar   4 egg yolks, beaten

Beat till well mixed. Beat egg whites till stiff. Fold in chocolate mixture. Pour over crumbs and freeze. This mixture will not freeze hard. Soften ½ gal. vanilla ice cream and spread over top and freeze till firm. Some crumbs may be kept for on top if desired. Cut in squares and serve.

Susanna Miller (Cook)

ICE CREAM SANDWICHES

3 eggs   1 c. cream
½ c. sugar

Separate eggs, beat egg yolks until light and thick. Add sugar and beat well. Beat cream until thick, last beat egg whites, fold all three together and put on graham cracker squares that have been put in a 9 × 13 pan. Top with another layer of graham cracker squares, freeze. Riches topping can be used instead of cream and only ¼ c. sugar.

Sharon Miller (Cook)

ICE CREAM SUNDAE

Add 4 c. sugar to 2 c. finely mashed fruit (fresh raspberries, strawberries, pineapple or cherries). Stir till sugar is dissolved as much as possible. Then add ½ bottle Certo and stir till well blended and thick. Store in refrigerator or freezer.

Laura Anna Miller (Grill Worker)

242

JELLO TAPIOCA

6 c. boiling water
pinch of salt
1 box (6 oz.) any kind jello

1 c. baby pearl tapioca
1 T. vanilla

Prepare jello as directed on package and put in pan to set. Cook tapioca in water with salt, then add 1 c. sugar, or more to suit taste. Cool. Then add: 2 c. topping (Riches) whipped, vanilla and cube jello and add to tapioca. Ready to serve.

Lydia Ann Miller (Cook)

LEMON CREAM DESSERT

1 c. graham cracker crumbs
3 T. butter, melted
1 can Eagle Brand milk

3 T. brown sugar
1 (6 oz.) lemonade concentrate
1 pkg. Dream Whip

Combine crumbs, sugar and butter for crust. Pat into 8" square pan. Beat lemonade and milk. Fold in whipped topping. Pour onto graham crust. Freeze.

Esther Hershberger

MAPLE SPONGE

First Part:

1 envelope Knox Gelatin
2 c. brown sugar
1 c. chopped crushed peanuts

1½ c. cold water
½ c. hot water

Second Part: **Custard**

½ c. sugar
1 T. flour
pinch salt

2 c. milk
2 egg yolks

Cook and cool.   Add the two parts together and add whipped cream.

Sue Miller (Manager)

ORANGE SHERBET DESSERT

2 sm. or 1 lg. box orange jello
¼ c. sugar
1 can mandarin oranges, drained
some small marshmallows

2 c. boiling water
1 c. Riches topping
1 pt. orange sherbet ice cream

Mix jello and sugar with water. When jello is starting to set fold in whipped topping and oranges. Then add orange sherbet and marshmallows.

Doris Yoder (Dishwasher)

OREO MINT DESSERT

Make two days ahead so marshmallows and mints will melt.

Crust:

20 crushed **Oreo cookies**, put in bottom of 9 × 12 cake pan.

Filling:

16 oz. Cool Whip
1¼ c. crushed dinner mints

2 c. miniature marshmallows

Mix and pour over crust. Sprinkle 8 crushed Oreo cookies on top.

Erma Bontrager (Manager of Country Cupboard)

TEACHER *(pointing to a deer at the zoo)*: "Curtis, what is that?"
CURTIS: "I don't know."
TEACHER: "What does your mother call your father?"
CURTIS: "Don't tell me that's a louse!"

ORANGE TAPIOCA PUDDING

2 boxes tapioca vanilla pudding
1 (3 oz.) box orange gelatin
3 c. water

Cook until thick. Cool completely, then add:

11 oz. can mandarin oranges, drained
13¼ oz. can crushed pineapple, drained
1 c. miniature marshmallows
1 pt. whipping cream, whipped or 8 oz. Cool Whip

Chill till set.

Lou Anna Yoder (Bakery)
Rosa Borntrager (Dutch Country Gifts)
Sharon Miller (Cook)

ORANGE BALLS

14 oz. box Vanilla Wafers (crushed)
1 box confectioners sugar
6 oz. can frozen orange juice (thawed)
1 c. chopped nuts

Mix together and form balls. Roll in coconut. Place in refrigerator until set. Place in candy tin or covered dish.

Mary Miller (Waitress)

OREO ICE CREAM DESSERT

1 lb. pkg. Oreo cookies, crushed
1 (8 oz.) Cool Whip, thawed
½ gallon vanilla ice cream, softened

Mix all together and put in 13 × 9 pan and freeze.

Marlene Eash (Cook)

PEANUT DELIGHT

1st layer: ⅔ c. chopped peanuts or pecans
               1 c. flour
               ½ c. butter

Blend and bake at 350° for 20 min. Cool.

2nd layer: ⅓ c. peanut butter (optional)
               1 (8 oz.) pkg. cream cheese
               1 c. powdered sugar
               2 c. Cool Whip

Cream together all of the above.

3rd layer: 1 box vanilla pudding
               1 box chocolate pudding or pistachio (instant)
               3 c. milk

4th layer: Top with Cool Whip, ⅓ c. peanuts and shredded Hershey bar.

Edna Borntrager (Head Cook, evening)
Mary Miller (Waitress)
Ella Bontrager (Cook)
Wilma Weaver (Waitress)
Rosie Eash (Waitress)

POPSICKLES

1 small box jello
2 c. boiling water
1 c. sugar

Stir until dissolved. Add 1 package Kool-Aid, same flavor as jello and 2 c. cold water.

Ruth Ann Bontrager (Busser)

PUMPKIN TORTE

24 graham crackers
⅓ c. sugar
½ c. margarine

Press in a 9" × 13" pan.

Add:

2 eggs, beaten
¾ c. sugar
8 oz. cream cheese

Mix and pour over graham crackers. Bake at 350° for 20 min.

Cook till thickened.

2 c. pumpkin
1 T. cornstarch
3 egg yolks
½ c. sugar

½ c. milk
½ t. salt
2 t. cinnamon

Add 1 package Knox gelatin dissolved in ¼ c. cold water. Add 3 beaten egg whites, fold into cooled mixture.

Lillian Miller (Cashier)
Elma Miller (Waitress)

Cut liver into strips like french fries. Coat the liver strips in a bag of seasoned cornmeal and cracker crumbs. Then fry it in deep fat. Only take a minute or two for frying—they are very tender.

PUMPKIN DESSERT

Crust: **(Optional Crust)**

1 c. flour	½ c. quick oats (uncooked)
1 c. coconut	½ c. brown sugar
¼ c. sugar	½ c. soft oleo
½ c. soft oleo	1 c. flour

Mix and press into 9×13 ungreased pan. Bake at 350° for 15 min.

Topping:

1 (1 lb. 3 oz.) can pumpkin	½ c. canned milk
4 eggs, beaten	2 t. pumpkin pie spice
1 t. vanilla	½ t. salt

Mix together and pour into baked shell. Bake at 350° for 40 min. Before serving, top with whipped cream.

Mary Miller (Waitress)

PROOF

If radio's slim fingers
Can pluck a melody
From night and toss it over
A continent or sea;
If the petaled white notes
Of a violin
Are blown across a mountain
Or a city's din;
If songs, like crimson roses,
Are culled from the thin blue air,
Why should mortals wonder
That God hears and answers prayer?

SPOONS TARNISHED BY EGGS—Spoons used for eggs get discolored and tarnished by the sulphur in the egg uniting with the silver as soon as it is moistened by saliva. This tarnish is easily removed by rubbing it with table salt or a little hartshorn (ammonia).

PUMPKIN DESSERT

1st layer: 1 c. flour
½ c. oleo
½ c. pecans

Mix the above together and press into 9×13 cake pan. Bake at 350° for 15 min. Cool.

2nd layer: 8 oz. cream cheese
1 c. powdered sugar
1 c. Cool Whip

Mix well and spread on first layer.

3rd layer: 1 c. pumpkin   dash of nutmeg
½ c. sugar   1 t. cinnamon
2 T. flour, heaping   1 t. vanilla
2 eggs   2 small boxes vanilla pudding (not
4 c. milk   instant)

Beat together well. Cook until thick. Stir occasionally until cool. Pour over layers in cake pan. Top with Cool Whip.

Cheryl Troyer (Cashier, Gift Shop)

PRETZEL TORTE

2 c. crushed pretzel sticks   1½ sticks margarine, melted
½ c. sugar

Line or sprinkle crumbs in a 9×13 pan. Bake 4-5 min. at 350°. Save a few crumbs for the top.

2 pkgs. Dream Whip topping   1 c. powdered sugar
8 oz. cream cheese

Whip Dream Whip, cream cheese, and powdered sugar. Put this mixture on top of crust. Cover with 2 cans of fruit filling . . . cherry, blueberry, etc. or prepare 3 oz. strawberry jello and add 1 pt. strawberries when partially set and pour over cheese mixture.

Lois Landis (Cook's Helper)
Edna Fern Schmucker (Bakery)

PARADISE DESSERT

Cream together:

¼ c. melted butter   1 c. powdered sugar
1 egg

Crush 18 graham crackers. Spread ⅓ of them in a dish. Pour in butter mixture. Use another ⅓ of crumbs on top. Then pour in mixture of:

1 c. cream, whipped   pinch of salt
1 c. drained fruit   ¼ c. chopped nuts
1 pkg. Philadelphia cream cheese   2 T. sugar
1 t. vanilla

Spread remaining crumbs on top and chill.

Ida Mae Schmucker (Pie Baker)

PINEAPPLE ORANGE CREME (low calorie)

1 c. graham cracker crumbs
1 T. soft butter
½ c. nonfat dry milk
½ c. well-chilled orange juice
1 can (8 oz.) unsweetened crushed pineapple, drained

1 egg white
1 T. lemon juice
¼ c. sugar

Mix graham cracker crumbs and butter. Reserve ⅓ c. crumb mixture; press remaining crumb mixture in ungreased baking pan, 8×8×2.

In mixer bowl, beat dry milk, orange juice, beat for 3 minutes at high speed. Blend in sugar on low speed, about ½ minute. Fold in pineapple. Pour into pan; sprinkle with reserved crumb mixture. Freeze at least 8 hours. Makes 9 servings (110 calories each).

Barbara Bainter (Cleaning Service)

RASPBERRY FREEZE

¼ c. honey
1 (8 oz.) pkg. cream cheese
1 (10 oz.) pkg. frozen raspberries, partially thawed

1 c. banana slices
2 c. miniature marshmallows
1 c. heavy cream, whipped

Gradually add honey to cream cheese, mixing until well blended. Stir in fruit; fold in marshmallows and whipped cream. Pour into 9" square pan. Freeze. Place in refrigerator 30 min. before serving. Makes 9 servings.

Variation: Pour mixture into ten 5 oz. paper cups; insert wooden sticks in center. Freeze. Frozen salads should "temper" in the refrigerator before serving, so they thaw slightly for a more edible consistency.

Sue Miller (Manager)

RICE KRISPY DESSERT

¼ c. corn syrup   3 T. butter
2 T. firmly packed brown sugar

Cook on low heat until it boils. Add 2½ c. Rice Krispies and press mixture into a 9″ pie pan.

¼ c. peanut butter   3 T. corn syrup
¼ c. Hershey syrup

Mix together and spread on crust. Place in freezer until hard. Fill with one quart of soft vanilla or chocolate ice cream. Let stand at room temperature for 10 min. before serving.

Ginger Yoder (Waitress)

If you don't want your children to hear what you're saying, pretend you're talking to them.

RHUBARB DELICIOUS

1 c. flour   ½ c. butter or oleo
5 T. powdered sugar   ½ c. chopped nuts

Mix above ingredients and press into ungreased 9×9 pan. Bake 15 min. at 350°. Beat 2 egg yolks, add 1½ c. sugar, ¼ c. flour, ¾ t. salt and 2 c. finely chopped rhubarb. Pour into baked crust and bake 35-40 min. more at 350°. Then whip the 2 egg whites, sweeten to taste, spoon on top and return to oven until lightly browned. Cool and serve.

Norine Borkholder (Cook)

STRAWBERRY PINEAPPLE JELLO

1 can (8¼ oz.) crushed pineapple in syrup, drained
¼ c. chopped pecans
½ c. sour cream
1 T. sugar
1 (3 oz.) pkg. strawberry flavor gelatin
1 c. boiling water
2 c. ice cubes
1½ c. sliced strawberries, chilled

Combine pineapple, pecans, sour cream and sugar, set aside. Dissolve gelatin in boiling water. Add ice cubes and stir constantly until gelatin starts to thicken, about 3 to 5 min. Remove any unmelted ice. Fold in strawberries. Spoon half the gelatin mixture into 6 or 8 parfait glasses. Add pineapple mixture and top with remaining gelatin. Chill until set, about ½ hour. Garnish with additional strawberries.

Barbara Bainter (Cleaning Service)

SWEETHEART PUDDING

Crust: Mix and put ¾ of it in bottom and sides of an oblong baking dish.

20 graham crackers, crushed fine   ½ c. soft butter
½ c. brown sugar

Custard: Mix together and cook:

3½ c. milk   ½ c. sugar
3 egg yolks   1 t. vanilla
4 T. flour

Pour into prepared dish.

Meringue: 3 egg whites (stiffly beaten)
         ¼ t. cream of tartar

Put over custard and add remaining crumbs. Brown in oven for 20-25 min. at 350°.

Alma Hershberger (Bakery)
Doris Miller (Waitress)
Mary Esther Lehman (Busser)

When serving cream soup, beat for a few seconds with your egg beater before heating and you'll have soup that's every so wonderfully smooth.

STRAWBERRY PRETZEL DESSERT

2 c. crushed pretzels
3 T. sugar
¾ c. melted margarine
1 pkg. whipped topping
2 c. mini marshmallows

2½ c. boiling water
½ c. powdered sugar
1 (8 oz.) pkg. cream cheese
1 (6 oz.) strawberry gelatin
1 (10 oz.) pkg. frozen strawberries

Mix first 3 ingredients in 9×13 pan. Bake 15 min. at 350° (will look bubbly). Set aside to cool. Cream cheese, softened. Add powdered sugar. Prepare whipped topping, fold into cream cheese and powdered sugar. Fold in marshmallows. Spread over baked layer. Dissolve gelatin in boiling water. Stir in strawberries. Chill until slightly thickened. Spread over cream cheese layer. Chill. This is good to make the day before. Serves 16 to 20.

Rosa Miller (Bakery)
Edna E. Bontrager (Cook)
Ruth Elaine Miller (Waitress)
Sharon Miller (Cook)
Luella Yoder (Cook)

When slicing a warm, baked ham, place several thicknesses of paper towels under the cutting board—this catches the juices. When finished, you can just roll up towels and toss in trash.

STRAWBERRY-SOUR CREAM CREPES

12 crepes
⅓ c. sugar
confectioners' sugar

2 c. sour cream
2 c. sliced strawberries

Make the crepes using the Sweet Crepe Batter. Set aside. Beat together the sour cream and sugar. Fold in the strawberries. Fill each crepe with the mixture and fold over. Sprinkle with confectioners' sugar and serve. Serves 6.

Sweet Crepe Batter:

2 eggs
2 egg yolks
½ c. water
¾ c. milk
1¼ c. plain flour

½ t. salt
2 T. sugar
1¼ T. melted butter or
    vegetable oil
1 T. brandy

Beat the eggs with the egg yolks, then mix with the water and milk beating by hand or in an electric blender. Sift together the flour, salt and sugar. Gradually add to the egg and milk mixture. Add the melted butter or vegetable oil and the brandy. Blend thoroughly. If mixing by hand, pour the batter through a sieve. Set aside and allow to stand for at least an hour before using. If the mixture is too thick, add a little milk and mix well. Pour one or two T. of the batter (depending on the size of the pan) in the center of a hot lightly oiled frypan. Tilt the pan to spread the batter and cook until the top is dry. Turn over and cook on the other side for 15 seconds. Makes 12.

Rhoda Troyer (Typist)

If you eat soup with a plastic spoon, it will cool faster. Metal spoons retain the heat.

TAPIOCA PUDDING

5 c. water (hot)
¾ c. white sugar
2 eggs (beaten)
1 T. melted browned oleo

1 c. tapioca
1 c. brown sugar
½ c. cold water
1 t. vanilla

Add tapioca to water and cook till clear. Add ½ cold water, sugar and egg mixture. Add oleo and vanilla. When cool add about 2 c. whipped cream. Also pineapple and bananas if desired.

Susanna Miller (Cook)

MILKY-WAY ICE CREAM (1 gallon)

3 large Milky Way candy bars (Snickers or Musketeers may also be used)
2 cans Eagle Brand milk

In double boiler, put your candy bars and 1 c. of milk till melted; remove from heat and add Eagle Brand milk. Fill your can with milk and freeze.

Edna Borntrager (Head Cook, evening)

ICE CREAM (1½ gallons)

3 qt. milk
3 pt. cream
2 t. flour

4 eggs
3 c. sugar

Beat eggs, add 1 qt. milk. Cook in double boiler. When hot, add sugar and flour. Cook for 5 min. stirring often so it will be smooth. Cool, add remaining milk and cream. Cream may be beaten stiff. Freeze.

Rose Schrock (Baker)

BUTTER PECAN ICE CREAM

3 T. cornstarch
3 eggs
3 qt. milk
1 T. butterscotch flavoring

3 c. sugar (1½ white and 1½ brown)
1 can Eagle Brand milk
1 t. maple flavoring
1 c. pecans

Boil together until thick (not long). Cool and then freeze.

Amanda Troyer (Waitress)

BUTTER PECAN ICE CREAM

2 qts. milk
6 eggs
3 T. butter (browned)
salt

2½ c. brown sugar
2 T. cornstarch
vanilla
pecans

Bring milk to a boil. Mix other ingredients and stir into milk. Add pecans when partly frozen.

Bertha Miller (Dutch Country Gifts)

BANANA PUNCH

6 c. water   3 c. sugar

Bring to boil for 1 min. Set aside.

Combine following:

5¾ c. pineapple juice   2½ c. orange juice
¼ c. lemon juice or "Real Lemon"

Cut up 5 bananas, add some of the above fruit juices to bananas and mix well to make a puree (or till mixture is like soup).

Add all above ingredients together then freeze until needed. Then about 8 hours before serving time, thaw fruit mixture, make sure club soda is chilled. Just before serving add 2 (28 oz.) bottles of club soda, 7-Up or Ginger Ale and mix well. Serves 50 (4 oz.) servings.

Doretta Mast (Dishwasher)

FROZEN FRUIT ICE

Stir well:

2 c. boiling water
2 c. sugar

Add:

1 (12 oz.) frozen orange juice
1 juice can of water
1 can #2 crushed pineapple with juice
2 large bananas (diced)
maraschino cherries (optional)
1 (12 oz.) Sprite or 7-Up (optional)

Mix well. Put in freezer. Stir every 2 hours until frozen. Delicious.

Betti Kauffman (Hostess)
Mary Miller (Waitress)
Fannie Yutzy (Pie Baker)

FRUIT SLUSH

2 c. sugar
6 oz. can orange juice concentrate
20 oz. can crushed pineapple

3 c. water
2 bananas

Mix sugar and water till sugar is dissolved, then cool. Mix orange juice as directed on can and add mashed bananas and stir in pineapple. You may add any other fruit you want.

Freeze in little individual cups. Allow to thaw till slushy before serving.

Rosa Borntrager (Dutch Country Gifts)
Ruth Elaine Miller (Waitress)
Mary Esther Miller (Bakery)

RECIPE FOR SPICED CIDER

1 gal. cider
1 c. orange juice
1 t. allspice
1 t. cloves

3 cinnamon sticks
1 T. lemon juice
sugar to taste

Simmer 6-8 min.

PUNCH

2 small cans frozen lemon juice
2 (46 oz.) cans pineapple juice
2 (46 oz.) cans orange juice

2 qts. lemon lime sherbet
2 qt. ginger ale

Mary Jane Bontrager (Cook)

Father looking over his son's report card: "One thing is in your favor. With these grades you couldn't possibly be cheating."

A REFRESHING DRINK

2 gallons water
2 c. sugar

1 (27 oz.) can Tang

Add:

2 gallons water
2¼ to 2½ c. sugar

2 c. lemon juice

Makes 4 gallons.

Alma Hershberger (Bakery)

RHUBARB PUNCH

2 quarts rhubarb

Cover with water. Boil 10 min. then put in blender or drain juice.

2½ c. sugar   2 T. strawberry jello

Dissolve jello in 2 c. hot water

2 c. pineapple juice   ½ c. Real Lemon

When ready to serve, put in Sprite or 7-Up. If you use soda when cooking rhubarb, it takes less sugar.

Ellen Miller (Cashier-Gift shop)

RUSSIAN TEA

3 T. cloves   1 c. sugar
3 T. allspice   1 (12 oz.) and 1 (6 oz.) can
1 c. water   frozen orange juice
3 t. tea or 4 tea bags   juice of 1 lemon
1½ c. water

Boil cloves and allspice in 1 c. water. In another pan, boil 3 t. tea or 4 tea bags in 1½ c. water until strong. Mix 1 c. sugar in large pan with both cans of frozen orange juice. Add the juice of one lemon. Add tea and spices. Fill with cold water to make 1 gallon.

Lois Landis (Cook's Helper)

TOMATO JUICE COCKTAIL

1 gallon tomato juice   2 t. celery salt
2½ T. sugar   1 t. Worcestershire sauce
4 t. salt   ¼ t. Tabasco sauce
1 t. onion salt

Mix all together and can the same as tomato juice.

Karen Nissley (Busser)

Soups, Pickles & Relishes

HELPFUL HINTS

A handful of dry laundry detergent scattered in garbage cans after cleaning will help repel flies and other insects.

Salt, flour, seasoning, spices, butter, and all solids are always measured level.

CORN MEAL TO REMOVE GREASE—Some housewives prefer to use crumpled pages of newspapers to get rid of grease in pots and pans, lard bucket, and slop pail. Be sure the grease is soft, and then toss heaping spoonful of cornmeal into vessel. It does an amazingly good clean-up job.

WIDE RUFFLES AT BOTTOM OF KITCHEN APRONS—These stand out just enough from the dress to catch any stray drops that may be spilled making a better shield for the skirt than a plain apron.

HOW TO TAME A ROCKING CHAIR—Some rocking chairs have a tendency to ambulate all over the floor when someone sits and rocks in one of them. To stop it, glue a good strong velveteen ribbon onto the rockers with fish or carpenter's glue. The width of the ribbon should be such that about 1/8th inch of space is left on each side of it when in position. Light bootweb also serves well. Or try nylon velvet ribbon.

CARPETS MARKED BY FURNITURE—To restore the pile in places where rugs have been pressed flat by furniture legs, remove the furniture and lay a wet towel, folded two times, over the spot. Then steam it gently with a hot iron. This will tend to lift the pile but not unless you hold the iron lightly.

Old age is golden I have heard it said,
But sometimes I wonder as I get into bed—
My "ears" on the dresser, my "teeth" in a cup,
My "eyes" on the table until I wake up.
Ere sleep comes each night I say to myself,
"Is there anything else I should lay on the the shelf?"
Yet I am happy to know as I close the door,
My friends are the same as in days of yore.

Soups, Pickles & Relishes

BLUEBERRY SOUP

⅓ c. sour cream
2 T. sugar

10 oz. pkg. frozen blueberries,
partially thawed
lemon slices, for garnish

Blend sour cream, blueberries and sugar in blender on low speed until smooth. Garnish with lemon slices. Serves 2.

Sherry Bell (Waitress)

CREAM OF BROCCOLI SOUP

6 T. butter
5 T. flour
2 c. milk
dash of pepper

1 T. finely chopped onion
1 c. chicken broth
¾ t. salt
1 (10 oz.) box broccoli, thawed

Saute butter and onion. Blend in flour, gradually add broth, milk, salt and pepper, stirring until smooth. Cook till thickened. Puree broccoli in blender. Add to mixture and heat 3 or 4 min.

Sharon Boley (Head Waitress)

 Try flavoring canned cream of chicken soup with a dash of curry.

The sleep of a labouring man is sweet, whether he eat little or much: but the abundance of the rich will not suffer him to sleep.

Eccl. 5:12

CREAM OF TOMATO SOUP

1 T. finely chopped onion
2 T. butter
3 T. flour
2 t. sugar

1 t. salt
⅛ t. pepper
2 c. tomato juice
2 c. cold milk

Sauté onion in butter. Stir in flour, sugar, salt, and pepper. Cook until smooth and bubbly, stirring constantly. Remove from heat.

Gradually stir in tomato juice. Bring to a boil, stirring constantly. Boil 1 minute, then stir this hot tomato juice mixture into cold milk. Heat rapidly to serving temperature and serve immediately.

Makes 4 servings.

Esther Hershberger

CABBAGE SOUP

1 t. butter or margarine
1 t. vegetable oil
5 c. coarsely shredded cabbage
1 c. carrot slices (½" thick)
¾ c. thinly sliced onions
1 small turnip, cut in pieces
½ c. celery, sliced

1 c. potatoes, peeled and cubed
4 c. water
2 c. chicken or turkey broth
1 t. salt
¼ t. dried thyme leaves
¼ t. pepper
¼ t. dried marjoram leaves

In a large (4-6 qt.) saucepan, heat the butter and oil over moderate heat. Add vegetables. Cook 4-5 minutes until cabbage begins to wilt. Add remaining ingredients and bring to a boil. Stir, lower heat, cover and let simmer for 40 minutes.

Mary Rose Yoder (Cook)

CREAM OF CABBAGE SOUP (approximately 2 gallons)

Steam:

3 medium heads of cabbage, chopped

Saute in large saucepan until yellow.

¾ c. margarine   ¾ c. chopped onions

Blend in ¾ c. flour. Add:

9 c. chicken broth   6 c. milk
1 T. Worcestershire sauce   Cabbage and cooking water

Cook until mixture thickens slightly. Add 3 c. shredded cheese.

Sue Miller (Manager)

CREAMY POTATO SOUP

8 slices bacon, cut up   1 c. onion
2 med. potatoes   1 c. water
1 can cream of chicken soup   1½ c. milk
salt   pepper
chopped parsley

In 3 quart pan, fry bacon to crisp. Add onion, cook 2-3 min. Pour off fat. Add water and potato cubes, simmer until potatoes are tender. Stir in soup, milk, salt, pepper and parsley. Heat to serve—do not boil.

Roberta Lantz (Bakery Cashier)

Before frosting an angel food cake, chill cake in the refrigerator. Frosting goes on easy and no mess.

DELICIOUS CHILI

Fry together:

2½ lbs. hamburger
1 T. chili powder, rounded
½ t. pepper

½ c. chopped onions
3 t. salt

Stir in:

1 c. flour
1 qt. catsup
2 qt. kidney beans

3 qt. water
1 c. brown sugar

Cook till hot.

Edna Nissley (Waitress)

EGG DROP SOUP

6 c. chicken broth
½ c. chopped celery

½ c. chopped onions
½ T. sugar

Simmer together for 2 hours. Add:

6 T. thickening with 1 c. water. Beat 1 egg slightly and stir in slowly. Serve immediately.

Ruth Elaine Miller (Waitress)

Wrap green tomatoes in newspaper and store in a cool, dark place and they ripen nicely.

HAMBURGER SOUP

2 T. shortening
½ c. chopped onion
2 c. tomatoes
2 medium carrots, diced
¼ c. rice

1 lb. hamburger
2 c. cubed potatoes
½ c. celery, chopped
2 t. salt
1/8 t. pepper

Brown meat and onion lightly, in shortening in a large kettle. Add the other ingredients and 1½ quarts water. Simmer slowly for an hour. Put in jars and cold pack 1 hour. Add milk or water when you open jars, and heat.

Esther Nisley (Pie Baker)

Maple syrup is not only good on pancakes, heat it and try on ice cream.

MINESTRONE SOUP

1 c. dry beans
5 c. water
3 T. oleo or oil
1 c. chopped onions
1 c. celery
1 c. diced potatoes
1 c. sliced carrots
1 lb. canned whole tomatoes,
  undrained

2 T. parsley
1 clove garlic
2 t. salt
¼ t. oregano
¼ t. black pepper
¼ t. red pepper
¼ t. thyme
4 beef bouillon cubes

Combine beans and water. Cover and simmer until tender. Add remaining ingredients. Bring to a boil and simmer until vegetables are tender, about 30 min. One cup uncooked maccaroni may be added along with vegetables.

Betty Graber (Waitress)

WINTER SQUASH SOUP

2 onions, chopped   1 clove garlic, crushed
1 c. celery   3 T. oleo

Saute vegetables until golden. Blend in 2 T. flour, then add:

3 c. chicken broth   2 c. cooked squash, mashed
1 c. milk or cream   2 T. chopped parsley
salt and pepper to taste

Bring to a boil, stirring constantly, then simmer 10 min. Makes 6 (1 cup) servings. (Options: ¼ t. nutmeg and winter savory and rosemary.)

Esther Nisley (Pie Baker)

TRAMP SOUP

1 medium onion, cut fine
4 medium potatoes, cubed
1 lb. sausage, cut up

Put together in pan with a little water and salt. Cook until well done. Add 1 quart milk, bring to a boil and serve with crackers.

Mary Rose Yoder (Cook)

VEGETABLE SOUP

½ bushel tomatoes   2 heads cabbage
12 ears sweet corn   1 qt. carrots
1 qt. lima beans   1 qt. green beans
2 bunches celery   6 small onions
2 peppers   2 handfuls salt

Cook for 2½ hours. Cold pack for 20 min. Makes 9 quarts.

Ada A. Schrock (Bakery)

ZUCCHINI BISQUE

2 c. chopped zucchini
1 c. water
½ c. tomato juice
1 T. chopped onion

1 chicken bouillon cube
1/8 t. basil
1 (8 oz.) pkg. cream cheese,
    cubed

In saucepan, combine ingredients except cream cheese. Cover; simmer 20 min. Pour into blender. Add cream cheese; blend until smooth. Return to saucepan; heat thoroughly. Six (½ c.) servings.

Sue Miller (Manager)

 Frequent naps prevent old age, especially if taken while driving.

CINNAMON CUCUMBERS

2 gal. large cucumbers
8½ qts. water

2 c. lime

Peel, seed and cut cucumbers in bite-size pieces. Soak in water and lime for 24 hours. Drain and wash, then soak in cold water for 3 hours. Place in large kettle and simmer for 2 hours in the following solution:

1 c. vinegar
1 small bottle red food coloring

1 T. alum
water to cover

Drain off liquid. Make a syrup of the following ingredients:

8 sticks cinnamon
10 oz. red hot cinnamon candy
3 c. water

3 c. vinegar
1 t. salt
10 c. sugar

Bring to a boil. Pour over cucumbers and let stand overnight. Drain and reheat this syrup every 24 hours for 3 days. On the fourth day, heat juice, put into jars and seal.

Lou Anna Yoder (Bakery)

BANANA PICKLES

Peel and take out seeds of pickles. Cut in strips and pack in jars.

Bring to a boil:

1 c. vinegar
2 c. water
3 c. sugar

1 t. salt
1 t. tumeric
1 t. powdered mustard

Pour over pickles. Cold pack for 10 min. Makes 3 quarts.

Ruth Schlabach (Busser)

DILL PICKLES

Put 2 heads of dill in a quart can. Fill with pickles. Pickles may be left whole. Put 2 or 3 garlic buds on top and ½ t. alum.

BRINE - Do not heat - mix up cold:

2 quarts water
½ c. salt
1½ c. vinegar

Pour over pickles—cold pack till boiling point. Do not let boil. Remove cans right away. Be sure you have can lids very hot before you put them on the cans to get a better seal.

Edna Nissley (Waitress)

Bride to New Husband: "There you are, Darling, my first meal cooked just the way you'd better like it."

FREEZER PICKLES

2 qts. small unpeeled pickles, sliced thin
2 onions, sliced thin
2 T. salt

Rub salt through pickles and onions. Let stand for 2 hours.

Boil until clear:

1½ c. sugar
½ c. white vinegar
½ t. celery seed

Let cool. Drain and rinse pickles and onions well. Pour sugar mixture over pickles and onions. Put in freezer containers and freeze. Makes 2 quarts.

Edna E. Bontrager (Cook)

FREEZER PICKLES

25 medium pickles
10 onions

Do not peel pickles, but slice thin. Add diced onions and place in salt water, refrigerate 6 or 8 hours. Take out and drain well.

Brine:

5 lbs. sugar   1 c. vinegar
2 c. water

Mix, heat until sugar is dissolved only. Cool. Mix with pickles, onions. Place in freezer boxes and freeze. Makes 6 quarts. Brine can be reused. "You will receive lots of compliments!"

Optional - 3 c. vinegar instead of water.

Ruth Schlabach (Busser)
Edna Schrock (Cook)
Susanna Miller (Cook)

ICICLE PICKLES

1 c. sugar   1 qt. vinegar
¼ c. salt (scant)   1 t. celery seed

Mix well. Slice cucumbers lengthwise and let soak in ice water for
2 or 3 hours. Pack into jars with slices of onion (1 medium onion per
quart jar). Add alum the size of a pea to each jar. Heat vinegar mixture
to boiling and pour into jars and seal.

Leora Kauffman (Purchasing)

MIXED PICKLE

Prepare about equal amounts of each:

red kidney beans   string beans (yellow or green)
lima beans   carrots
sweet corn   cauliflower
onions   celery

Boil each separately and salt to taste. Prepare some pickles and peppers,
leaving them raw. Put all ingredients in one large pan. Mix well. Mix
together 2½ qt. vinegar, 8 c. sugar, 2 T. celery seed, 1 box cinnamon
bark, and 3 T. tumeric. Heat and thicken with 2 T. cornstarch mixed
with a small amount of water. Pour over mixed vegetables. Mix and
pack into jars. Put in hot water bath for 5 min.

Erma Bontrager (Country Cupboard Manager)

REFRIGERATOR PICKLES

6 c. sliced cucumbers   1 c. vinegar
1 c. sliced onions   1 t. celery seed
1 c. sliced green peppers   2 c. sugar
2 T. salt

Mix together and store in refrigerator. Ready to use in 24 hours. Keeps
for 1 year.

Martha Miller (Cook)

ZUCCHINI BREAD AND BUTTER PICKLES

1 large onion, sliced
6 c. sliced zucchini
¼ c. salt
2 c. cider vinegar

1 c. sugar
1 t. tumeric
1 t. mustard seed
1 t. celery seed

Slice onion and zucchini 1/8" thick and place in large bowl. Salt thoroughly. Cover and allow to rest overnight. Combine remaining ingredients and bring to a rolling boil. Add zucchini and onion to pickling solution. Bring to a boil. Reduce heat and simmer for 15 min. Pack pickles into hot sterilized pint jars. Fill to ½" of top with pickling solution. Seal and process in a boiling water bath for 10 min. Makes 3 pints.

Mary Rose Yoder (Cook)

CURT: "They tell me you're the man who invented spaghetti. Where did you ever get the idea for it?"
RANDY: "Out of my noodle."

FRESH TOMATO RELISH

4 tomatoes, coarsely chopped
1 c. chopped green peppers
2 t. sugar
1 t. celery seed

2 medium onions, sliced
4 T. vinegar
1 t. salt
¼ t. black pepper

Combine tomatoes, onions and green peppers. Stir together vinegar, sugar, salt, celery seed and pepper. Stir into tomato mixture and chill thoroughly. Keep refrigerated. Drain before serving.

Edna Nissley (Waitress)

GREEN TOMATO RELISH

4 qt. ground green tomatoes
3 large onions (chopped)
1 red pepper (chopped)
4 green peppers (chopped)
4 qts. cold water
1 c. salt
½ t. dry mustard

3 c. vinegar
1 c. boiling water
3 c. sugar
1 T. celery seed
2 T. mustard seed
1 t. tumeric

Soak ground tomatoes, onions, and peppers in the cold water with salt for 3 hours. Rinse and drain well. Combine remaining ingredients and boil 3 min. Then add the ground tomatoes, etc. Simmer 10 min. Pack in sterilized jars and seal. Process for 5 min. in hot water bath. Makes 10 quarts.

Barbara Bainter (Cleaning Service)

EGOTIST—One who is always me-deep in conversation.

ZUCCHINI RELISH

12 c. ground zucchini squash
5 T. salt

4 c. ground onions

Let set overnight. Rinse off and squeeze excess water out. Add the following:

2½ c. vinegar
1 T. dry mustard
1½ t. celery seed
½ t. black pepper

6 c. sugar
¾ t. tumeric
1 green pepper
1 red pepper

Let everything cook for 30 min. DO NOT OVER COOK. Spoon into hot jars and let seal. Makes 7 pints.

Elsie Miller (Grill Cook)

PICKLED BOLOGNA

Heat together:

1½ c. vinegar
½ c. water
¼ t. salt

2 bay leaves
1 T. pickling spice

Cut up one medium onion and layer with a ring of bologna in a wide mouth, ½ gallon jar. Cover with heated mixture. Leave at room temperature a few days. Refrigerate once jar has been opened.

Leora Kauffman (Purchasing)

PICKLED TONGUE

2 qts. vinegar
1 small red pepper
1 bay leaf

2 T. horseradish, grated
1 t. whole black pepper
1 t. whole allspice

Bring to a boil and pour over tongue that has been cleaned, boiled and sliced into jars.

Leora Kauffman (Purchasing)

PICKLED RED BEETS

4 c. sugar
4 c. water
3 cinnamon sticks

4 c. vinegar
2 t. salt
2 doz. whole cloves

Bring to boil. Cook and skin beets. Place in boiling syrup and heat. Pack into sterilized jars and seal.

Variation:

½ c. sugar, 1 c. vinegar and spices, if desired. Prepare as above.

Erma Bontrager (Country Cupboard Manager)

SWEET PICKLED BEETS

½ c. sugar
½ c. vinegar
½ c. water

1 t. pickling spice
1 t. salt

Simmer for 5 min. Strain and pour over beets. Cook 8 or 9 medium red beets and strip off the skins. Slice into clean jars alternately with onion slices. Pour hot vinegar mixture over and seal jars.

Leora Kauffman (Purchasing)

Jellies, Jams & Misc.

A little boy who had spent a week at a dude ranch told his mother excitedly:
"Mom, I even saw a man who makes horses."
"Are you sure?" asked his mother.
"Yes," he replied. "He had a horse nearly finished when I saw him, and he was just nailing on the feet."

HOMEMADE HAPPINESS

Posies on the window sill
Wafting perfume lightly.
Yellow canary starts to trill
Sweet and shrill and spritely.
A white, bright wash gaily flapping;
A freshly scrubbed kitchen floor;
A spicy apple pie baking,
A neighborly knock at the door.
A husband's smile; a youngster's yell.
A baby's hug and soft, moist kiss
Put them all together—they spell
To the homemaker, HAPPINESS!

Where is the greatest place in the world? Right here!
Right where you are.
Build your life on a strong foundation
Right where you are.
Surround yourself with lifelong friends.
Right where you are.
Get involved in building a community.
Right where you are.
Let your roots grow deep. Watch your life stand tall.
Right where you are.

WAITRESS: "We have practically everything on the menu."
DINER: "So I see. Can you bring me a clean one?"

CUSTOMER: "Waiter, this food is terrible. I want to talk to the owner of this restaurant!"
WAITER: "You can't. He's out to lunch."

Jellies, Jams & Misc.

WATERMELON RIND PRESERVES

1½ qts. prepared watermelon rind
2 qts. cold water
1 T. ground ginger
¼ c. lemon juice
4 T. salt
1 thinly sliced lemon
4 c. sugar
7 c. water

TO PREPARE RIND:

Trim green skin and pink flesh from thick watermelon rind; cut into 1" pieces. Dissolve salt in 2 qts, water and pour over rind. Let stand 5 to 6 hours. Drain; rinse and drain again. Cover with cold water and let stand 30 min. Drain. Sprinkle ginger over rind; cover with water and cook till fork tender. Combine sugar, lemon juice and 7 c. of water. Boil 5 min. add rind and boil gently for 30 min. Add sliced lemon and cook till melon rind is clear. Pack in boiling hot into hot jars, leaving ¼" head space. Adjust caps. Process 20 min. in boiling water bath. Makes 6½ pints.

Mary Esther Miller (Bakery)

APPLE BUTTER

4 gal. apple snitz, not peeled
1 gal. Karo (light)
6 lbs. sugar

Put all in a lard can and let set overnight. Next morning cook 3 hours, do not open till done. Work thru ricer, then season with cinnamon, heat and put in jars. Makes 10 quarts.

Susanna Miller (Cook)

GRAPE BUTTER

1 lb. sugar   1 lb. whole grapes

Cook for 20 min. Strain and beat 10 min. Ready to go. Very good!

Mabel Hershberger (Cashier)

HONEY BUTTER

½ c. butter   1 c. honey

Butter and honey should be at room temperature. Cream butter, gradually add honey, beating until light.

Lois Landis (Cook's Helper)

RHUBARB JAM

2 c. rhubarb, cut up
2 c. sugar
8 oz. crushed pineapple

Combine all ingredients and bring to a boil. Simmer for 15 min. Stir in 1 pkg. strawberry jello and refrigerate to set.

Elsie Miller (Grill Cook)

DANNY: Why does your grandmother read the Bible so much?''
DAVID: ''I think she's cramming for her finals.''

TOMATO PRESERVES

¾ c. water
1 piece ginger root
2 thinly sliced lemons

1 T. mixed pickling spices
4 c. sugar
1½ qts. small, firm yellow, green or red tomatoes, peeled

So, do not core tomatoes, tie spices in a cheesecloth bag; add to sugar, lemon and water. Simmer 15 min. Add tomatoes and cook gently until tomatoes become clear, stirring occasionally to prevent sticking. Cover and let stand 12-18 min. in a cool place. Heat to boiling and pour into hot jars, leaving ¼" head space. Remove spice bag from syrup. Boil syrup 2-3 min. or longer if too thin. Pour boiling hot, over tomatoes; leaving ¼" head space. Remove air bubbles. Adjust caps. Process 20 min. in hot water bath. Makes 6½ pints.

Mary Esther Miller (Bakery)

STRAWBERRY JAM

5 c. prepared berries
7 c. sugar
1 box pectin

Yields approximately 8 cups.

Sue Miller (Manager)

RHUBARB JAM

4½ c. prepared rhubarb
6½ c. sugar
1 box pectin

Yields approximately 8 cups.

Sue Miller (Manager)

APRICOT JAM

5 c. prepared apricots
¼ c. lemon juice
7 cups sugar
1 box pectin

Yields approximately 8 cups.

Sue Miller (Manager)

BLUEBERRY JAM

4 c. prepared berries
2 T. lemon juice
4 c. sugar
1 box pectin

Yields approximately 5⅔ cups.

Sue Miller (Manager)

CHERRY JAM

4 c. prepared cherries
¼ c. lemon juice
5 c. sugar
1 box pectin

Yields approximately 6 cups.

Sue Miller (Manager)

GOOSEBERRY JAM

5½ c. prepared berries
7 c. sugar
1 box pectin

Yields approximately 8¾ cups.

Sue Miller (Manager)

Blend all ingredients together, allow to stand 1½ hours before serving.

RED RASPBERRY JAM

5 c. prepared berries
7 c. sugar
1 box pectin

Yields approximately 8 cups.

Sue Miller (Manager)

PEACH JAM

4 c. prepared peaches
2 T. lemon juice
5½ c. sugar
1 box pectin

Yields approximately 6½ cups.

Sue Miller (Manager)

TOMATO JAM

3 c. prepared tomatoes
¼ c. lemon juice
4½ c. sugar
1 box pectin

Yields approximately 5 cups.

Sue Miller (Manager)

COOKED JAM DIRECTIONS AND RECIPES

For maximum protection against mold growth and to obtain light seals, use jars with 2-piece lids and process in a boiling water bath after filling. If the boiling water bath is omitted, jars must be sterilized.

1. Locate and mark off fruit recipe on chart below. Check 8 oz. jars for defects. Because containers are not filled to the rim, one more container than the specified cup yield may be needed.

If jams will be placed in a boiling water bath, wash, scald and drain jars, or use automatic dishwasher with very hot rinse water. Keep hot.

If jams will not be placed in boiling water bath, wash jars and sterilize in boiling water for 10 minutes. Keep hot. Wash lids and place in a small container. Cover with boiling water shortly before placing on filled jars. Always use new lids.

2. Prepare fruit as directed in recipe.

3. Measure amount of prepared fruit specified in recipe ingredient listing, pack solidly in cup. If measure is slightly short, add water. Place measured fruit in 6 or 8 quart saucepot. Add lemon juice, if listed.

4. Measure sugar and set aside. DO NOT REDUCE SUGAR.

5. Stir Sure-Jell fruit pectin into prepared fruit. (Saucepot must be no more than ⅓ full to allow for a full rolling boil).

6. Bring to a full boil over high heat, stirring constantly. At once stir in sugar. Stir and bring to a full rolling boil (a boil that cannot be stirred down). Then boil hard 1 minute, stirring constantly. Remove from heat.

7. Skim off foam with large metal spoon. Immediately ladle into hot jars, leaving ¾" space at top. With a damp cloth, wipe jar rims and threads clean.

8. Immediately cover jars with hot lids. Screw bands on firmly.

9. Place in boiling water bath, carefully setting jars on rack in canner or large saucepot of boiling water. Water should cover jars by 1 to 2 inches. Cover canner and return the water to a boil, then boil 5 minutes. (At high altitudes, increase boiling time by 1 minute for each 1,000 feet above sea level.

10. Let jam stand to cool. Check seals. Jar lids should be slightly concave or remain so when pressed. Remove bands from jars. Store jam in a cool dry place. (Small amounts of unsealed jam may be covered and stored in the refrigerator).

CHIP DIP

1 lb. cottage cheese or 2 c. sour cream
1 c. Hellmann's mayonnaise
1 pkg. Hidden Valley Ranch salad dressing mix.

Mix together.

Edna Fern Schmucker

CURRY DIP

1 pint mayonnaise
3 T. chili sauce
3 t. curry owder
¼ t. salt

¼ t. pepper
1 T. garlic powder
1 T. grated onion
1 T. Worcestershire sauce

Mix all ingredients together and chill. Keeps indefinitely in refrigerator. Delicious dip for shrimp or raw vegetables.

Jil Kauffman (Waitress)

DILLY DIP

1 c. sour cream
1 T. Beau Monde seasoning
1 T. parsley flakes

1 c. cottage cheese or mayonnaise
1 T. dill weed
1 T. minced onions

Blend all ingredients together, allow to stand 1½ hours before serving. Eat with celery, carrots, chips, etc.

Alice Weaver (Waitress)
Mary Rose Yoder (Cook)

ENCHILADA DIP

2 lb. hamburger
¾ c. chopped onions
1 c. chopped celery
1 lb. shredded Cheddar cheese

1 can cream of mushroom soup
1 can cream of celery soup
1 jar enchilada sauce

Brown hamburger and add all other ingredients together in crock pot. Cook for 2-3 hours. Serve hot with tortilla chips or doritos.

Lyle Coblentz (Dishwasher)

FRUIT DIP

2 c. pineapple juice   ½ c. sugar
2 T. clear jell   8 oz. pkg. cream cheese
9 oz. Cool Whip

Cook pineapple juice, sugar and clear jell until thick. When cool, add cream cheese and Cool Whip. Mix together until creamy. Serve with sliced apples, bananas, oranges and grapes. Apples and bananas soaked in diluted lemon juice won't turn brown.

Rosetta Herschberger (Waitress)

MEXICAN DIP

1 lb. hamburger   ½ large onion or flakes
½ c. catsup   1 can refried beans
chili powder   1 t. salt

Simmer, add 1 c. grated Velveeta cheese. Bake at 350° for about 20 min. or just simmer on stove top awhile. Dip Doritos or Tostitos.

Betti Kauffman (Cashier-Hostess)

PHILLY AVOCADO DIP

1 (8 oz.) pkg. cream cheese   1 T. finely chopped onion
2 medium avocados, peeled,   ½ t. salt
  mashed   dash of Worcestershire sauce
1 T. lemon juice

Combine softened cream cheese and avocado, mixing until well blended. Add remaining ingredients; mix well. Serve with corn or tortillla chips and vegetable dippers. Makes 2 cups.

Sue Miller (Manager)

SHRIMP DIP

1 large cream cheese
4 T. mayonnaise
2 T. minced onion

1 can shrimps, mashed
2 t. lemon juice
dash Worcestershire sauce

Salt and pepper to taste. Great for chips and crackers.

Betty Graber (Waitress)

VEGETABLE DIP

⅔ c. mayonnaise
1 t. dry onions
1 t. seasoned salt
1 t. accent

⅔ c. sour cream
1 t. dry parsley
1 t. dill seed
2 drops Tabasco sauce

Mix all together and let set a couple hours.

Susanna Miller (Cook)
Lyle Coblentz (Dishwasher)

VEGETABLE DIP

1 pkg. Hidden Valley Ranch mix
½ c. mayonnaise or Miracle Whip
2 c. cottage cheese

Mix well. Serve with celery, cauliflower, carrots, chips, etc.

Edna E. Bontrager (Cook)

VEGETABLE DIP

1 c. Hellmann's mayonnaise
1 T. dry onion flakes
1 t. dill weed
½ t. accent

1 c. sour cream
1 t. Lawry's seasoned salt
½ t. Worcestershire sauce

Mix together and chill.

Laura Bontrager (Bakery)

VEGETABLE DIP

1 (8 oz.) cream cheese
1 c. real mayonnaise
2 beef bouillon cubes
garlic salt, to taste

onion salt, to taste
chipped ham
dash hickory smoke

Mix together. Put in tight container. Chill.

Rosa Miller (Bakery)

CHEESE SPREAD

2 lb. Chef's Delight cheese
¼ c. oleo

2 c. milk

Melt over low heat, spread on crackers or bread.

Esther Nisley (Pie Baker)

HOT CHEESE DIP

1½ lb. Velveeta cheese
3 t. minced onion

4½ oz. can deviled ham
3 c. mayonnaise

Melt cheese and blend in the rest of the ingredients. Serve warm as a dip with fresh vegetables or serve cold with crackers. Serves 100.

Esther Nisley (Pie Baker)

CORN CHILI

1 lb. ground beef
½ c. chopped onion
1 T. chili powder
1 t. salt
1 (28 oz.) can tomatoes, undrained

1 (16 oz.) can kidney beans,
 undrained
1 (12 oz.) can corn, undrained
1 c. barbecue sauce

In Dutch oven, brown meat; drain. Add onion and seasonings; cook until onion is tender. Stir in remaining ingredients. Cover; simmer 20 min. 8 servings.

Serve with an assorted fruit and cheese tray and heated rolls.

Sue Miller (Manager)

TINY HAM STUFFED TOMATOES

Begin early in day. Makes 20 appetizers.

1 pint cherry tomatoes
2 (2¼ oz.) can deviled ham
2 T. sour cream

2 T. horseradish
parsley for garnish

Thinly slice tops from cherry tomatoes. Remove pulp. Drain shells on side on paper towels. In small bowl, combine ham, sour cream and horseradish. Fill tomato shells and refrigerate. To serve, garnish with parsley.

Sherry Bell (Waitress)

CHEESE BALL

8 oz. Philadelphia cream cheese
½ tube soft smoked cheese
¼ t. garlic salt
1 t. onion flakes
1 t. Worcestershire sauce

½ t. Lawry's seasoned salt
1 pkg. dried beef, ground up
1 t. dried parsley
½ c. nuts, chopped

Mix all ingredients except parsley and nuts. Chill in freezer for 1 hour, until cold and stiff. Roll in nuts and parsley.

Wilma Schlabach (Dessert Counter)
Ruth Elaine Miller

NUTTY CHEESE BALL

8 oz. cream cheese
1 c. finely chopped pecans
1 t. chopped onion

4¼ oz. drained, crushed pineapple
1/8 c. chopped green peppers
½ t. seasoned salt

Form in ball and roll in ¼ c. chopped pecans.

Lydia Ann Miller (Head Cook)

HERBED MUSHROOMS

1 lb. small mushrooms	1½ t. sugar
⅓ c. cider vinegar	1 t. salt
2 T. salad oil	4 oz. jar pimentos, diced and
1½ t. Italian seasoning (fine)	drained

Trim rough ends of mushroom stems, rinse, pat dry. In large bowl, gently mix mushrooms with remaining ingredients. Serve with toothpicks.

Begin 1-3 days ahead. 12 servings.

Sherry Bell (Waitress)

BOLOGNA

100 lbs. beef	75 lbs.	50 lbs.	25 lbs.
3 oz. pepper	4½ T.	3 T.	1½ T.
1 lb. brown sugar	¾ lb.	½ lb.	¼ lb.
3¾ lb. tender quick	2¾ lb.	1¾ lb.	1 lb.
1 lb. salt	¾ lb. (scant)	½ lb.	¼ lb.
1 oz. saltpeter	4½ t.	2 t.	1½ t.

Grind and mix, then grind again. For 50 lbs. add 2 quarts water when mixing. Let stand 3 days. Just before putting on lids, put 1 t. liquid smoke on top of quart can. Cold pack for 1 hour.

Ida Weaver (Cook)

CANNED CABBAGE

1 head cabbage, shredded	½ c. onions, chopped
2 c. sugar	½ c. vinegar (scant)
2 t. salt	peppers (optional)
1 t. celery seed	

Mix together and let set for ½ day. Pack into jars. Cold pack for 7 min. Do not overcook. Serve like coleslaw.

Martha Miller (Cook)
Mabel Hershberger (Cashier)

CANNED GRAPE JUICE

Pick grapes off stems and wash. Put 1 c. grapes and ½ c. sugar in 1 quart jar and fill up with warm water. Cold pack for 20-25 min. This is ready to drink.

Elsie Miller (Grill Cook)

CANNED MANGOES

I peck mangoes — red and green and yellow. Clean and put in cold water. Let come to a boil, but don't boil. Drain, put in jars and cover with boiling syrup.

Syrup:

1 c. white Karo
½ t. salicylic acid

4½ c. white sugar
1 quart vinegar—not too strong

Boil this all together and pour boiling hot water over mangoes and seal.

Mabel Hershberger (Cashier)

For instant dessert, spoon canned, crushed pineapple on ice cream and top with melted marshmallows.

CANNED STRAWBERRIES

7 c. water
5 c. sugar

¾ c. minute tapioca

Cook until clear. Mix 4 T. clear jel with 1 c. water and add to above mixture. Continue cooking until thick. Add 4 quarts whole or chopped strawberries. You may either boil for 5 min. and can or put in jars and cold pack for 15-20 min.

Mary Yoder (Bakery)

CORN TO FREEZE

8 c. corn (cut off the cob)
2 t. salt
1 stick butter

2 c. water
2 T. sugar

Cook 5 to 7 minutes, then cool quick and freeze.

Doretta Mast (Dishwasher)

CHEESE

2½ gallon skimmed milk. Let sour until very thick. Then set in refrigerator or cool place for 5 hours. Then set on burner and heat ½ hour, not boiling but too hot to stand to put a hand in. You can stir occasionally. Heat till curds are a little firm. Drain through cheesecloth, drain till real dry, spread on paper toweling, let dry 1 hour. Crumble fine, then add 2 t. soda. Heat ½ c. butter. Then add the curds which should be 5½ c. or more. Stir constantly till smooth on low heat. Cheese should all melt, then add 1 c. hot sweet cream or milk and 3 t. salt. Stir well and pour in mold. Makes about 2 pounds.

Susie Bontrager (Cook)
Elsie Miller (Grill Cook)

NEVER FAIL MAYONNAISE

2 egg yolks
1 c. salad oil
¼ c. vinegar
2 T. lemon juice

1 t. salt
1 dash red pepper
½ c. sugar

Put these ingredients in a large mixing bowl, but do not beat. Make a white sauce by melting 2 T. butter—adding ⅓ c. flour. When this is blended, add 1 c. water. Cook while stirring, pour while hot into above ingredients. Beat with eggbeater until ingredients are all blended. Cool and store. Makes 1 full pint.

Martha Miller (Cook)

PIZZA SAUCE

½ bushel tomatoes   2-3 garlic buds
3 lb. onions   2 hot peppers

Juice tomatoes, grind garlic, onions and peppers in blender. Add 1 pint cooking oil, cook together for ½ hour.

Add:

8 small cans tomato paste   1 T. oregano
1½ c. sugar   1 T. sweet basil
½ c. salt

Simmer together till it comes to a boil. Put in cans and cold pack for an hour. Delicious!

Arlene Miller (Waitress)
Elsie Miller (Grill Cook)

Diets are for people who are thick and tired of it.

TOMATO CATSUP

4 quarts tomato juice   1 T. cinnamon
2 T. salt   ½ t. red pepper
3 c. sugar   1 t. ground mustard
1 T. mixed pickle spice   2 c. vinegar
3 small onions

Put altogether and cook 1 hour. Then thicken with 2½ T. cornstarch, moistened with water. Cook 10 min. longer and bottle. (Tie spice, mustard and onions all together in bag and place in strained tomatoes, sugar, and vinegar while it cooks (1 hour). Makes about 7 to 8 bottles.

Ada Schrock (Cook)

TOMATO CATSUP

Cook onions and peppers in tomatoes if you like.

1 gallon plus 1 pint tomato juice
1 c. vinegar
3 c. sugar
6 t. salt

In cloth bag put:

2 T. ground mustard
2 t. cinnamon
1 t. black pepper
½ t. cloves
½ t. allspice

Cook 3 hours or till thick enough.

Susie Bontrager (Cook)

SPAGHETTI SAUCE

1 quart tomato juice
1 t. celery salt
1 t. garlic powder
1 t. chili powder
1 T. brown sugar

1 t. Lawry's season salt
½ t. oregano
dash of Tabasco
1 t. onion powder or
   chopped onions

Simmer approximately 1 hour or until thick.

Rosa Borntrager (Dutch Country Gifts)

Cheddar cheese grates better if placed in the freezer for ten to fifteen minutes before grating.

SPAGHETTI SAUCE TO CAN

Cook down tomato juice to 2 gallon puree. Dice 4 large onions and 4 green peppers and simmer with the tomatoes. Put thru blender and add:

4 T. garlic salt	1 t. salt
2 T. chili powder	1 t. pepper
2 T. Lawry's season salt	1 t. oregano
½ c. sugar	¼ t. Tabasco

Return to stove and simmer for 30 min. Put in jars and seal.

Rosa Borntrager (Dutch Country Gifts)

STEAK SAUCE

⅓ c. wine vinegar	¼ c. catsup
2 T. oil	2 T. soy sauce
1 T. Worcestershire sauce	1 t. mustard
1½ t. salt	¼ t. pepper
½-1 T. garlic salt	

Mix well and refrigerate.

Charlotte Miller (Waitress)

YOGURT

Take 2 quarts of milk and heat to 180°. Cool to 110°. Add 1 can of Eagle Brand milk and ½ c. plain yogurt for starter. Put in cups and keep it between 90 and 105°. If it gets hotter than 110°, it kills the yogurt starter. Then more is needed. Takes 3 to 5 hours to thicken. Works better on a sunny day. (Heating to 180° is necessary only if using unpasteurized milk. If pasteurized, just heat to 110 ° and process.

Edna Nissley (Waitress)

CREAMED CELERY

12 qt. celery—scant 1 qt. water to cook
2 c. sugar
½ or ¾ c. vinegar
1½ T. salt
¼ lb. butter

Cook until soft, then mix together:

3 T. flour
2 c. brown sugar
1 can Carnation milk

2 c. white sugar
1 pt. cream

Laura Bontrager (Bakery)

TO DRY SWEET CORN:

1 gallon corn (cut from cob)
½ c. sugar
½ c. cream
¼ c. salt
a little butter

Mix all in a kettle and heat for about 30 min. Keep stirring so it doesn't burn. Then put on a drier, or it can be put in the oven for several hours on a cookie sheet with the oven turned to lowest temperature. Keeps indefinitely.

Leora Kauffman (Purchasing)

ALOE SALVE

3 large T. vaseline. Cut up 2″ long aloe vera stalks and heat. Do this twice more and strain. Add the amount of sulphur you can get on a dime and stir till almost cold. Add ½ t. oil of wintergreen and pour into jar.

Very healing for an open sore.

Mabel Hershberger (Cashier)

EASY BAKING POWDER

You can make baking powder by combining:

2 T. cream of tartar 1 T. cornstarch
1 T. baking soda

Sift ingredients and store in airtight container, use the same as purchased baking powder.

Edna Schrock (Cook)

GIANT BLOWING BUBBLES

1 c. liquid detergent ½ gallon water
4 oz. glycerin   1 T. sugar

Mix ingredients together. Use plastic pop can holder or a wire twisted into a circle. Have fun!

Edna Schrock (Cook)

Want a different tasting meatloaf? Try pouring peach or apricot juice over the loaf just before it is done.

HOMEMADE PLAY DOH

½ c. salt   1½ c. water
2 T. powdered alum 1 T. cooking oil
2 c. flour

Dissolve salt in water on slow heat. Add food coloring, alum, oil, and then flour. Work until not sticky. Keeps well.

Rosa Borntrager (Dutch Country Gifts)

RECIPE FOR CLEANER

This homemade cleaner can be used on windows, chrome, painted surfaces in the bath and kitchen.

Combine:

1 pint rubbing alcohol
1 T. household ammonia

1 T. dishwashing liquid
1 gallon water

Add a drop or two of blue food coloring for a more professional look. Will clean as good as any you can buy and it's a lot cheaper. Store in a gallon jug and be sure to add a label.

Edna Schrock (Cook)

Index

MISC.

PICKLES & RELISHES

PIES

303